Private Selves

Data protection has become such a key area for law – and for society at large – that it is important to understand exactly what we are doing when we regulate privacy and personal data. This study analyses European privacy rights focusing especially on the General Data Protection Regulation, and asks what kind of legal personhood is presupposed in privacy regulation today. Looking at it from a deconstructive angle, the philosophical foundations of this highly topical field of law are uncovered. By analysing key legal cases in detail, this study shows in a comprehensive manner that personhood is constructed in individualised ways. With its clear focus on data protection and individual rights, the book will be of interest to those trying to understand current trends in European Union law.

Susanna Lindroos-Hovinheimo is Professor of Law at the University of Helsinki. She is the author of *Justice and the Ethics of Legal Interpretation* (2012).

Cambridge Studies in European Law and Policy

The focus of this series is European law broadly understood. It aims to publish original monographs in all fields of European law, from work focusing on the institutions of the EU and the Council of Europe to books examining substantive fields of European law as well as examining the relationship between European law and domestic, regional and international legal orders. The series publishes works adopting a wide variety of methods: comparative, doctrinal, theoretical and inter-disciplinary approaches to European law are equally welcome, as are works looking at the historical and political facets of the development of European law and policy. The main criterion is excellence, that is, the publication of innovative work, which will help to shape the legal, political and scholarly debate on the future of European law.

Books in the Series

Fissures in EU Citizenship: The Deconstruction and Reconstruction of the Legal Evolution of EU Citizenship
Martin Steinfeld

The Boundaries of the EU Internal Market: Participation without Membership
Marja-Liisa Öberg

The Currency of Solidarity: Constitutional Transformation during the Euro Crisis
Vestert Borger

Empire of Law: Nazi Germany, Exile Scholars and the Battle for the Future of Europe
Kaius Tuori

In the Court We Trust: Cooperation, Coordination and Collaboration between the ECJ and Supreme Administrative Courts
Rob van Gestel and Jurgen de Poorter

Beyond Minimum Harmonisation: Gold-Plating and Green-Plating of European Environmental Law
Lorenzo Squintani

The Court of Justice of the European Union as an Institutional Actor: Judicial Lawmaking and Its Limits
Thomas Horsley

The Politics of Justice in European Private Law: Social Justice, Access Justice, Societal Justice
Hans-W Micklitz

The Transformation of EU Treaty Making: The Rise of Parliaments, Referendums and Courts since 1950
Dermot Hodson and Imelda Maher

Redefining European Economic Integration
Dariusz Adamski

Human Rights in the Council of Europe and the European Union: Achievements, Trends and Challenges
Steven Greer, Janneke Gerards and Rosie Slowe

Core Socio-economic Rights and the European Court of Human Rights
Ingrid Leijten

Green Trade and Fair Trade in and with the EU: Process-Based Measures within the EU Legal Order
Laurens Ankersmit

New Labour Laws in Old Member States: Trade Union Responses to European Enlargement
Rebecca Zahn

The Governance of EU Fundamental Rights
Mark Dawson

The International Responsibility of the European Union: From Competence to Normative Control
Andrés Delgado Casteleiro

Frontex and Non-refoulement: The International Responsibility of the EU
Roberta Mungianu

Gendering European Working Time Regimes: The Working Time Directive and the Case of Poland
Ania Zbyszewska

EU Renewable Electricity Law and Policy: From National Targets to a Common Market
Tim Maxian Rusche

European Constitutionalism
Kaarlo Tuori

Brokering Europe: Euro-Lawyers and the Making of a Transnational Polity
Antoine Vauchez

Services Liberalization in the EU and the WTO: Concepts, Standards and Regulatory Approaches
Marcus Klamert

Referendums and the European Union: A Comparative Enquiry
Fernando Mendez, Mario Mendez and Vasiliki Triga

The Allocation of Regulatory Competence in the EU Emissions Trading Scheme
Jospehine van Zeben

The Eurozone Crisis: A Constitutional Analysis
Kaarlo Tuori and Klaus Tuori

International Trade Disputes and EU Liability
Anne Thies

The Limits of Legal Reasoning and the European Court of Justice
Gerard Conway

New Governance and the Transformation of European Law: Coordinating EU Social Law and Policy
Mark Dawson

The Lisbon Treaty: A Legal and Political Analysis
Jean-Claude Piris

The European Union's Fight against Corruption: The Evolving Policy towards Member States and Candidate Countries
Patrycja Szarek-Mason

The Ethos of Europe: Values, Law and Justice in the EU
Andrew Williams

State and Market in European Union Law: The Public and Private Spheres of the Internal Market before the EU Courts
Wolf Sauter and Harm Schepel

The European Civil Code: The Way Forward
Hugh Collins

Ethical Dimensions of the Foreign Policy of the European Union: A Legal Appraisal
Urfan Khaliq

Implementing EU Pollution Control: Law and Integration
Bettina Lange

European Broadcasting Law and Policy
Jackie Harrison and Lorna Woods

The Transformation of Citizenship in the European Union: Electoral Rights and the Restructuring of Political Space
Jo Shaw

The Constitution for Europe: A Legal Analysis
Jean-Claude Piris

The European Convention on Human Rights: Achievements, Problems and Prospects
Steven Greer

Social Rights and Market Freedom in the European Constitution: A Labour Law Perspective
Stefano Giubboni

EU Enlargement and the Constitutions of Central and Eastern Europe
Anneli Albi

Private Selves

Legal Personhood in European Privacy Protection

Susanna Lindroos-Hovinheimo
University of Helsinki

CAMBRIDGE
UNIVERSITY PRESS

CAMBRIDGE
UNIVERSITY PRESS

University Printing House, Cambridge CB2 8BS, United Kingdom

One Liberty Plaza, 20th Floor, New York, NY 10006, USA

477 Williamstown Road, Port Melbourne, VIC 3207, Australia

314–321, 3rd Floor, Plot 3, Splendor Forum, Jasola District Centre, New Delhi – 110025, India

79 Anson Road, #06–04/06, Singapore 079906

Cambridge University Press is part of the University of Cambridge.

It furthers the University's mission by disseminating knowledge in the pursuit of education, learning, and research at the highest international levels of excellence.

www.cambridge.org
Information on this title: www.cambridge.org/9781108478885

DOI: 10.1017/9781108781381

First published 2021

A catalogue record for this publication is available from the British Library.

ISBN 978-1-108-47888-5 Hardback

To my Dad

Privacy is about nothing less than trying to live both as a member of a variety of social units - as a part of a number of larger wholes - and as an individual - a unique, individuated self.

Christena Nippert-Eng, *Islands of Privacy*

Contents

Series Editors' Preface

We are delighted to welcome *Private Selves: Legal Personhood in European Privacy Protection* by Susanna Lindroos-Hovinheimo to the *Cambridge Studies in European Law and Policy series.*

This book combines, in an original way, careful doctrinal analysis of the positive law on privacy within the framework of the European Union with jurisprudential insights into the nature of legal personhood and legal subjecthood, drawing on a range of sources within the field of continental philosophy. It suggests itself as a contribution to critical legal studies within the framework of European Union law. This offers a novel research-led insight into an important and topical area of European law, focused in particular on the relatively recent introduction of the General Data Protection Regulation (GDPR; the new personal data regulation), which has fundamentally altered the legal landscape in this domain.

While the doctrinal analysis on its own is already an important contribution to knowledge, the book's most important insights come in relation to the concept of privacy. Lindroos-Hovinheimo acknowledges that privacy is undoubtedly a difficult concept to analyse. It is also hard to get away from thinking that privacy is, in modern society, constantly under threat. She suggests re-thinking privacy in ways that try to overcome the obvious tension between the individual and the community/ies in which they live. Privacy is – according to Lindroos-Hovinheimo – a potential bridge between individuals and the community. It is less an individual entitlement, although obviously individuals, especially vulnerable individuals, are to be cherished and protected, but rather a relation, and a way of being *in a community*. The book is thus a critique of the individualism that seems inherent in most (legal) privacy protection, and a plea for a different kind of thinking that overcomes the individual/community dichotomy within most liberal thinking about privacy.

Jo Shaw
Laurence Gormley
Mark Dawson

Acknowledgements

This book has not been written by me. It has not been an individual endeavour. The work has been done with the help of many friends. Toomas Kotkas is a rock on which I lean. His comments on the manuscript were essential. Samuli Hurri and Ari Hirvonen have likewise given me strong support. Suvi Sankari has been an enormous help by discussing intricacies of EU law, among other things. Ida Koivisto I thank for her friendship, but above all for writing company across Europe. Päivi Korpisaari is an energising force, with whom I have enjoyed discussing privacy law for years. Pia Letto-Vanamo and the Faculty of Law have supported my research in generous ways, for which I am very grateful. Chris Tomlins invited me to Berkeley for a break when I needed it, which enabled me to concentrate on writing. Jo Shaw gave me feedback on a very early plan for this book, and it helped me realise what I am trying to do. The clarity and focus required to complete the book was offered by Gothenburg colleagues and other participants in a lovely seminar in Varberg 2018. I want to thank Merima Bruncevic, Matilda Arvidsson, Jannice Käll, Eva-Maria Svensson, Tormod Otter Johansen, Emilios Christodoulidis, Andreas Philippopoulos-Mihalopoulos and Fiona Macmillan for their helpful comments. I am also grateful to the participants of the Fundamental Rights Online research seminar held in Helsinki in 2019, especially Beate Roessler, Tuomas Ojanen, Bilyana Petkova, Marta Maroni and Anette Alén-Savikko. The Fundamental Rights, Privacy and Security (FUPS) community in Helsinki has given me lots of inspiration and I want to thank in particular Tobias Bräutigam and Jens Kremer for their support.

I have had invaluable help from research assistants Miikka Hiltunen, Enna Hakala and Linda Sydänmaanlakka. Christopher Goddard's meticulous proofreading has been an enormous asset. I am also very grateful for Barbara Eastman's editorial help, which has been invaluable, as has CUP's.

Finally, I want to thank my family, without whom I could never do anything at all.

Table of Cases

CJEU

Asociación Nacional de Establecimientos Financieros de Crédito (ASNEF) and Federación de Comercio Electrónico y Marketing Directo (FECEMD) *v.* Administración del Estado, Joined Cases C-468/10 and C-469/10, EU:C:2011:777.

Camera di Commercio, Industria, Artigianato e Agricoltura di Lecce *v.* Salvatore Manni, Case C-398/15, EU:C:2017:197.

ClientEarth and Pesticide Action Network Europe (PAN Europe) *v.* European Food Safety Authority, Case C-615/13, EU:C:2017:197.

Criminal proceedings against Bodil Lindqvist, Case C-101/01, EU:C:2003:596

Deutsche Post AG *v.* Hauptzollamt Köln, Case C-496/17, EU:C:2019:26.

Digital Rights Ireland Ltd *v.* Minister for Communications, Marine and Natural Resources and Others and Kärntner Landesregierung and Others, Joined Cases C-293/12 and C-594/12, EU:C:2014:238.

European Commission *v.* The Bavarian Lager Co. Ltd., Case C-28/08P, EU:C:2010:378.

Fashion ID GmbH & Co. KG *v.* Verbraucherzentrale NRW e.V., joined parties Facebook Ireland Limited, Landesbeauftragte für Datenschutz und Informationsfreiheit Nordrhein-Westfalen, Case C-40/17, EU:C:2019:629.

František Ryneš *v.* Úřad pro ochranu osobních údajů, Case C-212/13, EU:C:2014:2428.

GC and Others *v.* Commission nationale de l'informatique et des libertés (CNIL), Case C-136/17, EU:C:2019:773.

Google LLC, successor in law to Google Inc. *v.* Commission nationale de l'informatique et des libertés (CNIL), Case C-507/17, EU:C:2019:772.

Google Spain SL and Google Inc. *v.* Agencia Española de Protección de Datos (AEPD) and Mario Costeja González, Case C-131/12, EU:C:2014:317.

Maria Psara and Others *v.* European Parliament, Joined Cases T-639/15 to T-666/15 and T-94/16, EU:T:2018:602.

Maximillian Schrems *v.* Data Protection Commissioner, Case C-362/14, EU:C:2015:650.

Michael Schwarz *v.* Stadt Bochum, Case C-291/12, EU:C:2013:670.

Patrick Breyer *v.* Bundesrepublik Deutschland, Case C-582/14, EU:C:2016:779.

Peter Nowak *v.* Data Protection Commissioner, Case C-434/16, EU:C:2017:994.

Rechnungshof and Others *v.* Österreichischer Rundfunk and Others, Joined Cases C-465/00, C-138/01 and C-139/01, EU:C:2003:294.

Scarlet Extended SA *v.* Société belge des auteurs, compositeurs et éditeurs SCRL (SABAM), Case C-70/10, EU:C:2011:771.

Sergejs Buivids, Case C-345/17, EU:C:2019:122.

Tietosuojavaltuutettu *v.* Satakunnan Markkinapörssi and Satamedia Oy, Case C-73/07, EU:C:2008:727.

Tietosuojavaltuutettu, intervening parties Jehovan todistajat – uskonnollinen yhdyskunta, Case C-25/17, EU:C:2018:551.

Unabhängiges Landeszentrum für Datenschutz Schleswig-Holstein *v.* Wirtschaftsakademie Schleswig-Holstein GmbH, Case C-210/16, EU:C:2018:388.

Verbraucherzentrale Bundesverband e.V. *v.* Planet49, Case C-673/17, EU:C:2019:801.

Volker und Markus Schecke and Hartmut Eifert *v.* Land Hessen, joined party Bundesanstalt für Landwirtschaft und Ernährung, Joined Cases C-92/09 and C-93/09, EU:C:2010:662.

ECtHR

Bărbulescu *v.* Romania, ECHR:2017.

Magyar Helsinki Bizottság *v.* Hungary, ECHR:2016.

Peck *v.* United Kingdom ECHR 2003-I.
Roman Zakharov *v.* Russia ECHR 2015-VIII.

Supreme Court of Canada

R *v.* Sharpe, [2001] 1 SCR 45; 2001 SCC 2.

Table of EU Secondary Law

Directive 95/46/EC of the European Parliament and of the Council of 24 October 1995 on the protection of individuals with regard to the processing of personal data and on the free movement of such data, OJ 1995 No. L281, 23 November 1995.

Regulation (EC) No 1049/2001 of the European Parliament and of the Council of 30 May 2001 regarding public access to European Parliament, Council and Commission documents, OJ 2001 No. L145, 31 May 2001.

Regulation (EU) No 952/2013 of the European Parliament and of the Council of 9 October 2013 laying down the Union Customs Code, OJ 2013 No. L269, 10 October 2013.

Regulation (EU) 2016/679 of the European Parliament and of the Council, of 27 April 2016, on the protection of natural persons with regard to the processing of personal data and on the free movement of such data, and repealing Directive 95/46/EC (General Data Protection Regulation), OJ 2016 No. L119, 4 May 2016.

Directive (EU) 2016/680 of the European Parliament and of the Council of 27 April 2016 on the protection of natural persons with regard to the processing of personal data by competent authorities for the purposes of the prevention, investigation, detection or prosecution of criminal offences or the execution of criminal penalties, and on the free movement of such data, and repealing Council Framework Decision 2008/977/JHA, OJ 2016 No. L119, 4 May 2016.

Regulation (EU) 2018/1807 of the European Parliament and of the Council of 14 November 2018 on a framework for the free flow of non-personal data in the European Union, OJ 2018 No. L303, 28 November 2018.

OTHER INSTITUTIONAL SOURCES

Article 29 Data Protection Working Party, 'Guidelines on Consent under Regulation 2016/679', WP259rev.01, 28 November 2017.

Commission, 'Proposal for a Regulation of the European Parliament and of the Council concerning the respect for private life and the protection of personal data in electronic communications and repealing Directive 2002/58/EC (Regulation on Privacy and Electronic Communications)', COM (2017) 10 final.

Commission, 'Proposal for a Regulation of the European Parliament and of the Council on European Production and Preservation Orders for electronic evidence in criminal matters', COM (2018) 225 final.

Canadian Criminal Code RSC 1985 c C-46.

Introduction

This book analyses privacy law, with a focus on legal personhood. The key question that forms the narrative of the book is this: What kind of persons does European Union (EU) law think we are?

Privacy and personal data protection are areas that demonstrate current social and political tensions. From a societal perspective, this field of law renders itself useful for enquiries into some of the main issues in contemporary European life. It reflects how we see the private and public divide, and it regulates the way we communicate with each other, both online and off.

Privacy is now very much on the global political agenda. The law reflects a general worry shared widely in politics, philosophy, the arts and popular culture: that privacy is under threat. This sense of something being lost, or soon to be lost, has become ever stronger.

The most important reason to study privacy and personal data regulation lies in the specific nature of this field, where legal practice is forced to continually develop both the definition of privacy and the conception of the person that privacy rights are meant to protect. Here, in difficult cases, the European courts face the thankless task of outlining various aspects of what it means to be a private person in the connected, digitalised and globalised world.

There is no unambiguous definition of privacy to be found in European law – or in American law for that matter – or in legal philosophy. The openness of the concept makes it such an interesting instrument in legal regulation. As a result, European case law offers compelling material that can be studied to point towards dominant legal constructions of personhood.

In order to keep the research confined to reasonable proportions, I have had to limit the material that will be used. My focus is on EU law with special attention to the case law of the European Court of Justice (ECJ). Even though the Member States are components of the Union with their own legislation contributing to the way EU law develops, I will not discuss them in this study. The Member State courts, which function as important arbiters of justice in the Union, will also be left aside. The EU Court in Luxembourg will be our main concern and, hence, the material that will be read consists predominately of judgments given by this court. The other transnational European Court, the European Court of Human Rights (ECtHR), will not be studied in detail either.

This book is focused on the European Union and its legal system for a reason. The law has been changing. A shift of emphasis has been occurring, though gradually. Where the law of the EU used to be primarily concerned with free movement and trade, it has become increasingly attentive to the human beings who are its subjects. New fields of EU law that have developed as a result deserve the attention of scholars.

Privacy and personal data protection are areas enjoying increasing legal attention. They attest to the more general development, where fundamental rights are gaining more weight in the legal fabric of the Union. The most significant event in this field of law is the new personal data regulation (General Data Protection Regulation; GDPR), which became applicable in 2018.

In the EU, data protection is sometimes seen as a right of its own, and sometimes as a subcategory of the right to privacy. Indeed, the relationship between the two is not clear.[1] Both case law from the ECJ and academic scholarship show ambivalence in this regard. The difficulties are partly due to the fact that privacy itself is notoriously hard to define. It encompasses, for instance, the right to private life, domestic privacy, privacy in public premises, as well as informational privacy.

How exactly the new Regulation on data protection influences the law remains to be seen. It is certain, though, that it will have an impact on European societies. It emphasises a commitment to personal data protection as a fundamental right. Introducing the possibility to impose significant administrative fines for infringements, the GDPR has also

[1] On data protection and privacy generally, see e.g. Federico Ferretti, 'Data Protection and the Legitimate Interest of Data Controllers: Much Ado about Nothing or the Winter of Rights?' (2014) 51 *Common Market Law Review* 843–68; and Juliane Kokott and Christoph Sobotta, 'The Distinction between Privacy and Data Protection in the Jurisprudence of the CJEU and the ECtHR' (2013) 3 *International Data Privacy Law* 222–8.

made a telling gesture directed to private and public actors alike that privacy and personal data need stronger protection.

This is why it is so important to study privacy and data protection, especially in the EU setting. Because of the GDPR, the Union has become de facto – if not also *de jure* – the most important global regulator of privacy.[2] What the EU does is now followed with keen interest, and occasional dread, all across the globe.

From an internal Union point of view, on the other hand, I feel that it is worthwhile studying the connection between the kind of legal personhood that is emerging in fundamental rights protection and the problems in solidarity and equality that the Union as a polity continues to face. It may just be that legal constructions of personhood are linked with certain understandings of community.

The critique developed in this book engages with the kinds of presuppositions about personhood that are embedded in privacy protection in the EU. The aim is not, therefore, to criticise privacy rights per se. Nor is the book proposing that European legislators or courts should protect privacy less. The aim is only to give an account of the preconditions that are at work in privacy protection, as regards legal understandings of personhood.

Questioning protection of privacy and personal data is controversial, and not very common in critical legal research.[3] Much more often, critically minded scholars tend simply to promote more privacy in an attempt to salvage values such as human dignity and freedom against either multinational industry interests or, say, the interests of governments to enhance security and control.[4] These views are acknowledged in this book and no attempt is made to undermine them. Nevertheless,

[2] The Brussels effect is arguably quite potent in this area of law. See Anu Bradford, 'The Brussels Effect' (2012) 107 *Northwestern University Law Review* 1–68.

[3] Nevertheless, in feminist legal theory this has been done. See e.g. Janice Richardson, *Law and the Philosophy of Privacy* (Oxon, New York: Routledge, 2016). For a general critique of rights and neoliberalism, see e.g. Susan Marks (ed.), *International Law on the Left: Re-Examining Marxist Legacies* (Cambridge: Cambridge University Press, 2008); or Samuel Moyn, *Not Enough: Human Rights in an Unequal World* (Cambridge, MA: Belknap Press, 2018).

[4] See e.g. Austin Sarat (ed.), *A World without Privacy: What Law Can and Should Do?* (Cambridge: Cambridge University Press, 2015); Viktor Mayer-Schönberger and Kenneth Cukier, *Big Data: A Revolution That Will Transform How We Live, Work, and Think* (New York: Hachette, Eamon Dolan/Mariner Books, 2014); or Daniel J. Solove, *Understanding Privacy* (Cambridge, MA: Harvard University Press, 2008) for views on what kind of privacy regulation is needed.

there is a need for greater in-depth analysis of the ways in which human beings are constructed through privacy rights.

The ideal way to organise the relationship between individuals and communities is the broader political problem involved in this research. This is an age-old issue that still today lurks behind the law. Differing answers make continual appearances in the form of legal questions that the European courts need to solve. In its own way, the book contributes to one of the fundamental debates in political and legal philosophy. It considers the relationship between the individual and the community by analysing some of the philosophical underpinnings of privacy and personal data law.

Main Objective: Deconstructing Private Personhood

A deconstructive gaze inspires this book. This kind of critical work on privacy has been done before, although not in as much detail. The starting point is an acknowledgement that privacy is not a pre-political space for individual freedom but a constituted notion that reproduces social power relations.[5]

Critical voices typically question the understanding of privacy as developed in the liberal paradigm. This liberal understanding is seen as: 'insufficient to grasp the forms of domination that emerge in the course of digital restructuring of interpersonal communication. Technological innovations are deeply entangled with socio-economic power relations and this raises questions about digital age privacy in a radical new way.'[6] The conditions of our social environment – including all the power relations we are entangled in – shape us, and they shape our privacy needs as well. Being embedded in a society, we may suffer domination even without knowing it but also, at times, contribute to dominating practices. Privacy rights are by no means a neutral instrument in all of this. They create social relations and are in turn created by them.

Following Marxist intuitions, one can see the legal right to privacy as genuinely ambivalent. Even though it may enable domination, the right to privacy can have emancipating and liberating functions, too. Few

[5] Sandra Seubert and Carlos Becker, 'The Culture Industry Revisited: Sociophilosophical Reflections on "Privacy" in the Digital Age' (2019) 45 *Philosophy and Social Criticism* 930–47 at 930.

[6] Seubert and Becker, 'The Culture Industry Revisited', 931.

critical theories, therefore, question the value of privacy altogether, nor will that be done here.

The main argument of the book is developed through a reading of case law from the ECJ in combination with an analysis of regulatory sources, especially the GDPR. Presuppositions of personhood portrayed in these are neither uniform nor unambivalent. Nevertheless, both the case law and the interpretations that can be made of the GDPR show certain tendencies towards individualist views. The book considers whether these developments in the law can pose a threat to community values, such as solidarity and equality.[7]

The philosophical roots of the study lie in the deconstruction of the subject in late-modern philosophy. Different ways of questioning subjectivity were developed by Michel Foucault in his hermeneutics of the subject, as well as by Jacques Derrida in his deconstruction of prevailing patterns of thought. Both philosophers' work is guided by a mistrust of liberalism and includes attempts to address the inequality-producing mechanisms of global capitalism.

This continental philosophical tradition forms the theoretical framework for the analysis undertaken in this book. However, it draws predominantly on contemporary political philosophy, namely the works of Jacques Rancière, Roberto Esposito and Jean-Luc Nancy, in order to scrutinise how the individualising practices of the self are becoming normalised by various aspects of privacy law. Nancy's thinking is especially valuable because it enables ways of conceptualising community without succumbing to unifying or totalitarian ideas. A pluralistic community, where rights are respected without individualising undertones, becomes possible in this philosophy.

Legal scholarship on the EU has lately evolved in new directions. In addition to doctrinal research on existing norms, their content and systematisation, it now encompasses approaches and methods acquired from social and human sciences. Additionally, a growing volume of critical legal research has begun to emerge. This book situates itself in this kind of scholarship, which exhibits disillusionment with the content and application of EU law, even though it does not question the integration project as such. The worry is that if the Union favours questionable views of personhood – views that are insufficiently

[7] For a similar approach, though more theoretical, see Einar Øverenget, 'Heidegger and Arendt against the Imperialism of Privacy' (1995) *Philosophy Today* 430–44.

recognised while nevertheless embedded in the law – it will not be able to fulfil its sociopolitical potential.

Several sociologists and philosophers have raised concerns with individualism and a heightened focus on the personal in Western societies. Richard Sennett, Zygmunt Bauman, Esposito, Rancière and Nancy belong to those who have undertaken fundamental work in this regard and are important for the research done here The book also engages with contemporary debates in EU legal theory. In this area, for instance, Alexander Somek has put forward arguments against individualism, although from a slightly different point of view. Arguably, however, not enough attention has been paid to the legal person that is being constructed in EU law.[8]

In the field of personal data protection, a thorough and critical evaluation of the politics of personhood is clearly needed. This area of law remains generally under-theorised, too. A lot of research is currently being done on the GDPR, but most of it does not analyse the GDPR's philosophical underpinnings or its sociopolitical outcomes. The focus is usually on doctrinal analysis of the instrument.

Critical legal research has strong roots in legal realism, as well as Marxism. Both traditions have provided inspiration for this book, too. It is indebted to them in many ways. However, the legacy of realism and Marxism is often incorporated into critical scholarship on EU law in ways that focus on the gap between the ideal and actual practice. Thus the critique concerns the ways in which law fails to live up to its promises, and falls short of delivering the good that it claims to.

This book, however, takes a slightly different approach. The aim is to deconstruct not only the practice, but the ideal, too. This is where the critique of individualism is located: both on the level of what the law produces, but also on the level of its promises. One of the main suggestions will be to show that the ideal of privacy, as it has been understood in liberal Western legal thinking, has its fundamental problems as well.

The book does not aim at promoting any normative claim. However, the critique of privacy rights will be situated within a normative framework in the last chapters of the book. By doing so, I will approach conclusions of an ethical or an ideological nature. The main arguments will end up with the thought that privacy rights are valuable because

[8] One notable exception being Loïc Azoulai, Ségolène Barbou des Places and Etienne Pataut (eds.), *Constructing the Person in EU Law: Rights, Roles, Identities* (Oxford: Hart Publishing, 2016).

they can protect our co-existence. This means, however, that their primary target should not be the immunisation of private individuals. Privacy is not valuable because it enables a life left in peace but because it protects lives lived in common.

I also suggest, after a careful reading of case law, that privacy rights should not be used to trump all other rights. Protection of people as social beings means that other rights need careful balancing in all cases. The weight of privacy claims requires evaluation on a scale of many values, not just individualist ones.

An Outline of EU Privacy Rights

Reading the more recent accounts of privacy, both legal and philosophical, one notices similarities between many of them. Regardless of various points of emphasis, most theorists tend to end up with the same conclusions: no definition of privacy is to be found, nor any one value that the right to privacy protects. Many writers nevertheless go on to claim that a more nuanced view is needed. Several scholars list all the different aspects of privacy that need to be taken into consideration in philosophy, political theory and law.

This book does not attempt such a task. It neither presupposes nor denies one theoretical definition of privacy. The book starts off with the legal material that is available and tries to conceptualise personhood as it emerges from that material.

The most important regulatory sources for privacy and personal data protection in Europe are the European Convention on Human Rights (ECHR), the EU Charter of Fundamental Rights (the Charter) and the General Data Protection Regulation (GDPR). The focus of this study is on EU law and, hence, the ECHR or its corresponding legal praxis are not studied in detail, even though interpretations by the European Court of Human Rights do play a role in the development of EU law as well.

Data protection, or informational privacy as it is sometimes called, is being regulated in new – and stronger – ways. The GDPR includes some significant changes to this area of law. Other legal reforms are also being made and show that questions of data protection traverse many areas of European society.[9]

[9] See e.g. the Police Directive (Directive (EU) 2016/680 of the European Parliament and of the Council of 27 April 2016 on the protection of natural persons with regard to the processing of personal data by competent authorities for the purposes of the prevention, investigation, detection or prosecution of criminal offences or the execution of criminal

The main primary law source at Union level is Article 16 of the Treaty on the Functioning of the European Union (TFEU), which gives the mandate to the Union to introduce regulation in data protection. Protection of privacy rights also has strong legal support in the Charter. In contrast to the ECHR,[10] the Charter includes separate provisions for protection of private and family life and for protection of personal data.[11]

According to Article 7 of the Charter, everyone has the right to respect for their private and family life, home and communications. Article 8, on the other hand, stipulates that everyone has the right to protection of personal data concerning them. Such data must be processed fairly for specified purposes and on the basis of the consent of the person concerned or some other legitimate basis laid down by law. Article 8 also states that everyone has the right of access to data that has been collected concerning them, and the right to have it rectified.

Regulation of privacy rights in the EU is a complex field partly because it incorporates EU law as well as older conceptions of privacy stemming from the Member States' constitutional systems. Complexities in the application of different rules derive especially from the fast pace with which the law has been changing. The GDPR is meant to function as *lex specialis* and therefore has wide application. Other instruments have been passed or are in the process of being passed to support and complement it. To complicate matters further, even though the GDPR is a regulation, many of its articles leave room for national implementation in the Member States, which results in slightly different legal regimes across Europe.

penalties, and on the free movement of such data, and repealing Council Framework Decision 2008/977/JHA, OJ 2016 No. L119, 4 May 2016). See also ePrivacy reform: Commission, 'Proposal for a Regulation of the European Parliament and of the Council concerning the respect for private life and the protection of personal data in electronic communications and repealing Directive 2002/58/EC (Regulation on Privacy and Electronic Communications)', COM (2017) 10 final; eEvidence: Commission, 'Proposal for a Regulation of the European Parliament and of the Council on European Production and Preservation Orders for electronic evidence in criminal matters', COM (2018) 225 final; etc., which are under preparation at the time of writing.

[10] The ECHR differs from the Charter in that it does not include a separate article that would protect personal data. Informational privacy, in many of its aspects, has been developed in the Strasbourg court's case law through interpretational devices.

[11] On the development of the right to personal data protection in the EU, see Gloria González Fuster, *The Emergence of Personal Data Protection as a Fundamental Right of the EU* (Cham: Springer, 2014).

The GDPR

Extensive data protection reform started in the EU in 2012 and the General Data Protection Regulation[12] became applicable in late May 2018. Although the GDPR did not completely revolutionise the field, bearing in mind that many of the main principles and rules include extensions or specifications of its preceding Data Protection Directive[13] (DPD), the GDPR did introduce new norms. The aim of the Regulation is to increase legal certainty through harmonisation and to afford more efficient protection for data subjects.

There are, of course, also economic purposes. The Regulation aims at safeguarding the free flow of personal data throughout the Union, thus enhancing the development of a strong single market. However, because of the many requirements that the Regulation places on processing personal data, it also shows genuine concern for fundamental rights, as well as an attempt to catch up with the law in action as developed by the ECJ.[14] It remains to be seen how the two goals of strengthening citizens' fundamental rights and facilitating business will operate in tandem, or collide, in future applications of the Regulation.

The legal nature of the Regulation is slightly complex. It includes elements of fundamental rights regulation and, when interpreted as such, many of its specifics will make sense. On the other hand, it also includes elements that resemble EU consumer law, for instance a strong emphasis on data subjects' control and consent. It also displays features

[12] Regulation (EU) 2016/679 of the European Parliament and of the Council, of 27 April 2016, on the protection of natural persons with regard to the processing of personal data and on the free movement of such data, and repealing Directive 95/46/EC (General Data Protection Regulation), OJ 2016 No. L119, 4 May 2016.

[13] Directive 95/46/EC of the European Parliament and of the Council of 24 October 1995 on the protection of individuals with regard to the processing of personal data and on the free movement of such data, OJ 1995 No. L281, 23 November 1995.

[14] The ECJ has for some years been very active in interpreting privacy and personal data protection cases in a manner that has strengthened their position as fundamental rights of the Union. Landmark cases, which we will discuss further on, include Case C-131/12, *Google Spain SL and Google Inc.* v. *Agencia Española de Protección de Datos (AEPD) and Mario Costeja González*, EU:C:2014:317; and Case C-362/14, *Maximillian Schrems* v. *Data Protection Commissioner*, EU:C:2015:650. In the latter case the court re-affirms its view that the Directive must be interpreted in light of the Charter: 'It should be recalled first of all that the provisions of Directive 95/46, inasmuch as they govern the processing of personal data liable to infringe fundamental freedoms, in particular the right to respect for private life, must necessarily be interpreted in the light of the fundamental rights guaranteed by the Charter', para. 38.

of EU competition law origins, such as administrative fines that can be ordered for significant breaches of personal data protection.

In essence, the Regulation works so that it lays down rules on the protection of natural persons with regard to the processing of personal data (the rights element) but it also expresses the need to allow for free movement of personal data (the internal market element).

'Personal data' is defined in a similar way as in the previous Directive. This definition has become commonplace in European personal data law and receives support from settled case law. Personal data means *any information relating to an identified or identifiable natural person.* The natural person is in this context called a 'data subject'. In order for data to be regarded as personal, it is enough that a data subject can be identified, directly or indirectly, for instance by reference to a name, an identification number, location data, an online identifier or to factors specific to physical, physiological, genetic, mental, economic, cultural or social identity.

The decisive factor for data to be regarded as personal, and for the GDPR to apply to its processing, is whether or not the data relates to an identified or identifiable individual.[15] Processing of such data is lawful according to the Regulation only under certain circumstances. These include, for instance, situations where the data subject has consented to processing, and situations where processing is necessary for some other reason that is specified in the Regulation.[16] Processing is therefore possible on grounds other than the data subject's consent but, also in these instances, there are transparency requirements. The subject has a right to know what data is processed. In a nutshell the general idea is the same as Warren and Brandeis formulated in their groundbreaking definition of a legal right to privacy:[17] individuals shall be granted the right to govern information about themselves.[18]

[15] Art. 4.

[16] Art. 6.

[17] See Samuel D. Warren and Louis D. Brandeis, 'The Right to Privacy' (1890) 4 *Harvard Law Review* 193–220.

[18] Whether the Regulation will be an effective instrument in terms of protecting individuals against gathering of Big Data is debatable. Big Data refers to data that is gathered and processed in mass quantities combining various kinds of information and analysed by computer algorithms. The individual is not central to this process. For a critical account see e.g. Bart van der Sloot, 'Do Data Protection Rules Protect the Individual and Should They? An Assessment of the Proposed General Data Protection Regulation' (2014) 4 *International Data Privacy Law* 307–25.

When personal data protection is interpreted as a fundamental right, which is what the EU Court often does, then interpretation of the GDPR follows a rather clear logic. Considering whether an action is allowed or not, the starting point is to decide if it falls under the material and territorial scope of the Regulation. Both of these are wide.

The second step in applying the rules requires an analysis of whether the processed data amounts to personal data. Here again the definition is wide. If any natural person can potentially be identified from the data, then the GDPR applies. If that is the case, then processing of that data is only allowed in accordance with the rules laid down in the GDPR.

When the Regulation applies in a situation, it stipulates that data may only be processed on lawful grounds. These are consent, contract, legal obligation, protection of vital interests of the data subject or of another natural person, public interest or exercise of official authority and legitimate interest. Even though data is processed on one of these grounds, which are listed in Article 6, the Regulation still requires processing to be done in certain ways. These are stipulated as the basic principles of data protection, which include for instance data minimisation and purpose limitation. These principles correspond with the rights of the data subject towards controllers and processors, that is, the right to data portability, access, erasure and so on. Read in this way, the Regulation forms a logical and - mostly - systematic whole.

The ECJ's Interpretation Practices

Arguably, the European Court of Justice has played a major role in shaping data protection into a proper fundamental right - a right that is enforced in both the private and the public sectors.[19] In prominent cases, the court has balanced data protection against other rights and consequently strengthened data protection. Moreover, other landmark cases have resulted in more thorough definitions of the different actors' duties and responsibilities vis-à-vis individuals.

[19] See e.g. Joined Cases C-465/00, C-138/01 and C-139/01, *Rechnungshof and Others* v. *Österreichischer Rundfunk and Others* EU:C:2003:294, Case C-212/13, *František Ryneš* v. *Úřad pro ochranu osobních údajů*, EU:C:2014:2428 and Case C-398/15, *Camera di Commercio, Industria, Artigianato e Agricoltura di Lecce* v. *Salvatore Manni*, EU:C:2017:197.

Before examining the Court's reasoning, a few words might be helpful on the interpretative difficulties pertaining to the old DPD as well as the current Regulation. As is well established in EU legal scholarship, the EU forms a legal system *sui generis*, and interpretation of that system, as performed by the EU Courts, follows its own logic.[20] In order to understand the outcome of a specific case, it is thus necessary to know the methods of reasoning used by the ECJ. In its case law, contextual, teleological and systemic arguments tend to rank higher than semantic ones.[21] Hence, when interpreting data protection rules, it is critical to determine the context, as well as the *telos*, or purpose, of the legal instrument being interpreted.

What, then, is the context?[22] The most evident context for data protection seems to be fundamental rights protection. Secondary law, such as the DPD and now the GDPR, add detailed provisions on the protection of a right expressed in primary law.[23] The ECJ has held that the provisions of the DPD and now the GDPR, inasmuch as they govern the processing of personal data liable to infringe fundamental freedoms, in particular the right to respect for private life, must necessarily be interpreted in the light of the fundamental rights guaranteed by the Charter.[24] Hence, it is the Charter that guides interpretation of secondary legislation in this field.

[20] See e.g. Joxerramon Bengoetxea, *The Legal Reasoning of the European Court of Justice: Towards a European Jurisprudence* (Oxford: Clarendon Press, 1993); Gunnar Beck, *The Legal Reasoning of the Court of Justice of the EU* (Oxford: Hart Publishing, 2012); and Suvi Sankari, *European Court of Justice Legal Reasoning in Context* (Groningen: Europa Law Publishing, 2013).

[21] Koen Lenaerts and Jose A. Gutierrez-Fons, 'To Say What the Law of the EU Is: Methods of Interpretation and the European Court of Justice' (2014) 20 *Columbia Journal of European Law* 3–61; and Elina Paunio and Susanna Lindroos-Hovinheimo, 'Taking Language Seriously: An Analysis of Linguistic Reasoning and Its Implications in EU Law' (2010) *European Law Journal* 395–416.

[22] Contexts are notoriously difficult to define, but it is possible to argue for the choice of one primary context over another. On the indeterminacy of contexts, see e.g. Jacques Derrida, *Limited Inc* (Evanston, IL: Northwestern University Press, 1988), p. 136.

[23] See Hielke Hijmans, *The European Union as Guardian of Internet Privacy: The Story of Art 16 TFEU* (Cham, Heidelberg, New York, Dordrecht and London: Springer, 2016), p. 66. According to Hijmans, the right to privacy represents a normative value, whereas the right to data protection includes a legal structure that enables individuals to claim that data should be processed fairly and lawfully. Hence, privacy may be understood as a principle-based right and data protection as a rule-based right.

[24] See judgments in Joined Cases C-465/00, C-138/01 and C-139/01, Rechnungshof and Others v., *Österreichischer Rundfunk and Others*, EU:C:2003:294, para. 68; Case C-131/12, *Google Spain and Google*, EU:C:2014:317, para. 68; and Case C-212/13, *Ryneš*, EU:C:2014:2428, para. 29.

The purpose of the legislation has repeatedly been expressed by the ECJ as a leading interpretational principle. During the time of the Directive, the Court announced that 'according to settled case law of the Court, the provisions of a directive must be interpreted in the light of the aims pursued by the directive and the system which it establishes'.[25] This statement was recently repeated by the Court in the *Buivids* judgment from 2019.[26]

But the *telos* of data protection is a tricky question. Arguably, it is the issue that lies at the heart of some of the most difficult interpretation situations concerning the GDPR. Generally, when legal rules are unclear, or their applicability to the facts of a case is uncertain, the aim of the rules can help to guide the interpreter towards a sound interpretation. If the context is fundamental rights protection, it would be reasonable to define the *telos* accordingly. However, as already pointed out, the GDPR (just like the DPD) has *two* aims: to protect individuals' right to protection of their personal data *and* to ensure the free flow of data and thus promote the functioning of the internal market. The tension between these two aims, which can be in competition, is inscribed in the text of the GDPR. It causes what Orla Lynskey has called the 'split personality' of data protection regulation.[27]

The ECJ has nevertheless eased the burden of legal decision makers by developing case law in a coherent and mostly predictable way.[28] It has made choices that can, at times, be seen as creative, but have nevertheless clarified the law and increased legal certainty. This it has done by focusing on the context – data protection as a fundamental right – and thereby prioritising the *telos* of protecting individuals' data rights over the free flow of data. This is the background against which the ECJ's case law may become easier to understand.

Not all of the Court's case law concerns grand issues. In many judgments, the argumentation revolves around technicalities rather than

[25] Case C-73/07, *Tietosuojavaltuutettu* v. *Satakunnan Markkinapörssi and Satamedia Oy*, EU:C:2008:727, para. 51 and the case law cited.

[26] Case C-345/17, *Sergejs Buivids*, EU:C:2019:122, para. 49.

[27] Orla Lynskey, 'From Market-Making Tool to Fundamental Right: The Role of the Court of Justice in Data Protection's Identity Crisis', in Serge Gutwirth et al. (eds.), *European Data Protection: Coming of Age* (Dordrecht: Springer, 2013), pp. 59–84.

[28] For a critique of current data protection law, see Audrey Guinchard, who recently argued that the ECJ has not been successful in its proportionality analyses. Audrey Guinchard, 'Taking Proportionality Seriously: The Use of Contextual Integrity for a More Informed and Transparent Analysis in EU Data Protection Law' (2018) 24 *European Law Journal* 434–57.

value judgements or politico-ethical choices. Hence, the cases can be divided into two types: definitions cases and balancing cases. I propose this distinction in order to highlight how the Court has argued, what features it has chosen to focus on, and in what way it has solved the legal questions. The Court makes a case into the case it becomes, emphasising for instance a fair balance of rights or a new definition of data protection details.

Several judgments, such as the early but significant *Lindqvist*[29] and the more tech-related *Breyer*,[30] for instance, can be seen as definitions cases. *Digital Rights Ireland*[31] also falls into this general category. The main issues that the Court decided to consider in these were definitional. The Court considered that the central questions in these cases concerned the meaning of certain concepts in the Directive, or the correct understanding of the rules on scope and applicability. In these definitions cases, judgments usually aim at clarifying the interpretation of specific articles in the legal instruments.

Balancing cases, on the other hand, are cases where the ECJ clearly recognises the need to balance data protection, and sometimes privacy more generally, against other rights and freedoms.[32] In these judgments, the main focus of the Court's reasoning lies not in classifying, interpreting and clarifying legal texts, but rather in evaluating the appropriate strength of privacy rights compared to other rights and values.[33]

Google Spain[34] is a prime example of a balancing case, even though the judgment also defines certain aspects of controllership. In *Google Spain*, the focal question was whether a person's right to be forgotten could override the public's right to information, a clear balancing exercise

[29] Case C-101/01, *Criminal proceedings against Bodil Lindqvist*. EU:C:2003:596.

[30] Case C-582/14, *Patrick Breyer* v. *Bundesrepublik Deutschland*, EU:C:2016:779.

[31] Joined Cases C-293/12 and C-594/12, *Digital Rights Ireland Ltd* v. *Minister for Communications, Marine and Natural Resources and Others and Kärntner Landesregierung and Others*, EU: C:2014:238.

[32] An intriguing discussion on balancing in data protection law has been published in the *European Data Protection Law Review*. See Raphael Gellert, 'On Risk, Balancing, and Data Protection: A Response to van der Sloot' (2017) 3 *European Data Protection Law Review* 180–6; and Bart van der Sloot, 'Ten Questions about Balancing' (2017) 3 *European Data Protection Law Review* 187–94.

[33] Occasionally these cases also revolve around the idea of the essence of rights. An example is Case C-362/14, *Schrems*, EU:C:2015:650. For analysis, see e.g. Maja Brkan, 'The Concept of Essence of Fundamental Rights in the EU Legal Order: Peeling the Onion to Its Core' (2018) 14 *European Constitutional Law Review* 332–68.

[34] Case C-131/12, *Google Spain and Google*, EU:C:2014:317.

where privacy was ultimately considered to outweigh other rights. Another example of a rather straightforward balancing judgment is *Bavarian Lager*,[35] where the Court compared the values of privacy against transparency.

Both types of case are of interest in our investigation into the private person. It is my starting point that both give evidence as to the ways in which the person is constructed in privacy protection. Of course, technical details may occasionally be less rewarding for this undertaking, but sometimes they, too, reveal interesting features of how the Court sees the person. Balancing cases tend to give more immediate evidence of the aims and values that the Court emphasises in its interpretive endeavours. But both kinds of cases do presuppose some kind of person as the objective of privacy protection. And that person can have many different features.

Two Examples: *Wirtschaftsakademie* and *Jehovan Todistajat*

The GDPR became applicable in May 2018. During the summer of 2018, the Court gave two judgments that have had an influence on various issues in data protection law. The first was the *Wirtschaftsakademie* judgment,[36] which provides important clarification of the responsibilities of different data processing parties with regard to individuals' rights.

The outcome of the case was that organisations providing services via a Facebook fan page are co-responsible for data that is processed by Facebook. Conversely, the social media platform was found to be responsible for (at least some of) the processing it performs at the request of another party. The questions were problematic not least because they concern the gathering of information with the help of cookies, which is a much-debated issue in data protection.

The ECJ delivered its second post-GDPR judgment, *Jehovan todistajat*,[37] soon afterwards. Here, the Court was faced with the task of analysing door-to-door data collection by preachers from the Jehovah's Witness Community. This case concerned a more old-fashioned scenario devoid of complicated technological issues. Nevertheless, here too the case

[35] Case C-28/08 P, *European Commission* v. *The Bavarian Lager Co. Ltd.* EU:C:2010:378.

[36] Case C-210/16, *Unabhängiges Landeszentrum für Datenschutz Schleswig-Holstein* v. *Wirtschaftsakademie Schleswig-Holstein GmbH*, EU:C:2018:388.

[37] Case C-25/17, *Tietosuojavaltuutettu, intervening parties Jehovan todistajat – uskonnollinen yhdyskunta*, EU:C:2018:551.

raised difficult questions about data protection and associated responsibilities. The two rulings provide an introduction to the recent reasoning tactics of the court. After having looked at these it is possible to move forward to an in-depth analysis of privacy constructions in EU law.[38]

While the two decisions differ in some respects and deal with partly different questions, the general lesson that can be learned from both is that the ECJ takes data protection very seriously. In both cases, it sets the tone for GDPR interpretation in a privacy-friendly key.

The judgments in *Jehovan todistajat* and *Wirtschaftsakademie* still concern the old Directive. Both deal in their respective ways with the definition of the 'controller', who is the entity responsible for ensuring that data protection rules are followed.[39] However, the way personal data is gathered, processed and stored is different in the two cases, as are many other facts.

The architecture of the DPD was similar to the Regulation now applicable: in order for the rules of data protection to apply, the situation must be of a certain kind. Firstly, the data being processed must be personal data. Secondly, the processing of such data, that is, collection, storage, movement or even deletion, can only be performed on certain conditions and in certain ways. Moreover, it is necessary in every data processing situation to ascertain which party bears the main burden for ensuring that individuals' personal data is protected.

The parties handling personal data can occupy the role of controller, which is the technical term for the party who bears the main responsibility for data protection. However, they can also occupy the role of processor, who is responsible in a more limited capacity. The definition of these roles is key to understanding data protection rules. It needs to be clear in the myriad forms in which personal data is collected, stored, used, sold, exchanged and deleted in various technological situations.

[38] The discussion of these two cases is based upon an article by Susanna Lindroos-Hovinheimo, 'Who Controls Our Data? The Legal Reasoning of the European Court of Justice in Wirtschaftsakademie Schleswig-Holstein and Tietosuojavaltuutettu v Jehovan todistajat' (2019) 28 *Information & Communications Technology Law* 225–38.

[39] The question of who should carry the responsibility for data protection in complex networks of data flows is extremely significant also because the GDPR introduced the system of administrative fines. It will become increasingly important to be able to define who the liable party is when data protection breaches are considered.

Personal Data on Facebook Fan Pages

The main legal issue in *Wirtschaftsakademie* concerns the distribution of responsibility in a situation where many different actors participate in processing data. Who is the data controller in these scenarios? Both the Directive and the Regulation have similar rules on controllership. The main rule is simple: the controller is the party who decides how processing is performed. According to Article 4 of the GDPR, 'controller' means the natural or legal person, public authority, agency or other body that, alone or jointly with others, determines the purposes and means of the processing of personal data. Of particular relevance to the case at hand is that the controller may operate 'alone or jointly with others'.

The controller can, moreover, decide to outsource processing activities to other parties. These are called processors. According to said Article 4, 'processor' means a natural or legal person, public authority, agency or other body that processes personal data on behalf of the controller. From this definition, it follows that a processor acts in accordance with the orders of the controller. If processors were to perform their own independent data processing as well, they would become controllers for that processing.

It is vital to discern and distinguish the roles in which each party operates because it is the controller who bears a larger part of the responsibility for ensuring that personal data is protected. This is emphasised throughout the GDPR but is especially evident in Article 24, which defines the responsibility of the controller.[40] The protection of individuals' privacy is constructed in such a manner that the person ('data subject') and the controller form the primary relationship that data protection rules are intended to regulate.[41] This idea is prominent throughout data protection law.

Even though the rules concerning the responsibilities of controllers are relatively clear in both the Directive and the Regulation, the same cannot be said of real-life situations. Today, data processing occurs in highly complex and (for lawyers at least) technologically obscure networks, where a large number of operators do various things with data. European Union legislation recognises that situations may occur where

[40] Article 24 stipulates, among other things, that the controller must implement appropriate technical and organisational measures to ensure and to be able to demonstrate that processing is performed in accordance with the Regulation.

[41] Also the processor has responsibility for its own operations, under e.g. Art. 28 GDPR.

data is processed by many controllers and processors simultaneously. Nonetheless, the legal definition and classification of such labyrinthine data flows is challenging, and it is for this purpose that the Court's decision in *Wirtschaftsakademie* is useful.

The parties in the German proceedings were the data protection authority of Schleswig-Holstein and the private company Wirtschaftsakademie Schleswig-Holstein. The company's Facebook fan page offered educational services, but neither Wirtschaftsakademie nor Facebook informed visitors to the page that Facebook, by means of cookies, collected and subsequently processed personal data concerning them. Wirtschaftsakademie nonetheless argued that it was not responsible for the processing performed by Facebook. The dispute found its way to the Bundesverwaltungsgericht (Federal Administrative Court), which decided to refer several questions to the EU Court for a preliminary ruling.

Advocate General Bot, when considering the case, focused on the fact that cookies were used in data processing. Hence, at the beginning of his opinion, he located the case in a particular context:

> The background to the present case is the phenomenon known as 'web tracking', which consists in the observation and analysis of the behaviour of Internet users for commercial and marketing purposes. Web tracking helps identify the centres of interest of Internet users, through observation of their browsing habits. This is referred to as behavioural web tracking and it is usually carried out with the aid of cookies.[42]

The Advocate General observed that web tracking was not completely prohibited by the Directive. Nevertheless, the collection of user information for statistics and marketing purposes needed to fulfil certain conditions in order to be compatible with the Directive. The Advocate General drew the clear conclusion that this kind of data processing was forbidden unless the data subject consented.[43] The new Regulation does not introduce differences in this matter, although it does include more definition on the criteria for consent.

According to the Advocate General, the next step in deciding the case was to identify the controller.[44] The questions that were referred to the

[42] Case C-210/16, *Wirtschaftsakademie Schleswig-Holstein*, Opinion of AG Bot, EU:C:2017:796, para. 4.

[43] Case C-210/16, *Wirtschaftsakademie Schleswig-Holstein*, Opinion of AG Bot, EU:C:2017:796, para. 9.

[44] Case C-210/16, *Wirtschaftsakademie Schleswig-Holstein*, Opinion of AG Bot, EU:C:2017:796, para. 11.

ECJ presupposed that Wirtschaftsakademie *was not* the controller for the operations performed by Facebook. The Advocate General, however, disagreed with this. His interpretation, which has significant ramifications for future application of data protection law, was that Wirtschaftsakademie and Facebook should be regarded as *mutually responsible* for the protection of data: 'Wirtschaftsakademie must, in my opinion, be regarded as jointly responsible for the phase of the data processing which consists in the collection by Facebook of personal data.'[45]

This interpretation may seem rather radical given the Advocate General's acknowledgement that Wirtschaftsakademie was primarily a user of Facebook – a fan page administrator. Nevertheless, he concluded that such a fan page administrator can also be regarded as responsible for collection of personal data performed by Facebook.[46]

The Advocate General thus argued for a broad definition of the concept of 'controller', the most important reason being that such a broad definition would ensure effective and complete protection of data subjects. Here the context and the *telos* of data protection law were mobilised. In deciding which party or parties are controllers, it was thus necessary to consider what interpretation would provide maximum protection for individuals.

When considering the responsibilities of the parties, the decisive factor was not agreement that might have existed between the two companies; rather, it was their actual roles. The administrator of the fan page played a predominant role in determining how data was processed by Facebook. It participated in determining the means and purposes of data processing and therefore had de facto influence over it. Moreover, the idea that both parties were controllers was supported by the fact that Wirtschaftsakademie and Facebook pursued closely related objectives. Wirtschaftsakademie wished to obtain statistics that required the processing of personal data, and that same data processing also enabled Facebook to target the advertising that it publishes on its network.[47]

45 Case C-210/16, *Wirtschaftsakademie Schleswig-Holstein*, Opinion of AG Bot, EU:C:2017:796, para. 42.
46 Case C-210/16, *Wirtschaftsakademie Schleswig-Holstein*, Opinion of AG Bot, EU:C:2017:796, para. 53.
47 Case C-210/16, *Wirtschaftsakademie Schleswig-Holstein*, Opinion of AG Bot, EU:C:2017:796, paras. 53–60.

The conclusion was that both companies shared responsibility for the data processing performed by Facebook. However, the Advocate General nonetheless observed that 'the existence of shared responsibility does not imply equal responsibility. On the contrary, the various controllers may be involved in the processing of personal data at different stages and to differing degrees.'[48] This point is significant and may prove especially important in future cases.

The Advocate General's opinion may be seen as a clear indication of teleological interpretation. It corresponds to the aim of protecting individuals' personal data, which is the primary purpose of the Directive as well as the Regulation. In so doing, he follows earlier interpretations by the Court. Hence, his reasoning also reveals an attempt to add coherence to a rapidly evolving area of EU law. The most important principle in this area is the strong protection of individuals' data, which may often override other interests. There is, however, little balancing to be seen in the Advocate General's opinion. The definition of controllership is developed explicitly to ensure the protection of individuals.

The Court agreed with the Advocate General on most issues. However, it began by defining the context of the case as explicitly that of fundamental rights protection. Where the Advocate General had begun his opinion with a discussion of cookies, the Court commenced its analysis by arguing that fundamental rights and freedoms were at the heart of the case: '[I]t must be recalled that, as is apparent from Article 1(1) and recital 10 of Directive 95/46, the directive aims to ensure a high level of protection of the fundamental rights and freedoms of natural persons, in particular their right to privacy, with respect to the processing of personal data.'[49] As for the responsibility of the two companies, the Court agreed with the Advocate General: they were jointly responsible. The fact that an administrator of a fan page uses a platform provided by Facebook in order to benefit from its services did not exempt the administrator from the obligation to ensure protection of personal data. The Court also noted in passing that fan pages hosted on Facebook could also be visited by non-Facebook users without a user account on that social network. In these instances, the fan page administrator's responsibility for processing personal data may be even

[48] Case C-210/16, *Wirtschaftsakademie Schleswig-Holstein*, Opinion of AG Bot, EU:C:2017:796, para. 75.

[49] Case C-210/16, *Wirtschaftsakademie Schleswig-Holstein*, EU:C:2018:388, para. 26.

greater, as merely visiting the homepage automatically triggers the processing of their personal data.

The Court concluded, as did the Advocate General, that the existence of joint responsibility does not necessarily imply equal responsibility. Both operators may be responsible, but in different ways and to different degrees because the 'operators may be involved at different stages of that processing of personal data and to different degrees, so that the level of responsibility of each of them must be assessed with regard to all the relevant circumstances of the particular case'.[50]

In the reasoning of the Court, the strongest argument for the conclusion of joint responsibility was that it ensured complete protection of rights, the idea being that if both operators were not considered responsible in such a situation, gaps might appear in the protection of individuals' rights and freedoms. Hence, broad definitions of controller, as well as the broad application of joint controllership, advance the *telos* of data protection law.

Following the typology above, it is evident that *Wirtschaftsakademie* is predominantly a definitions case, as very little balancing occurred either in the Advocate General's or in the Court's reasoning. The Court's analysis was first conceptualised with the clear purpose of protecting data subjects' rights, and a definition of the various operators' roles and responsibilities was made within that framework. Nonetheless, even though the case can be classed as a definitions case, it is by no means only an insignificant technical case. On the contrary, through its definitions of key concepts, the Court drew important lines that affect the legal relationship among individuals, companies and social media service providers.

However, if the Court had considered the balancing of individuals' rights against the interests of the operators, its reasoning could have been even more helpful for data protection lawyers. Hence, it is still unclear when and how operators' interests may override any of the personal data rights established by the Directive and the Regulation.

The Court's reasoning in *Wirtschaftsakademie Schleswig-Holstein* is not particularly extensive.[51] Instead, the judgment is concise and the analysis follows a clear and logical form. Moreover, it conforms to the Advocate General's views on many issues. As such, the judgment helps

[50] Case C-210/16, *Wirtschaftsakademie Schleswig-Holstein*, EU:C:2018:388, para. 43.

[51] For analysis, see also Nicolas Blanc, 'Wirtschaftsakademie Schleswig-Holstein: Towards a Joint Responsibility of Facebook Fan Page Administrators for Infringements to European Data Protection Law' (2018) 4 *European Data Protection Law Review* 120–6.

clarify the way the concept of 'controller' and the idea of joint controllership should be understood in future cases, and the result is satisfying in this respect. In this judgment, as in many preceding it, data subjects' fundamental right to informational privacy is the compass by which data processing rules are to be navigated.

Both the Advocate General and the Court itself began their reasoning by defining the context of the case. The context then led to the choice and definition of the legal issues to be solved. Only some of the questions posed to the Court were discussed in detail, and the Court also disagreed with the referring court's understanding of the roles of the operators. Through these choices, the Court delivered a judgment on the issues that it deemed important.

The judgment is interesting in the light of current political pressures. Facebook and social media giants more generally are occasionally seen as the most pressing privacy threat, perhaps with good reason. Scandal after scandal seems to show that these companies cannot be trusted and should be strongly regulated. Nevertheless, the Court seems relatively immune to such fears, as it clearly stated that Facebook was not to be held solely responsible for the data that it processed. Instead, companies that use Facebook's services are also liable for the data processing that Facebook performs.

Jehovan Todistajat: Religious Communities Are Not Exempt from Data Protection Regulation

Next, we shall look at the *Jehovan todistajat* ruling, which is also a Grand Chamber decision. The main issue is very similar to that of *Wirtschaftsakademie*: the scope of protection of personal data and the actors responsible for that protection. Both cases serve as an introduction to the logic of data protection law in the EU. Through them, we see how the law works in two rather different real-life scenarios. It becomes apparent that data protection issues encompass all areas of our lives, an observation that is supported by the other cases read throughout this book.

The *Jehovan todistajat* case concerns the Jehovah's Witnesses, a religious community that preaches door-to-door. Members of the community gather notes about the people that they have visited, with the data consisting, among other things, of the names and addresses of those contacted as well as information concerning their religious beliefs and their family circumstances. This information is collected as a memory aid and is stored in order to be retrieved for another visit. This is done without the knowledge or the consent of the persons concerned.

The religious community was the defendant in this case, where the main proceedings took place in Finland. The national Data Protection Supervisor (*Tietosuojavaltuutettu*) was the applicant. According to the referring court, the case required consideration of the rights to both privacy and personal data protection and also freedom of religion and association as guaranteed by the Charter and the European Convention for the Protection of Human Rights and Fundamental Freedoms and by the Finnish Constitution. In its decision, however, the ECJ paid little attention to freedom of religion.

The first two questions concerned the scope of application of the Data Protection Directive. Of particular relevance was whether the activity of door-to-door preaching could be considered a purely personal or household activity and thereby outside the scope of application of the Directive. Such a household exemption is also included in the new Regulation. In turn, questions three and four, which were relevant if the Directive was to be applied, concerned the definition of controller, as the referring court was unsure whether the Jehovah's Witnesses Community should be regarded as a controller of the data processing.

According to the household exemption in Article 3(2) of the DPD, the Directive does not apply to the processing of personal data performed by a natural person in the course of a purely personal or household activity. Hence, if the data collection performed by the Jehovah's Witnesses Community or its preachers had been seen as a purely personal activity, as suggested by the defendant, the data protection rules in the Directive would not have applied at all. Here, the religious circumstances of the case make it particular, as, in effect, the ECJ had to decide whether the fact that the data had been collected in a *preaching situation* was relevant.

The ECJ noted that personal data was collected by members of the Jehovah's Witnesses Community with the intention of spreading the faith. Therefore, data collection from preaching door-to-door occurred outside the private setting of the community. Furthermore, according to the facts of the case before the Court, some of the data collected by the members of the community was sent to the congregations, which compiled lists from the data of persons who no longer wished to receive visits. Thus, the Court observed that in the course of their preaching, community members had made at least some of the data collected accessible to a potentially unlimited number of persons.[52] In other words, the data had not remained within any household.

The Court also stated that although door-to-door preaching activities were protected by Article 10(1) of the Charter as an expression of faith, this did not imply that the activity had an exclusively personal or household character.[53] Thus, the court concluded that the household exemption did not apply in this case.[54]

On the basis of this reasoning, as well as on certain more technical considerations concerning the way the community had filed the data, the court held that the Directive applied to the activities of the Jehovah's Witnesses. Therefore all the data protection rules and principles of the Directive needed to be respected in regard to the data processing activities. However, the Court still needed to decide which party was responsible for the data processing. The third question posed by the referring court asked whether a religious community may be regarded as a controller in respect of processing performed by its members. The religious community claimed that only individual members who engaged in preaching had access to the data that they gathered.

Here the Court's argumentation centred on whether the Jehovah's Witnesses Community could be considered a controller only if it had taken specific measures, such as the issuing of written instructions or orders about the collection of data. Here, the answer was no. The community was assigned controller status because the purpose of door-to-door preaching was to achieve the aims of the community. Moreover, the Court paid attention to the fact that preaching was de facto organised, co-ordinated and encouraged by the community.[55] Thus, whether the community had provided members with specific guidelines or orders was not decisive.

[52] Case C-25/17, *Tietosuojavaltuutettu, intervening parties Jehovan todistajat – uskonnollinen yhdyskunta*, EU:C:2018:551, paras. 44–5.

[53] The defining case for interpreting the household exemption is *Lindqvist* from 2003, Case C-101/01, *Lindqvist* EU:C:2003:596. Advocate General Mengozzi engages in an interesting comparison between *Lindqvist* and *Jehovan todistajat*. Funnily enough, the facts in *Lindqvist* also happened to have a religious connection. See Opinion of Advocate General Mengozzi delivered on 1 February 2018. Case C-25/17, *Tietosuojavaltuutettu, intervening parties Jehovan todistajat – uskonnollinen yhdyskunta*, EU:C:2018:57, Opinion of AG Mengozzi, para. 34.

[54] Case C-25/17, *Tietosuojavaltuutettu, intervening parties Jehovan todistajat – uskonnollinen yhdyskunta*, EU:C:2018:551, para. 51.

[55] Case C-25/17, *Tietosuojavaltuutettu, intervening parties Jehovan todistajat – uskonnollinen yhdyskunta*, EU:C:2018:551, paras. 70–1.

The Court referred to *Wirtschaftsakademie Schleswig-Holstein* and repeated the formula developed there: through a broad definition of the concept of 'controller', effective and complete protection of persons can be ensured. This functional interpretation of controller status quite naturally led to the conclusion that both the community and the members were to be regarded as controllers and thus jointly responsible for processing data. While leaving the referring court to verify the specific circumstances, the Court ultimately held that a religious community was a controller jointly with its members who engage in preaching door-to-door if the community encouraged, co-ordinated and organised the activity, even if the community did not have access to the data.[56] The existence of joint responsibility, however, does not necessarily imply equal responsibility. Thus, in this case too, it was necessary to assess the level of responsibility of each party with regard to all the relevant circumstances.[57]

According to the definitions versus balancing typology, it seems clear that *Jehovan todistajat* is a rather clear-cut definitions case. This is remarkable for two reasons: firstly, there were no difficult technological solutions for the Court to untangle, only notes made with pen and paper. This was not a complex, high-profile platform capitalism case. Nevertheless, the case demonstrated that challenging data protection issues can arise in quite mundane circumstances. Moreover, the Court found it necessary to deliver a well-argued decision – in Grand Chamber no less – on what data protection law required in the situation.

Secondly, it is worth noting that the case *could have become a balancing case* if the Court had so wished. As it was, the judgment contained little discussion on freedom of thought, conscience or religion, as defined in Article 10 of the Charter. Nor was the Court overly concerned with the autonomy of religious organisations, which is protected under Article 17 TFEU. However, the Court did mention, in passing, that a religious community's responsibility as a controller could not be challenged by appealing to the principle of the organisational autonomy of religious communities. This is because the universal obligation to comply with EU law on the protection of personal data cannot be regarded as interference in the organisational autonomy of such communities.[58] Hence,

[56] Case C-25/17, *Tietosuojavaltuutettu, intervening parties Jehovan todistajat – uskonnollinen yhdyskunta*, EU:C:2018:551, paras. 73, 75.

[57] Case C-25/17, *Tietosuojavaltuutettu, intervening parties Jehovan todistajat – uskonnollinen yhdyskunta*, EU:C:2018:551, paras. 66–7.

[58] Case C-25/17, *Tietosuojavaltuutettu, intervening parties Jehovan todistajat – uskonnollinen yhdyskunta*, EU:C:2018:551, para. 74.

the Court placed little importance on whether data is processed in relation to religious activities; data protection rules apply just as they would in any other activity. Consequently, no real balancing between data protection and religious rights occurred in the Court's ruling.

The Court did not, for instance, consider whether promulgation or maintenance of a faith or religious belief was hindered by the need of all religious communities and preachers to comply with data protection rules – such considerations seemed more or less irrelevant in the eyes of the Court. This is noteworthy because it demonstrates the strong protection currently enjoyed by data protection in the Union. Thus, even though the GDPR does not apply to every activity, its scope is extensive indeed.

This judgment continues the Court's previous line of reasoning, upheld by legislators when drafting the GDPR, that the context in which data processing occurs – be it for commercial or other purposes – plays a minor role. Indeed, in this case, one could argue that the Court's argumentation would have been little different if the controllers had been companies or any other kind of organisations. Hence, the Court solidified existing data protection rules by delivering a judgment that was consistent with previous interpretations. Consequently, the judgment can be seen to add legal certainty.

Nonetheless, the reasoning of the Court fails to address a number of matters. For instance, by not engaging in a rigorous balancing of rights, which this case invited the Court to do, the Court avoided the most difficult issue: how far does the Directive and now the Regulation take data protection? And how should the aim of data protection be balanced with other interests and other rights?

Jehovan todistajat is an intriguing case because it includes a conflict between *two rights to private life*: the right to religious freedom or the freedom of religious organisations to operate, and the right to protection of personal data. Without engaging in any proper balancing, the Court held that religious freedom was still protected in the EU and was not infringed upon by the requirement that religious communities process data in accordance with data protection rules. Such an interpretation is by no means the only possible one. However, it clearly demonstrates the strength of the far more recent privacy right, namely the right to protection of personal data. Thus we see that even if this were a balancing case, it would not necessarily involve one right being weighed against another; instead, it could equally involve the collision of one aspect of a right with another aspect of the same right. In the EU today, it is likely that if one of these aspects is personal data protection, the Court tends to deem it the strongest.

What the two judgments show is that the general trend in EU law points towards strong data protection. The EU Court has become one of the main players in this development, although certainly not the only one. In both *Wirtschaftsakademie Schleswig-Holstein* and *Tietosuojavaltuutettu* v. *Jehovan todistajat*, it upheld its previous interpretations and continued on an already established route. The judgments themselves are therefore unsurprising. Nevertheless, their predictability in a situation where the law has recently changed is a reason to consider them noteworthy.

Courts, the Law and the Impossibility of Neutrality

All the DPD definitions upon which the Court has delivered judgments have tended to be broad, and these recent judgments are no exception. 'Personal data' and 'controller' are just a few of the concepts that are defined in broad terms in the interpretation practice of the Court, thereby granting data protection rules a very wide scope. This line of interpretation has been palpable for quite some time now, and, for that reason alone the outcome of these cases is predictable. Furthermore, in the *Jehovan todistajat* judgment, the Court also continued its habit of narrowly interpreting exceptions, in this instance the household exemption.

Furthermore, both cases indicate that a clear need existed to clarify the main definitions of data protection law, and the main issue involved is indeed important: the scope of protection of personal data and who is responsible for it. When read together, these judgments clarify the law a great deal, and in their wake it is clear that privacy is a strong fundamental right whose protection encompasses most areas of life.[59]

However, in the hands of the Court, these two cases became predominantly focused on definitions. Hence, the Court was able to avoid the most difficult issues in EU data protection law, the hardest of which being how to balance individuals' right to data protection with other rights and freedoms.[60] In both cases, context and *telos* became evident in

[59] Bilyana Petkova's understanding of privacy as a leading right in the EU is indeed compelling. Bilyana Petkova, 'Privacy as Europe's First Amendment' (2019) 25 *European Law Journal* 140–54.

[60] A reference to H. L. A. Hart's and Ronald Dworkin's differences may come to mind. Whereas Hart sees the law as comprising rules, Dworkin also recognises principles as

the reasoning of the Court. Both pointed in the same direction: ensuring that individuals' personal data rights are protected. When the cases were framed this way, the question of controllership morphed into the question of who should be defined as the controller in order for fundamental rights protection to be achieved.

After this introduction to data protection rules and the ECJ's reasoning, it is time to move on to the more philosophical parts of the book. To wrap up the discussion of the Court's argumentation practices, it can be said that the Court has sometimes tried to stick to the definition of data protection rules and their technical terms instead of engaging in balancing of rights and interests. It undoubtedly has many reasons for doing so, not least rebuttal of the critique of being an activist court.

The Court may not want to look like a political player in EU law. However, there may be no choice. Some of the privacy and data protection cases are very hard to solve because they necessarily require weighing different rights and interests. Law has its limits. When the essence of rights collide,[61] politics and ethics begin.

Likewise, when difficult cases are framed as definitions cases, the Court cannot escape making value judgements. For this reason, it would be better for transparency's sake to engage in outright balancing of rights and interests instead of sticking to definitions of various parts of data protection rules. The ideology behind privacy protection makes a difference either way.

The political atmosphere has been privacy-friendly in the Union for some years now. This shows clearly in legislation. It also shows in the Court's case law, especially in terms of the kinds of balancing decisions it occasionally has made. It is good that it shows, even though we might occasionally disagree on its merits.

In all the judgments that we will read during the following pages, the circumstances of the case and the main legal issues have been picked, categorised and interpreted by the Court. Their formulation and

a part of modern law. Principles, however, require balancing. It is not the case that interpreting and applying a rule would be easier than balancing principles, but it is different. And Dworkin does have a point in saying that principles are often needed in order to solve hard cases because these are often the kinds of cases where rules are not enough. In the two annotated cases, defining data protection rules was, perhaps, easier than balancing various rights and freedoms.

[61] See e.g. Brkan, 'The Concept of Essence of Fundamental Rights'; and Tuomas Ojanen, 'Making the Essence of Fundamental Rights Real: The Court of Justice of the European Union Clarifies the Structure of Fundamental Rights under the Charter' (2016) 12 *European Constitutional Law Review* 318–29; on the essence of rights.

classification is made by the Court itself, which also decides on the importance it grants them. The EU Court often holds on to teleological and context-dependent reasoning, but these are also chosen from several alternatives and their exact significance interpreted case by case. None of these choices can ever be completely neutral. All legal reasoning always displays some political or ethical choices, under which lies an understanding of the human being, as well as convictions about what kind of protection this person should be granted by the law.

1 Private Persons Are Made

Jacques Derrida noted years ago that psychoanalytic thinking has not found its way into law. Even though it may be commonplace in many areas of contemporary thought, it has scarcely even been noticed in the legal domain. What he specifically refers to is the unconscious. Legal thinking has not been able – or willing – to acknowledge its existence, nor to think through the consequences. The alterity at the heart of every person has not been taken seriously: 'the differentiation or the scission of agencies [instances], the fact that the ego is only one agency or can be a dissociated agency, all of this, with all the refinements and complications that this topic can induce, remains massively ignored in juridical discourse. Ignored in the very principle, at the very inception of law or right.'[1] There is certainly some truth to this. Not only privacy and personal data regulation, but law generally tends to presuppose a self-present individual who is in control of themselves and their actions. However, this inability of law to think of personhood in other ways should not be exaggerated.

What Is a Person, According to the Law?

It is not clear that Western legal thinking has ever endorsed one specific view of the person. Rather, personhood and its many features have been dealt with in various ways depending on the practical circumstances of a case, or the political goals of a particular legislation project. Hence, there is no uniform theory of the legal subject, nor any unambiguous

[1] Jacques Derrida and Bernard Stiegler, *Echographies of Television: Filmed Interviews* (Cambridge: Polity Press, 2002), p. 98.

conception of legal personhood on which to focus a deconstructive gaze.

The important question, therefore, does not necessarily lie in the law's inability to take the unconscious seriously, even though that may be one feature of privacy rights as well. There are ways in which the law constantly grapples with its own inadequacies and its outdated presuppositions. In the end, paraphrasing Rancière,[2] it can be said that it is not decisive what kind of knowledge the law builds upon, but what it does with that knowledge.

The person as a legal category is not a concept with a clear, real or true meaning, which jurisprudence could explain or practising lawyers apply. It is a concept like any other, that is, ambiguous, but even more ambiguous than some because it includes philosophical, ideological and biological connotations about what it means to be a human being. But a concept void of precise meaning is not a concept void of power. The legal person, and its relative, the legal subject, are fundamental categories for Western legal thought.[3] It is hard to see how law could operate without them. These concepts are of vital importance in organising the law: its norms, institutions and practices.

The flexibility of the legal person can be demonstrated for instance in the Canadian case of *R.* v. *Sharpe*[4] from 2001. Here, the Supreme Court of Canada decided that imaginary human beings are persons. This was a criminal law case, which concerned possession of child pornography. One problem was the definition of child pornography, which in Canadian legislation included the term 'person'. According to the Criminal Code, in order to constitute child pornography, a visual representation must show, depict, advocate or counsel sexual activity with a person.[5] The judgment includes a fascinating section that boldly asks whether the term 'person' applies only to actual, as opposed to imaginary, persons.

According to the judgment, not only actual persons are included in the definition. Because of the quality of contemporary technology, it can be very difficult to distinguish a real person from a computer creation. Interpreting the term 'person' in accordance with the purpose of the legislation, the Court said that the term 'person' should include

[2] Jacques Rancière, *The Method of Equality: Interviews with Laurent Jeanpierre and Dork Zabunyan*, Julie Rose trs. (Cambridge: Polity Press, 2016).

[3] For a recent analysis see Visa Kurki, *A Theory of Legal Personhood* (Oxford: Oxford University Press, 2019).

[4] *R* v. *Sharpe*, [2001] 1 SCR 45; [2001] SCC 2.

[5] Criminal Code RSC 1985 c C-46, s. 163.1(1).

visual works of the imagination as well as depictions of actual people.[6] Thus, the person might well be both an actual and an imaginary human being.[7]

The example shows that the legal person is a category used – that is, put to use – in law. It is a productive instrument. Production here works in many directions. The category of the person has effect in shaping the law and its operations, for instance when used to include and exclude legal participation. Only beings granted full personhood can have certain rights and privileges, for instance.

Law affects society when it upholds certain ways of understanding the person, while shutting out others. Simultaneously, law and the prevailing understandings of legal personhood are influenced by societal factors such as beliefs, values, policies and ideology. This is the other direction in which production works. Law is politics legalised, and politics is, of course, not neutral.

Existing theoretical approaches to the legal person can roughly be divided into two main groups.[8] In analytic theories, the legal person is more or less a pure, legal artifice. It is a concept used by lawyers for lawyering purposes, and it is not real, nor does it necessarily have to reflect anything in the real world. According to these conceptions, the legal person does not - and should not - depend on metaphysical or moral presuppositions about human beings.

The problems arising from analytical theories have to do with how an empty concept like this can be of use in the actual practices of the law. It is also worth asking whether the artificial legal person is really as pure a concept as it is claimed to be. Is it not necessary that the category of the legal person, as an instrument in organising legal life, gets filled with meaning that is not so clearly pure or neutral, thus necessarily gaining normative, moral or even political significance? It seems evident that some moral and metaphysical considerations - at least implied ones - are unavoidable.

The second approach can be called 'essentialist' for want of a better term. Essentialist theories claim that the legal person has some necessary characters. They may be considered natural, ontological or,

[6] See also Jannice Käll, *Converging Human and Digital Bodies: Posthumanism, Property, Law* (Gothenburg: University of Gothenburg, 2017).

[7] *R* v. *Sharpe*, [2001] 1 SCR 45; [2001] SCC 2, paras. 37–8.

[8] Inspired by Ngaire Naffine, although she distinguishes between three different theoretical positions. See Ngaire Naffine, 'Who Are Law's Persons? From Cheshire Cats to Responsible Subjects' (2003) 66 *Modern Law Review* 346–67.

especially in older versions, God-given. The legal person is here characterised through the morally relevant status of being a human being.[9] The problems related to this theoretical framework are different from those related to analytical theories. What kind of argumentation is required in order to define 'the person' by referring to the equally ambiguous 'human being'? This is what courts are forced to do in some human rights cases for instance, and the argumentation tends to come with awkward hesitancy. Naturally so because judges may understandably be reluctant to take upon themselves the task of defining what a human being is.

The general purpose that a legal system is seen to fulfil is intertwined with an understanding of personhood. Experts on public law tend to have a different view from private lawyers, for instance. The logic of the legal area in which one operates influences the way one thinks of the legal person. Naturally, an evaluation of law's success is dependent on these presuppositions as well.

For the purposes of deconstructing privacy law, it may not be useful to consider the person as a pure, empty or artificial category, nor as one that has essential characteristics pertaining to the ethics or metaphysics of the human being. The concept can rather be seen as a construct used in many ways. We can study its manifestations without subscribing to any theory of personhood.

Persons Are Made by Law

In 1973, Michel Foucault observed that academic Marxism tries to determine the way economic conditions are reflected and expressed in various areas of human life. This kind of analysis takes the economy as the dynamic force that affects everything in the superstructure: culture, knowledge, religious beliefs, tastes and fashions, even law. Foucault pays attention to an interesting defect in this way of thinking. Marxism assumes that the human subject is somehow given in advance and that the economic, social and political conditions of existence are imprinted on this already existing being.[10]

[9] See also Gadamer's interesting discussion of subject and person in, Hans-Georg Gadamer, 'Subjectivity and Intersubjectivity, Subject and Person' (2000) 33 *Continental Philosophy Review* 275–87.

[10] Michel Foucault, 'Truth and Juridical Forms', in Michel Foucault, *Power*, James D. Faubion ed., Robert Hurley et al. trs., *The Essential Works of Foucault 1954–1984*, 3 vols. (New York: New Press, 2000), vol. 3, pp. 1–2.

Foucault himself tries to analyse how social practices influence forms of knowledge, which in turn give rise to new forms of awareness, new concepts, new technologies, new objects and even new kinds of subjects.[11] He does not believe in a pregiven subject. Foucault excludes from his study the primacy of a subject of knowledge and replaces it with a subject that is formed historically.

A similar understanding traverses this book. It builds upon the hypothesis that there is no subject prior to social, economic, political and legal conditions. Most of the philosophical theories that the book engages with can, regardless of their differences, be reconciled with the idea of a constructed subject that changes over time.

The picture of a self-centred, autonomous and pregiven subject has been fading for a long time. Decisive cracks on its surface have been caused by psychoanalytic theories, late-modern philosophy, as well as certain versions of communitarianism. This theoretical background informs the analysis undertaken in this book, inviting suspicion over the kinds of person that are constructed in privacy law. An awareness of these cracks in the picture forms a contrast with the person that emerges from legal material. Throughout the book, it will be shown that the view of the person as an autonomous individual lies very much at the heart of contemporary regulation of privacy rights.

An analysis of the productive power of privacy rights requires that distance is taken from hegemonic discourses on privacy. Here, too, Foucault shows the way. In the *Birth of Biopolitics* (1979), he outlines one of his methodological starting points saying that he attempts to write a history of a phenomenon without accepting its a priori existence. This kind of method also informed his early enquiry into madness. The question was not whether madness exists. Rather, he attempted to examine history supposing that madness does not exist. This allowed him to find out what to make of the different events and practices that are organised around something that is thought to be madness.[12]

The most striking feature in today's understanding of privacy is, I argue, the overwhelming feeling shared by academics and the public alike that our privacy is under threat. So let us suppose that privacy has

[11] Foucault, 'Truth and Juridical Forms', vol. 3, p. 2.

[12] Michel Foucault, *The Birth of Biopolitics: Lectures at the Collège de France, 1978–1979*, Michel Senellart ed., Graham Burchell trs. (New York: Palgrave Macmillan, 2008), pp. 3–19.

not eroded, that a loss of privacy has not taken place, and that privacy has not been abolished. Let us for the moment put to one side the 'fact' that privacy is about to be lost. What kind of effects does this apparent and almost universally accepted state of affairs – loss of privacy – have? And conversely: what kind of societal conditions have produced the need to require more, and wider, protection of privacy?

The argument is not that it is an illusion that privacy is threatened, or that it would be an error to claim that privacy has been eroded. Rather, we can think of the dominant discourse on privacy as one regime of truth. It is one among many possibilities. Thus the question arises: How is this discourse visible in law and, on the other hand, how does law uphold this particular truth?

A set of practices and certain kinds of knowledge regimes have established current understandings of privacy. These practices, regimes and discourses are too many to be analysed in their entirety, but the effort to account for even some of them may nevertheless be useful. We may understand more, and better, what goes on in EU law once this enquiry has been made.

The privacy paradigms at work in law correspond to various conceptions of the person. This brings us to the key question of this book. It asks what kind of person goes together with current understandings of privacy and personal data protection. Throughout the analysis, I try to display the person with privacy rights, that is, the private person, as constructed. In order to do this, it is necessary to question the thought that there exists a pregiven person who has privacy, who can in some meaningful ways be private, and whose privacy claims are claims about fundamental rights that the law should recognise. What if a private person never existed as such but was drafted, recognised and created in various practices and counter-practices, of which the most important have been legal?

To sum up, there are two provisos to this study. Firstly, it does not recognise a priori the existence of a pregiven person. Secondly, it does not take at face value either loss of privacy, or the value of privacy, but sees both claims as discourses with corresponding legal practices, in which the subject *as a private person* is made.

Hence, in order to analyse the various, multilevel – and even conflicting – ways in which privacy and personal data regulation function in European societies, it is necessary to dispense with the idea of a pregiven subject. This is necessary for us to study how these specific legal practices exercise power in constitutive ways. As Foucault puts it:

> One has to dispense with the constituent subject, to get rid of the subject itself, that's to say, to arrive at an analysis that can account for the constitution of the subject within a historical framework. And this is what I would call genealogy, that is, a form of history that can account for the constitution of knowledges, discourses, domains of objects, and so on, without having to make reference to a subject that is either transcendental in relation to the field of events or runs in its empty sameness throughout the course of history.[13]

It would, of course, be useful also to look beyond the law for forms of power that shape, control and produce subjectivities.[14] Traditional juridical rules are only one example of a mechanism that shapes relations of power. The law can never control all actual power relations. But an analysis of legal regulation may have privileged value nevertheless. As Foucault notes in 'Truth and Juridical Forms', among all the different social practices that can be analysed for the purposes of locating the emergence of new forms of subjectivity, the most important are juridical ones.[15] This book focuses on those forms.

Inspired by Foucault, we can study the law in order to find out what kinds of subjectivities have become operative – or perhaps even dominant – recently. Foucault studies, for instance, penal law, that is, how wrongs and responsibilities are settled and how compensation and punishment are imposed on certain individuals. Enquiry into other forms of legal regulation can be just as fruitful.[16] For the purposes of studying subjectivities, we can take privacy and personal data regulation as areas that are both timely and representative.

The worry underlying my analysis in the EU setting is that the liberal economic paradigm, on which the integration project mostly rests, threatens to privatise not only services and administration, but people, too. Fundamental rights have been seen as the security break in this regard, or occasionally as the last instance of control for European societies. Fundamental rights prevent the state and other governing bodies from overstepping their limits.

The importance of rights is their ability to ensure the basic values of societies, such as equality and justice. Rights safeguard the common good against private interests or the aims of particular political groups.

[13] Michel Foucault, 'Truth and Power', in Michel Foucault, *Power*, James D. Faubion ed., Robert Hurley et al. trs., *The Essential Works of Foucault 1954–1984*, 3 vols. (New York: New Press, 2000), vol. 3, p. 118.

[14] See e.g. Foucault, 'Truth and Power', vol. 3, pp. 122–3.

[15] Foucault, 'Truth and Juridical Forms', vol. 3, p. 4.

[16] See e.g. Samuli Hurri, *Birth of the European Individual: Law, Security, Economy* (Oxon, New York: Routledge, 2014).

Lately, however, rights have been criticised for their impotence in terms of providing the practical results that they are meant to, as well as for their inability to resist neoliberalism.[17] Rights do not always deliver on their societal promises, the most important of these being equality. I will come back to the questions of equality at the end of the book.

My arguments in this book are not meant as an addition to this rights critique as such. The purpose is not to show what privacy rights fail to do, but rather to study the various things that they do all the time. The protection of privacy and personal data through legal means constructs personhood in a certain manner. These rights attest to some general tendencies in European law. Therefore, this book in essence studies how privacy and personal data regulation individualise the people of Europe.

What Do Privacy Rights Produce?

Drawing on the brief sketch of privacy and personal data protection presented above, I shall now offer a first glimpse into the various persons that are produced. I will discuss them all in more detail throughout the following chapters.

Several different kinds of persons can be discerned from the material. Distinguishing between their paradigmatic appearances is by no means easy as they often overlap. They also appear to have contradicting logics. Nevertheless, certain forms of personhood do emerge.

Firstly, emphasis on control of data, which traverses current privacy law, implies the existence of persons who control, can control and should control their data. The law seeks to empower, a measure that is informed by a specific view of personhood. Legal methods of empowering presuppose and seek to produce competent persons.

The empowered person is especially visible in the self-management ideology of the GDPR, where the consent of the data subject is emphasised.[18] The law presupposes that there exist persons who know themselves, and their own preferences and opinions. Hence, the law presupposes and continually produces an autonomous person.

[17] See e.g. Moyn, Not Enough: Human Rights in an Unequal World; and Marks (ed.), *International Law on the Left*.

[18] See e.g. J. C. Buitelaar, 'Privacy: Back to the Roots' (2012) 13 *German Law Journal* 171–202. Informational self-determination is the core value of privacy. It is grounded in dignity and autonomy. Understood this way, privacy can still function even in a networked society.

We can compare the data subject with another prevalent modern figure: the consumer. In many ways, the data subject leads a similarly confusing life to the consumer. Consumerist freedom means that we have the possibility to choose and to consume whatever we want. This freedom, however, turns into an obligation to choose. There are always innumerable options to buy, be and speak.[19]

Social media platforms have increased the burden for people to administer themselves and their image as the kind of person they want to be. This includes all kinds of life choices including physical appearance, education, sexual orientation, career and opinions. While this freedom is enhanced, the socio-economic conditions of one's life can seldom be chosen freely. The main characteristic of today's subject contains an odd combination of free beings who experience themselves as wholly responsible for their own social standing, and subjects whose social standing is beyond their control.[20]

Other people can form a potential threat, especially in networks. Sexual and racist harassment are just a few of the constant risks that haunt us. We also feel threatened by invasive surveillance mechanisms, as well as by various greedy businesses that prey on our personal data. In today's form of individuality, freedom is therefore combined with a psychological awareness of others as a threat. Subjectivity includes a perception of oneself as a potential victim.[21] Aware of the risks, we seek regulation to protect us in our individuality.

Privacy rights are often understood as shells in which we can feel secure in our own personhood. We aim to conceal our innermost secrets from the outside world. The whole idea of protecting personhood, however, downplays the fact that we are in many ways incomplete and unaware of our innermost selves. We are not even completely in control of ourselves, nor can we ever be fully autonomous. Still, discourses on privacy – also legal ones, as will be seen further on – presuppose that we are. Self-determination is one key value of privacy protection.

In this book I want to explore also the mirror image of the empowered person. Namely, privacy rights are interconnected with disempowerment. This observation builds upon an awareness of the smokescreen function of rights, which is basically a Marxist critique. The idea is that

[19] Slavoj Žižek, *Like a Thief in Broad Daylight: Power in the Era of Post-Human Capitalism* (London: Allen Lane 2018), pp. 5–8.
[20] Žižek, *Like a Thief in Broad Daylight*, pp. 5–8.
[21] Žižek, *Like a Thief in Broad Daylight*, pp. 5–8.

rights given by an authority deflect attention from rights taken away. Such other rights could be democratic – or economic, say in matters concerning the material conditions of one's life. As will be discussed in more detail later, the importance of privacy rights has grown in tandem with the postmodern developments of Western societies, where diminishing democratic legitimation for global capitalism is a prevalent issue.

The general framework, in which privacy rights are currently understood, is individualism in the sense of investment in one's own affairs. One feature of privacy rights - and their accompanying rhetoric - emphasises the individual as a self with their own unique feelings, beliefs, concerns and opinions. Such egocentrism often coincides with the fact that the political subject's gaze turns away from the other and away from common issues.

Another form of personhood that emerges from our material is the immune ego. With individualism comes a need to protect the self from outside intrusion. We shall explore the logic of immunisation as a way of describing privacy regulation. Privacy protects us from others. However, when driven too far, it can cause societal problems. Privacy as immunity can take individualisation to a level where common issues, and the common good, become secondary compared to everyone's own private concerns. Privacy as immunisation includes a distancing from others.

The law produces privacy itself. The legal understanding of privacy presupposes that there is something there behind the curtain, something private, a private person. With the production of the private person, however, the public person is also created.[22] The two forms, corresponding to two 'spheres', the private and the public, are arguably as old as Western legal thinking.

Today in the Union it is the time of the private sphere, which means that production of the legal person as a private person is predominant.

[22] The idea of production here is inspired by Karl Marx's analysis of capitalism. In the first part of *Capital* he describes the capitalist system and its various components from commodities to labour and different kinds of value mechanisms. One of his conclusions was that the system keeps recreating the possibilities for its continuing. It reproduces the relationship between the worker and the capitalist all the time by making the worker dependent on the capitalist economy for survival. The worker has to work, which enables the capitalist to gain from that work. As a whole, Marx says, capitalist production not only produces goods, or only surplus value. It produces the capitalist and the worker as well. See Karl Marx, *Capital: A Critique of Political Economy*, Friedrich Engels ed., Samuel Moore and Edward Aveling trs., 3 vols. (London: Penguin Books, 1992), vol. I, first part end of VII chapter 21.

The idea is that if private personhood is not protected, then everything, or at least too much, would be public. It is, however, extremely difficult to define where to draw the line between the private and the public. Even defining the two spheres is not easy. This fuzzy topic is a central problem in legal privacy and personal data protection. It is of practical concern for legislators as well as for judges, and thereby for everybody working with the law. Here, conceptual confusion produces very real problems.

It has been said that, in the EU, privacy has been understood primarily in the sense of something personal, relating to one's self, something intimate, instead of private as opposed to public.[23] This is arguably one reason why privacy rights have their individualising connotations in EU law. However, as recent case law shows, the good old dilemma of where to draw the line between what is private and what is public is still very much alive.

Privacy rights are often seen as a saviour against the perils of technological advancement, and there is certainly a lot of truth in this. But blaming technology can entail diverting blame away from somewhere else, that is, global capitalism. The many links between tech and money need to be analysed in more detail than I can do in this book in order for us to see all the different ways in which they operate in tandem. I draw on Shoshana Zuboff, who has argued that today's tech companies operate a form of surveillance capitalism, which is as ruthlessly exploitative as any earlier form.

Data protection in the EU has a double nature in this regard. Introducing the most severe and comprehensive system for data protection in the world, the Union has taken a firm stand on protecting the individual's rights against those of profit-seeking companies, whose sole aim is to make money with people's data. In this sense, it is clear that the Union is hammering away at least at some of the most rampant capitalist exploitation. The GDPR aims to secure people's rights through regulating the responsibility of controllers and processors who, if they fail to comply, face fines. The strength of the Regulation is on a par with the Union's competition rules, which are also motivated, at least in the main, by the welfare of consumers.

Moreover, the heavy responsibilities that data protection rules lay on controllers and processors means that protection of privacy also covers persons who are not active in seeking protection. By laying a large part

[23] Fuster, *The Emergence of Personal Data Protection*.

of the legal burden on parties who collect, store and use people's personal data, the GDPR also takes a vulnerable subject under its wing. Passive persons are protected regardless of their capability of – or even interest in – demanding respect for their rights. Hence, the law presupposes a vulnerable passive subject as well as an active one.

The ideological foundations of privacy regulation are not unambiguous. The law has many aims and is not only directed at protecting individuals. As we have seen, data protection also aims to secure the free flow of data within the internal market. The two aims of the GDPR are often at odds with each other, which occasionally makes teleological interpretation of the meaning of the Regulation quite difficult. Only time will tell which aim gets more weight in any future judgment, but for now the emphasis is on rights protection.

Nevertheless, even if the main focus of data protection is to develop rules for the benefit of people, the Regulation does harmonise the market and thus level the playing field for all companies to compete. The Regulation has the potential to clarify operating conditions, thus decreasing transaction costs and enabling profit-making from personal data. Therefore, one dominant form of personhood is without doubt the person formed by the economy.

Governing people and governing the economy are intrinsically linked in the historical development of the EU. Here, the European integration project has always been about prosperity. From this perspective, the Union's interest in upholding fundamental rights is a rather recent development. The four freedoms of the single market have been at the centre of attention, and indeed they still are: they form an integral part of the constitutional backbone of the Union.

Therefore, the dominant form of legal personhood in the Union setting has originally been the free-moving economic agent, and to some extent this still holds. In secondary law, this picture appears frequently, even when fundamental rights are considered. In personal data law, this is reflected in the enhancement of certain rights such as data portability, as well as the general aim of producing a single market in data. The free movement of persons from one EU country to another is protected. People are able to do their internet shopping in any Member State(s), as well as to move, work and enjoy themselves on social media within the EU and feel that their personal data is protected at all times.

The GDPR does attempt to facilitate the data subject's enjoyment of their free movement rights. To operate as a consumer, worker, investor or houseowner in the single market entails that one need not worry about how one's data is being processed. This trust in a fair and inviting market is partly created by regulating the free flow of data.

Privacy protection is also intertwined with political personhood. Privacy is often seen as a prerequisite for a functioning democracy. One cannot be a fully functioning citizen, for instance, without the protection of one's innermost thoughts, opinions, beliefs and the like. These values connected to privacy have a long history, and they are usually codified under the protection of private life more often, and earlier, than under the right to personal data protection.

Privacy rights can offer democratic legitimation for the whole political system. Privacy is a general requirement for rule-bound and democratically organised government. Totalitarian regimes do not tend to protect privacy.

The last production is a complicated one. This is the person who is neither completely individual, nor determined by otherness, but something in between.[24] This alternative will be developed in the last part of the book. One reason to have legal protection of privacy is perhaps because so much tends to be hidden from the individuals themselves. This idea goes against the bland picture of a person as an autonomous and thoroughly intelligible being. We can ask if privacy rights in fact imply an implicit admission of the incapability of persons to fully know themselves and understand the truth of themselves. Perhaps they also imply an admission of the difficulties human beings often have in sharing their lives and expressing themselves to others. In this way, privacy and the need to protect it can imply acknowledgement of the fundamental risks of miscommunication in human relationships.[25] These thoughts will be explored in relation to singular–plural personhood drawing on Nancy. I will argue that it would be helpful for the law to consider persons as both singular and plural when protecting privacy. That way, the individual-centred interpretation of privacy rights could be amended.

The book is divided into chapters according to the various kinds of persons that spring from the material. We first focus on empowered persons who are in control of themselves and their data. This view of personhood corresponds with the individualism of late-modern

[24] For an interesting alternative, see also Jannice Käll, 'A Posthuman Data Subject? The Right to Be Forgotten and Beyond' (2017) *German Law Journal* 1145–62.

[25] Maria Aristodemou, 'Freedom in the Free World: The Extimate Becomes the Law' (2016) 48 *International Journal of Law and Psychiatry* 85–91.

societies. The next chapter focuses on autonomy, which lies at the heart of privacy protection. In tandem with the autonomous person in control, we notice that privacy rights also protect the disempowered, passive and vulnerable person. We will ponder how the myth of the autonomous person haunts privacy and data protection law today. We then consider the construction of personhood according to the logic of immunisation. We will discuss the ways in which rights to privacy aim at protecting people through making them immune. The following chapter looks at the economic agent that privacy law constructs. Thereafter we will investigate whether privacy rights produce equal persons, hence moving into questions of political personhood. The next chapter analyses the person as a singular-plural being and seeks an understanding of privacy that protects people as members of a community. The concluding chapter considers the different aspects of individualism embedded in privacy rights while seeking alternative understandings, both theoretical and legal.

2 The Person in Control

The person of privacy law today is predominately a person who is in control of their data. As privacy has increasingly become defined in terms of data protection, the most emblematic picture of the private person is an empowered person, a person in control.

The principle of control traverses EU privacy law in many ways. That people should be able to have a say in the transmission and spread of information about themselves is one of the key values that privacy rights have been protecting all along. This goes for peeping toms as well as governmental spy institutions. However, the current data protection rules paint a nuanced, if at times contradictory, picture of control.

According to the GDPR, personal data can only be processed on the basis of one of the lawful grounds stipulated in Article 6. The list in the first paragraph starts with consent:

Article 6 Lawfulness of processing

1. Processing shall be lawful only if and to the extent that at least one of the following applies:
   (a) the data subject has given consent to the processing of his or her personal data for one or more specific purposes;
   (b) processing is necessary for the performance of a contract to which the data subject is party or in order to take steps at the request of the data subject prior to entering into a contract;
   (c) processing is necessary for compliance with a legal obligation to which the controller is subject;
   (d) processing is necessary in order to protect the vital interests of the data subject or of another natural person;
   (e) processing is necessary for the performance of a task carried out in the public interest or in the exercise of official authority vested in the controller;

(f) processing is necessary for the purposes of the legitimate interests pursued by the controller or by a third party, except where such interests are overridden by the interests or fundamental rights and freedoms of the data subject which require protection of personal data, in particular where the data subject is a child.

The list of lawful grounds in Article 6 is exhaustive and restrictive, according to the ECJ. Member States cannot, for instance, add new grounds for lawfulness or impose their own requirements that would amend the scope of one of these six grounds.[1] The list therefore includes all the grounds on which processing of personal data is allowed.

We see throughout the text of the Regulation that control is one of the guiding principles of informational privacy. Subjects' right to rule over their data is already protected in the way lawful processing is defined. In addition to consent, contract as a lawful ground for processing also points towards the view of persons as empowered individuals. Both consent and contract require active acceptance of data processing by the data subject.

It is noteworthy that the Regulation includes a more detailed definition of consent than the old Directive. Article 4 defines consent as 'any freely given, specific, informed and unambiguous indication of the data subject's wishes by which he or she, by a statement or by a clear affirmative action, signifies agreement to the processing of personal data relating to him or her'. It is the purpose of the Regulation, therefore, that the data subjects' wishes are to be respected.

The Regulation also specifies conditions for consent. According to Article 7, when processing is based on consent, the controller has to be able to demonstrate that the data subject has consented. In addition, it stipulates that if consent is given in the context of a written declaration that also concerns other matters, then the request for consent has to be presented in a manner that is clearly distinguishable from the other matters, in an intelligible and easily accessible form, using clear and plain language. In other words, the data subject has to be able to understand what they are consenting to.

[1] See Joined Cases C-468/10 and C-469/10, *Asociación Nacional de Establecimientos Financieros de Crédito (ASNEF) and Federación de Comercio Electrónico y Marketing Directo (FECEMD)* v. *Administración del Estado*, EU:C:2011:777, paras. 30, 32; See also Case C-582/14, *Patrick Breyer* v. *Bundesrepublik Deutschland*, EU:C:2016:779, paras. 61–4.

Furthermore, the data subject has the right to withdraw consent at any time. Before giving consent, the data subject must be informed of this right. The data subject's mind can change and the principle of control is relevant in such situations as well. There is symmetry here: it has to be as easy to withdraw consent as to give it.

The issue of consent came up in *Planet49*, where the ECJ delivered judgment in 2019. Here the Court stated, among other things, that to give consent involves the person giving an indication of their wishes. This clearly points to active, rather than passive, behaviour, according to the Court.[2] The issue here was whether a preselected tick in a checkbox on a web page could be a valid way of giving consent. The Court said 'no'. Consent given in the form of a preselected tick in a checkbox does not imply active behaviour on the part of a website user.

The Court argued, for instance, that Article 7(a) of the DPD provides that the data subject's consent may make processing lawful if the data subject has consented 'unambiguously'. Only active behaviour on the part of the data subject can fulfil that requirement.[3]

In the GDPR, active consent is required if processing is undertaken on the basis of consent. According to GDPR recital 32, giving consent can include ticking a box when visiting an internet website. However, the recital expressly precludes 'silence, pre-ticked boxes or inactivity' from being valid forms of consent. In other words, personal data can be processed only if the controller can make sure that the person actively agrees to processing.

As for the processing of special categories of data, such as data revealing political opinions, religious beliefs, sexual orientation or data concerning health, the main rule expressed in Article 9 of the GDPR is that consent is always needed for processing, even though other lawful grounds are possible as well. Therefore, in situations where data is sensitive, or one could say *extra-personal*, the Regulation emphasises consent even more.[4]

In its guidelines for consent under the new Regulation, the Data Protection Working Party has stressed that: 'If obtained in full

[2] Case C-673/17 *Verbraucherzentrale Bundesverband e.V.* v. *Planet49*, EU:C:2019:801, para. 52.

[3] Case C-673/17 *Planet49*, EU:C:2019:801, para. 54.

[4] Whether this applies in practice is another matter because for special categories of data the GDPR does in fact leave quite a wide margin for Member States to legislate.

compliance with the GDPR, consent is a tool that gives data subjects control over whether or not personal data concerning them will be processed. If not, the data subject's control becomes illusory and consent will be an invalid basis for processing, rendering the processing activity unlawful.'[5] Hence, consent is meant primarily as an instrument that enables the data subject's control over their data. Consent is a lawful ground for processing only if it ensures that control.

Problems with Consent

The basic understanding of the importance of control traverses case law as well. When considering the legal permissibility of web tracking in *Wirtschaftsakademie*, the Court underlined that individuals' control is the focus of data protection rules. Even though web tracking is not completely prohibited, the processing is forbidden unless the data subject has consented.[6]

Control has been fairly widely debated in legal literature on data protection. On the one hand, it has been regarded as an important value that privacy rights should protect. On the other, the emphasis on consent and other active measures of the data subject have been understood as de facto weakening the protection of individuals because the data subject may not always have the best abilities or resources to decide on the processing of data.

For instance, Bert-Jaap Koops has argued that the way data protection is regulated in the Union relies too much on informational self-determination. In fact, in the legislation process leading up the GDPR, there were attempts to move away from consent-centred regulation. These alternative voices were not successful, however, and the current Regulation relies heavily on consent, causing both practical and normative problems. Koops argues that relying on consent can have the tendency to weaken protection of personal data because few people are as informed – or as interested – in the complex activities where their data is processed.[7]

[5] Art. 29 Data Protection Working Party, 'Guidelines on Consent under Regulation 2016/679', WP259rev.01, 28 November 2017, p. 4.

[6] Case C-210/16, *Unabhängiges Landeszentrum für Datenschutz Schleswig-Holstein v. Wirtschaftsakademie Schleswig-Holstein GmbH*, Opinion of AG Bot, EU:C:2017:796, para. 9.

[7] Bert-Jaap Koops, 'The Trouble with European Data Protection Law' (2014) 4 *International Data Privacy Law* 250–61.

It has been noted in case law, too, that consent as a lawful ground for processing can in fact weaken the protection of individuals' privacy. In *Breyer* the Advocate General notes that consent constitutes a subjective justification for processing, whereas other grounds such as legitimate interest would provide for a more objective basis. The advantage of the latter is that it would necessarily require fundamental rights balancing and might, hence, bring about stronger protection of rights.[8]

The problems of consent and Big Data are also complex. With technological developments, it has become increasingly possible for controllers and processors to handle huge amounts of data. The sheer amount of data may bring about new kinds of risks in data protection. This change of scale can introduce a change of state because data processing is done in many new ways. For instance, by combining large amounts of data from different sources, it is near-impossible for anonymised data to remain anonymous. Data subjects may be identified when data sets are combined, even though the different sets do not include personal data in themselves.[9] This issue has been considered by the ECJ, for instance in *Digital Rights Ireland*.

In the GDPR framework, these problems have been addressed, even though it remains to be seen if the GDPR is up to the challenge of regulating rapid technological development in this regard. Some of the Regulation's main principles – for instance, purpose limitation, data minimisation, data accuracy and storage limitation in Article 5 – are potential instruments for dealing with Big Data. Additionally, Article 18 on the right to restriction of processing, as well as Article 22 on prohibitions concerning automated decision-making and profiling, may become important.

One main concern with Big Data is that data is abundant, sometimes even excessive, and information is constantly re-used. This undermines the foundational idea that self-determination is the main value of privacy and personal data protection, and that this is expressed through meaningful consent to data processing. Because of the complexities of Big Data processing, data subjects scarcely have the understanding to give meaningful consent. Moreover, Big Data undermines the very notion that the scope of data processing should be known and defined at the moment of data collection. Data is used in an unpredictable manner when analysts mine databases and, as a result, the specific

[8] See Case C-582/14, *Breyer*, Opinion of AG Campos Sánchez-Bordona, EU:C:2016:339.

[9] See Mayer-Schönberger and Cukier, *Big Data*, pp. 151–68.

uses of data cannot always be expected at the moment of data collection. Therefore, the data subject's consent may become an easy way to legitimise any sort of data processing and further re-use of information, even though consent would rarely cover the complete processing infrastructure.[10]

These problems related to actual possibilities for control have been widely acknowledged, as have issues relating to consent in situations where there is a power imbalance between the controller and the data subject. According to the Data Protection Working Party, imbalances of power are likely to occur in situations where data is processed by public authorities or employers, for instance. Because of this, consent can only be valid if the data subject is able to exercise a real choice.[11] As we can see, these formulations draw a picture of a subject who is, or at least can be, in control, and whose self-determinacy needs to be protected by law.

An alternative regulation strategy emphasises accountability for data users that collect, store and use personal data. This approach shifts the burden of responsibility from individuals to users of data. The most obvious reason for doing so is that users are the ones who most benefit from the data. Such a move from 'privacy by consent' to 'privacy through accountability' can solve some of the problems with consent.[12]

The GDPR includes elements that resemble the accountability approach: it regulates the responsibility of controllers and processors to quite a high degree. For instance, the idea that data protection should be built into all activities from an early stage finds expression in Article 25 on data protection by design and by default. The Regulation also develops the idea of accountability through placing a responsibility on controllers to undergo data protection impact assessments as stipulated in Articles 35 and 36.

Regardless of the responsibilities placed on controllers and processors, the law aims at enabling data subjects' empowerment. For instance Articles 13 to 21 of the GDPR define various rights that the data subject has in order to control how, when and if their personal data is being processed. The subject has the general right to know what data is being collected about them, as well as the right to restrict and even

[10] See Alessandro Mantelero, 'Regulating Big Data. The Guidelines of the Council of Europe in the Context of the European Data Protection Framework' (2017) 33 *Computer Law & Security Review: The International Journal of Technology Law and Practice* 584–602 at 587.

[11] Art. 29 Data Protection Working Party, 'Guidelines on Consent under Regulation 2016/679', WP259rev.01, 28 November 2017, p. 8.

[12] Mayer-Schönberger and Cukier, *Big Data*, pp. 171–5.

object to processing. These are not absolute rights but they are means by which the data subject's control is improved.

The right to access has also been seen as one of the cornerstones of data subjects' informational empowerment: 'EU data protection law offers individuals an arsenal of rights they can exercise against controllers. Among them, the right of access constitutes a cornerstone of data subjects' informational empowerment. The right allows individuals to monitor what personal data are held about them, how it is being processed and with whom it is shared.'[13] It is evident that one important feature of EU privacy law is the construction of an individual in control. Consequently, current privacy and personal data regulation follows a long-established path.

Control has been emphasised in legal scholarship for a long time. Alan Westin argues that privacy performs certain functions for individuals in democratic societies. He classifies these under four headings: personal autonomy, emotional release, self-evaluation, and limited and protected communication. Privacy, for him, is essentially an instrument for achieving individual goals of self-realisation.[14]

It is rare that any legal theorist or philosopher notes the problem of too much privacy. Westin, however, takes up this interesting detail:

> Too much privacy can be a result of social or physical conditions that lie largely beyond the individual's power to control. Thus, it can come from forced physical separation from society ... Or it may be the effect of life in complex, impersonal, industrial societies; many studies testify to the sense of rootlessness, anomie, and psychological isolation that this evokes.[15]

Be the issue too much or too little privacy, Westin's argument is that the core of the problem is usually lack of control.[16] Privacy is valuable as a capacity or ability for an individual to have a say in how much they interact with others, what they reveal about themselves and whom they reveal information to. In a free society, Westin argues, the choice of how much privacy anyone wants is left to the individual. Everyone then has the right to decide for themselves – 'with only extraordinary exceptions in the interests of society' – what, when and on what terms they reveal to the general public.[17]

[13] Jef Ausloos and Pierre Dewitte, 'Shattering One-Way Mirrors – Data Subject Access Rights in Practice' (2018) 8 *International Data Privacy Law* 4–28 at 4.

[14] Alan F. Westin, *Privacy and Freedom* (New York: Atheneum Publishers, 1967), pp. 35–43.

[15] Westin, *Privacy and Freedom*, p. 44.

[16] Westin, *Privacy and Freedom*, pp. 44–5.

[17] Westin, *Privacy and Freedom*, p. 46.

Individualisation As an Index of Late Modernity

Technological developments and new forms of media and surveillance appliances may be one reason why we need legal protection of privacy and personal data. A look at the deeper currents of contemporary societies will, however, reveal other meanings in our privacy debates. The pertinence of increased emphasis on privacy becomes intelligible when set against a backdrop of fundamental features of late-modern life.

I argue that one fruitful explanation for the prevalence of privacy concerns is to be found in the development of an ever more individualised society, where people have become independent actors instead of group members or citizens. This development corresponds to tendencies that see individuals in charge of their life and their fate. This kind of individualism makes human beings solely responsible for their own lives. The importance of control in data protection law rhymes well with such individualism.

The experience of an ever stronger need for privacy rights can thus be analysed as an indicator of a general individualisation process that is emblematic of late-modern Western societies. According to Zygmunt Bauman, individualisation – as well as the privatisation of public space – is symptomatic of liquid modernity, the contemporary landscape of society. With the turn from the political to the individual, and the demise of the citizen, we can notice the public space being colonised with the intimacies of private life. Interestingly enough, enhanced emphasis on privacy has emerged simultaneously.

According to Bauman, society generally offers shared meanings and liberation from thinking about physical forces. In an Aristotelian vein he considers societies as factories of meaningful life.[18] There is a continuous and never fully quenched thirst for life-meaning. In late modernity, where everybody is left with the task of creating the meaning of their own life, people have been made responsible for themselves but dependent on conditions that elude their grasp. There is no one to blame if their lives are not successful, not God, the government or the party. Blame can only be turned on the individual, not an institution. Bauman sees the results in rising political apathy and the colonisation of public space with the intimacies of private life.[19]

This development can be discerned in contemporary Western societies. The public, the political and the common have lost meaning. Our

[18] Zygmunt Bauman, *The Individualized Society* (Cambridge: Polity Press, 2001), pp. 2–3.

[19] Bauman, *The Individualized Society*, pp. 5–6.

hyper-individualised late-modern society lifts the person, defined without any constructive element from the community, to the highest level of the value hierarchy. Focus has now shifted to the autonomous self's own life story, which is often taken into the public space and made into a topic, or occasionally *the* topic, of public discussion. Simultaneously with this process, we see the rise of the right to privacy and data protection.[20]

Bauman sees individualisation today as a fate, not a choice.[21] We are all cast as individuals:[22] 'Casting members as individuals is the trademark of modern society. That casting, however, was not a one-off act like divine creation; it is an activity re-enacted daily. Modern society exists in its activity of "individualizing", as much as the activities of the individuals consist in the day-by-day reshaping and renegotiating of the network or their mutual entanglements called "society".'[23] What is noteworthy of the late-modern human condition is that the common troubles of individuals are not additive. They do not sum up to form a common cause.[24] The individual is now more than ever the citizen's worst enemy. Society, commonality and political action have lost their importance. What people demand of the public power, be that the state or some other authority such as the EU, is to defend human rights, which basically means the right for everyone to live their life as they please.[25]

The concerns of individuals as individuals fill the public space. Such a development is clearly visible in demands for privacy as voiced today. Claims for privacy and personal data protection can seldom be seen as a common cause that would bring people together as a political group. Understandably, in a world where much power has escaped the grasp of political authorities, flowing with the global currents of economy, there is growing disbelief that anything can be achieved collectively or that collective action can make a real change.[26] Belief in democracy has

[20] Other arguments about the individualist presuppositions of privacy have been put forward by Richard F. Hixton, *Privacy in a Public Society: Human Rights in Conflict* (Oxford: Oxford University Press, 1987), p. xv; and Steven J. Andre, 'Privacy As an Aspect of the First Amendment: The Place of Privacy in a Society Dedicated to Individual Liberty' (1988) 20 *University of West Los Angeles Law Review* 87–112 at 87, 89. See also Barrington Moore, Jr., *Privacy: Studies in Social and Cultural History*, reprint ed. (Armonk, NY: M. E. Sharpe, 1984), p. 267.

[21] Bauman, *The Individualized Society*, p. 46.

[22] Zygmunt Bauman, *Liquid Modernity* (Cambridge: Polity Press, 2000), p. 31.

[23] Bauman, *The Individualized Society*, p. 45.

[24] Bauman, *The Individualized Society*, p. 48

[25] Bauman, *The Individualized Society*, p. 49; and Bauman, *Liquid Modernity*, pp. 35–6.

[26] Bauman, *The Individualized Society*, pp. 53–5.

decreased and subjects as citizens have become impotent. Subjects are now above all individuals who increasingly often understand their fears, concerns, aspirations and life choices as their own private projects.

Bauman compares modern society with a caravan site. The place is open to everyone who has their own caravan and enough money to pay the rent. Guests come and go. None of them tends to take much interest in the site or the way it is run. What they mainly care about is that their allocated slots are large enough and otherwise fulfil their needs, and that the people in the neighbouring caravans do not make too much noise. When guests leave, according to their own itineraries and schedules, the site remains much as it was before their arrival:[27] 'What the drivers want from the site's managers is not much more ... than the right to be left alone and not interfered with. In exchange, they promise not to challenge the managers' authority and to pay the rent when due.'[28] With this echo of Warren and Brandeis' classic definition of privacy as a right to be let alone, it is rather evident that wide-ranging connections can be sought between the fate of the modern individual and increased regulation of privacy.

What may not be immediately visible in the caravan site metaphor is that the conditions under which people construct their individual existence and which decide the range and consequences of their choices are not within their own grasp.[29] It is understandable that people feel an urgent need to control at least their life stories when their abilities to control the material, physical and economic conditions of life are increasingly small. The site may no longer be one for caravans, but a technological site, a platform provided, a social medium.

Lives lived and lives told are interdependent. And the increasing need to control lives told is reflected in enhanced privacy demands. Thus increasing demands for privacy and protection of personal data can be explained as part of these liquid modern tendencies. They can be interpreted as an indicator of a wish to control narratives about ourselves, which is the only form of control left to late-modern human beings.

When more and more economic, social and political power has slipped from the fingers of nation states and their peoples, it is natural that there is a growing juridical will to master what little there is left to

[27] Bauman, *Liquid Modernity*, p. 24.
[28] Bauman, *Liquid Modernity*, p. 24.
[29] Bauman, *The Individualized Society*, pp. 6–7.

control. Even though the citizen has become impotent, individuals still have a say in shaping their life story through administering the publicity of their personal life.[30] The individual in control that transcends from personal data legislation correlates with this thought.

Individualism in Legal Theories of Privacy

To trace the reasons why privacy law looks as it does, we need to consider not only the sociological aspects of contemporary societies, but the theoretical basis on which privacy law rests.

European legal theory on privacy is influenced by American thinking, even though the legislative solutions achieved in Europe are rather different from those in the USA. The differences on the surface of the law have recently grown even more with the focus that the EU has given to protection of personal data. Nowadays privacy enjoys stronger protection in the EU than in the United States, and it has even been argued that privacy has become the leading right in Europe.[31] Still, legal scholarship draws on US sources to a surprisingly large degree.

Because legal theories of privacy have been developed mainly by American scholars, the ideology that privacy protection relies upon has an American background in the EU as well. For instance, Westin's *Privacy and Freedom* is still considered a classic in the field on both sides of the Atlantic and it has had quite an influence. In his work, the roots of privacy rights are clearly visible.

As Westin himself argues, American thought relies heavily on John Locke's version of liberalism. One striking feature that affected political thinking and the development of independent government in the USA in the 1970s was the concept of individualism, which included ideas of each person's worth, private religious judgement, private economic motives and direct legal rights for individuals.[32]

[30] The image of atomised individuals visiting sites but not caring for shared social structures can be contrasted with Martha C. Nussbaum and Saul Levmore's analysis of the Internet: 'In many ways the Internet has succeeded in remaking us as inhabitants of a small village. No one is a stranger either in the village or on the Internet; in both settings the savvy citizen knows how to process information.' Martha C. Nussbaum and Saul Levmore (eds.), *The Offensive Internet: Speech, Privacy, and Reputation* (Cambridge, MA: Harvard University Press, 2010), p. 1.

[31] See Petkova, 'Privacy as Europe's First Amendment'.

[32] Westin, *Privacy and Freedom*, p. 369.

An important feature of early American legal thought was the moral primacy of the private over the public sphere of society.[33] This comes with a conviction that things that are private and belong to individuals are more valuable than what is public, shared or held in common. To some extent this still applies to American legal thinking.

Westin upholds this view arguing, for instance, that a democratic society includes a fundamental belief in the uniqueness of the individual in basic dignity and worth. Individuality is sacred. However, Westin does notice a gap between what a person is and what they want to be, between what the world sees of them and what they know to be their more complex reality. Interestingly enough, Westin notes that the individual that individualism holds sacred is not altogether opaque. A person may have aspects that they may not – even themselves – fully understand. In this sense, every individual lives behind a mask.[34]

Even though the person emerging in European privacy law is by no means unambiguous, they still correspond predominately with individualistic views. This is curious considering that the roots of political theory in Europe are complex and not straightforward liberalist. The basis of philosophy - and the philosophy of law - lies in antiquity where, especially in the thought of Aristotle, the common good, the political sphere and the social values of society were emphasised. The classic canon of European legal theory is also filled with examples of theories that link law with societal values such as justice and the common good. Both dominant modern legal theoretical traditions, natural law theory and legal positivism place weight on general values and the good of the society. It is not possible in the present study to analyse the ideological history of European privacy law, though it would be very interesting to do so. Suffice it to say that the liberalist tradition seems to have influenced privacy theory, though the reasons for such a development are unclear.

It cannot be claimed that European privacy rights are defined by individualism through and through – but they are shaped by it. Individualist assumptions can be found both in legislative sources as well as in the interpretations of the EU Court. The method employed in this study, where legal sources are deconstructed, will reveal many inconsistencies in these assumptions. The contradictions found in the material are especially interesting. They show the many faces of legal

[33] Westin, *Privacy and Freedom*, p. 369.
[34] Westin, *Privacy and Freedom*, pp. 36–7.

personhood. They may also point towards conceptual weaknesses of individualism, which become visible as contradictions in legal practice.

Personal Data Is Always Data about an Individual

Individualisation of the late-modern variety and the person of privacy rights go hand in hand. This is seen, for example, in the way the current emphasis on personal data protection in the EU directs focus away from more traditional forms of privacy. Private life is one thing, data protection another. This split was glimpsed at in *Jehovan todistajat*. Data protection was the core issue in the case, so the Court naturally focused on that. But it is interesting that the other privacy right, namely freedom of religion, was all but neglected.

Individualism is heightened in data protection law because personal data refers by definition only to identified or identifiable individuals, whereas protection of private life can conceptually include protection of groups – such as families – from unwanted intrusion. The more traditional forms of privacy protection have been those of correspondence, the home and the private sphere of the household.[35] None of these aims solely at protecting the individual.

The definition of personal data as data about an individual has been the focus of certain ECJ judgments, most notably *Breyer*.[36] This case concerned interpretation of the Data Protection Directive in line with a request for a preliminary ruling from the Bundesgerichtshof (Federal Court of Justice, Germany). The national dispute took place between Mr Patrick Breyer and the Federal Republic of Germany concerning the registration and storage of the Internet Protocol (IP) address allocated to Mr Breyer when he accessed several internet sites run by German federal institutions.

Definition of personal data was relevant because the referring court asked essentially whether a dynamic IP address registered by an online media services provider when a person accesses a website that that provider makes accessible to the public constitutes personal data – with regard to that media services provider. In this case,[37] only a third party, namely the internet service provider, had the additional data necessary to identify Mr Breyer from the IP address. The address in

[35] See David Vincent, *Privacy: A Short History* (Cambridge: Polity Press, 2016).

[36] Case C-582/14, *Breyer*, EU:C:2016:779.

[37] In contrast to the earlier Case C-70/10, *Scarlet Extended SA* v. *Société belge des auteurs, compositeurs et éditeurs SCRL (SABAM)*, EU:C:2011:771.

question was a dynamic IP address, which is only a temporary address assigned for each internet connection and replaced when subsequent connections are made.

The Court noted, firstly, that a dynamic IP address does not constitute information relating to an 'identified natural person', since such an address does not directly reveal the identity of the natural person who owns the computer from which a website was accessed, or that of another person who might use that computer.[38]

However, the definition of personal data also includes the second component: personal data is data that relates to an 'identifiable' natural person. Here, the focus is on the online media services provider. Does a dynamic IP address, registered by an online media services provider, constitute personal data in relation to that service provider when the additional data necessary to identify users of the website of that service provider are held by the user's internet service provider? In this case, the website provider and the internet service provider held different sets of data and a natural person could not be identified by the IP address without combining these data sets.

The Court had to decide whether the possibility to combine a dynamic IP address with the additional data held by the internet service provider constitutes a means likely reasonably to be used to identify the data subject. As Advocate General Sánchez-Bordona pointed out in his opinion, a means likely reasonably to be used would not be involved if identification of the data subject was prohibited by law or practically impossible because it required a disproportionate effort in terms of time, cost and effort.[39]

The Court concluded that in *Breyer* it appeared that the online media services provider had the means that may likely reasonably be used in order to identify the data subject, with the assistance of other persons, namely the competent authority and the internet service provider. Hence, the definition of personal data needs to be interpreted as meaning that a dynamic IP address registered by an online media services provider constitutes personal data in relation to that provider, where the latter has the legal means that enable it to identify the data subject with additional data that the internet service provider has about that

[38] Case C-582/14, *Breyer*, EU:C:2016:779, para. 38.

[39] Case C-582/14, *Breyer*, Opinion of AG Campos Sánchez-Bordona, EU:C:2016:339, para. 68.

person.[40] The result is, therefore, that the term 'personal data' has wide applicability.

The broad definition of identified or identifiable individuals enables data protection in many different scenarios. Any data from which an individual can be identified with means likely reasonably to be used qualifies as personal data. The data does not need to be personal in any other sense, neither intimate in nature nor especially private in the sense of non-public. Most public information, such as people's names, is personal data. In this regard, the data protection rules apply to a vast amount of data processing.

However, as the concept of personal data is so exclusively linked to an individual, it is complicated to utilise data protection rules for the protection of groups. When an IP address can be traced, for instance to a certain physical address, it may still be impossible to ascertain which individual living on the premises has made the connection. If a person is identifiable, then data protection rules apply. If no individual person is identifiable, then a strict interpretation of the Regulation would entail that it does not apply at all. In this sense, data protection has narrower scope than more traditional forms of privacy rights – these are more flexible in terms of protecting the privacy of groups.

In the *Nowak*[41] judgment from 2017, the Court again considered the definition of personal data. Mr Nowak was a trainee accountant who took an accounting examination. After he had failed the exam for the fourth time, in autumn 2009, Mr Nowak challenged the result. The challenge was rejected in March 2010, after which he submitted a data access request seeking all the personal data relating to him. The organiser of the exam sent seventeen documents to Mr Nowak, but refused to send to him his examination script, on the ground that it did not contain personal data within the meaning of data protection legislation.

Mr Nowak took the dispute first to the data protection authorities, from where it eventually found its way to the Supreme Court of Ireland. Being unsure of whether an exam script constitutes personal data, the Supreme Court referred the question to the ECJ for a preliminary reference.

The ECJ reasoned, firstly, that the definition in the Directive entails that a candidate at a professional examination should be regarded as a natural person who can be identified, either directly, by name, or

[40] Case C-582/14, *Breyer*, EU:C:2016:779, paras. 48–9.
[41] Case C-434/16, *Peter Nowak* v. *Data Protection Commissioner*, EU:C:2017:994.

indirectly, through an identification number. It is not relevant whether an examiner can or cannot identify the candidate at the time when correcting and marking the examination script.[42]

In the *Nowak* judgment, the Court referred to its previous reasoning in *Breyer*. Personal data was defined in similar ways in both. Information is 'personal data' even though all the information enabling identification of the data subject would not be in the hands of one person.[43]

Considering the other components of the definition of personal data, the Court said that the concept of 'any information' needs to be given a wide interpretation. The definition of personal data:

> reflects the aim of the EU legislature to assign a wide scope to that concept, which is not restricted to information that is sensitive or private, but potentially encompasses all kinds of information, not only objective but also subjective, in the form of opinions and assessments, provided that it 'relates' to the data subject. As regards the latter condition, it is satisfied where the information, by reason of its content, purpose or effect, is linked to a particular person.[44]

The Court finally found that written answers by a candidate at an examination constitute information that is linked to them *as a person*. This is so because the content of those answers reflects the extent of their knowledge and competence and, sometimes, their intellect, thought processes and judgement. These are personal matters. In the case of a handwritten script, the answers also contain information about a person's handwriting.

In addition, the purpose of the exam answers is to evaluate the candidate's professional abilities and their suitability to practice the profession concerned, which makes the answers linked to the candidate. As regards the comments of an examiner with respect to the candidate's answers, it is, according to the Court, clear that also they constitute information relating to the candidate.[45]

It is interesting to note that the Court in this judgment also considers the personal data of groups, but only in passing. It argues that the same information may relate to a number of individuals and may be personal data for each of them. Such is the case with the examiner's comments, for instance. They are linked to the candidate but they can also

[42] Case C-434/16, *Nowak*, EU:C:2017:994, paras. 29–30.
[43] Case C-434/16, *Nowak*, EU:C:2017:994, para. 31.
[44] Case C-434/16, *Nowak*, EU:C:2017:994, paras. 34–5.
[45] Case C-434/16, *Nowak*, EU:C:2017:994, paras. 36–42.

constitute information relating to the examiner.[46] The same data can be personal data relating to many people.

The *pro and contra* argumentation that the Court engages in brings to the fore the overarching aim of protecting individuals' rights. The worry is that if information contained in a candidate's answers and in the comments made by the examiner were not classified as personal data, then that would entirely exclude information from the obligation of complying with all the principles and safeguards provided for in the Directive.[47] It is inherent in the logic of the Directive, and now the Regulation, that when something is considered personal data processing, then all the data protection rules normally apply. If an activity is not defined as such processing, then the rules do not apply at all. Hence, it is, according to the Court, important to keep interpretation of definitions broad for the sake of individuals' rights.

Recent attempts have been made in legal literature to take a step further from the individual-centred view towards considering, for instance, the privacy of groups or the privacy of other collectives. One central issue in data protection is that group profiles are often used, for instance in crime prevention and control, as well as in business, such as when banks consider loans.[48] When decisions are made on the basis of these group profiles, they may include discrimination. In order for data protection rules to become applicable in such situations, it is necessary that an individual be identifiable. The group itself does not enjoy protection of personal data, even though policies are based on group profiles that can be stigmatising or discriminatory.[49] Because of the definition of personal data, gaps may occur in data protection in these situations where no individual can be identified as such.

Alternative Perspectives from the ECtHR

The more traditional forms of privacy protection, such as protection of communication or protection of the home and of family life, may be

[46] Case C-434/16, *Nowak*, EU:C:2017:994, paras. 44–5.

[47] Case C-434/16, *Nowak*, EU:C:2017:994, para. 49. See also, on any information relating to a natural person who is identified or identifiable, Joined Cases C-92/09 and C-93/09, *Volker und Markus Schecke and Hartmut Eifert* v. *Land Hessen, joined party Bundesanstalt für Landwirtschaft und Ernährung*, EU:C:2010:662, para. 52; and Case C-291/12, *Michael Schwarz* v. *Stadt Bochum*, EU:C:2013:670, para. 26.

[48] See e.g. Mayer-Schönberger and Cukier, *Big Data*.

[49] See on collective interests of privacy e.g. Bart van der Sloot, *Privacy as Virtue: Moving beyond the Individual in the Age of Big Data* (Cambridge: Intersentia, 2017), p. 100.

more easily adaptable to the idea of privacy protecting a collective, although these rights are nowadays often seen in individualistic terms as well. A recent illustration of their complex nature is found from the case law of the Strasburg Court: the European Court of Human Rights.

The case of *Bărbulescu* v. *Romania*, in which judgment was delivered in Grand Chamber in 2017, is interesting because it concerns privacy of communication but also includes certain features that pertain to personal data protection. It needs to be recalled here, however, that the ECHR does not mention personal data protection as a privacy right. Nevertheless, the ECtHR does occasionally attune itself to an understanding of privacy protection very similar to that of the ECJ. Indeed, in *Bărbulescu* the ECtHR refers explicitly to the Union's data protection rules, as well as to the case law of its Luxembourg colleagues.

The facts of the case were as follows. The applicant had been employed by a Romanian private company. At his employer's request, for the purpose of responding to customers' enquiries, he created an instant messaging account using Yahoo Messenger. The employer's internal regulations prohibited the use of company resources for personal use. The regulations did not, however, contain any reference to the possibility for the employer to monitor employees' communications. The applicant had been informed of the employer's internal regulations and had signed a copy of them.

The employer recorded the applicant's Yahoo Messenger communications and the applicant was summoned by his employer. He was informed that his Yahoo Messenger communications had been monitored and that there was evidence that he had used the Internet for personal purposes, in breach of the internal regulations. Charts were attached indicating that his internet activity was greater than that of his colleagues. At that stage, he was not informed whether the monitoring of his communications had also concerned their content.

On the same day, the applicant informed the employer in writing that he had used Yahoo Messenger for work-related purposes only. The applicant was then shown forty-five pages of a transcript of the messages that he had exchanged with his brother and his fiancée during the period when he had been monitored. The messages related to personal matters and some were of an intimate nature. The transcript also included five messages that the applicant had exchanged with his fiancée using his personal Yahoo Messenger account; these messages did not contain any intimate information. The applicant then argued that the employer had committed a criminal offence by breaching the secrecy of correspondence. After this, the employer terminated the applicant's contract of employment.

The case eventually found its way to the Grand Chamber of the ECtHR. The Court had previously established case law according to which communications from business premises can be covered by the notions of 'private life' and 'correspondence'. The argument is that individuals have a reasonable expectation of privacy even in many situations outside the home.

Internet messaging services are, according to the Court, one form of communication that enables individuals to lead a private social life.[50] The Court paid attention to the fact that even though the applicant knew that personal activities were forbidden in the workplace, he was not informed that the employer would be monitoring both the flow and content of his communications.[51] It also transpired that the employer had monitored his personal Yahoo account, not only the one he used to answer customers. Considering all this, the Court noted that even though an employer restricts personal activities in the workplace, it cannot reduce private social life in the workplace to zero. Employees are still left with at least some reasonable expectation of privacy.[52]

In the end, the Court found that the domestic authorities had not afforded adequate protection of the applicant's right to respect for his private life and correspondence. They had failed to strike a fair balance between all the different interests involved in the case. Therefore, the Court found a violation of Article 8 of the Convention.[53]

The judgment is interesting for many reasons – both for what is said and for what is unsaid. Firstly, the Court's argumentation is only focused on the applicant's right to privacy but no mention is made of the fact that other peoples' privacy rights were infringed upon as well (for instance, the fiancée's). The case is framed according to one individual's claim: the applicant's.

This way, the case becomes an example of the individualist character of privacy rights: even when communication is protected, legal argumentation is only able to consider the rights of the individual whose case is to be decided. This is partly due to the procedural nature of these cases before the ECtHR, and it applies more or less at the ECJ as well.

[50] *Bărbulescu* v. *Romania*, ECHR:2017, paras. 73–4.
[51] *Bărbulescu* v. *Romania*, ECHR:2017, paras. 75–8.
[52] *Bărbulescu* v. *Romania*, ECHR:2017, para. 80.
[53] *Bărbulescu* v. *Romania*, ECHR:2017, para. 141.

It is noteworthy, however, that the ECtHR does not consider an individual in isolation. The Court maintains that there exists such a thing as *private social life*, which is protected even in workplaces. This innovative concept may perhaps be a way to operationalise privacy rights in a less individual-centred way if the social aspect of private life is emphasised. It can therefore be maintained that the Court here creates one possible opening for less individual-centred privacy rights.

It also becomes clear in this case that the argumentation is different from the ECJ's personal data jurisprudence. Focus lies on privacy rights understood as containing many different aspects. The ECJ's personal data case law, as we have seen, is often stricter in its argumentative technique, following very closely the relevant articles of the DPD or the GDPR. When there is no pressing need to balance other interests or rights, then the ECJ tends to refrain from doing so. The ECtHR takes more aspects into consideration and regularly engages in balancing different rights and interests.

When comparing the two courts' argumentative practice, we see that privacy cases at both are predominately framed as individual grievances. This affects the conceptualisation of privacy rights as the rights of individuals, not groups or other collectives.[54] Cases succeed if an individual applicant can show that their right has been infringed upon.[55] It follows that privacy issues are often conceptualised in these terms – by both lawyers and interest groups. This, in turn, affects the ways in which privacy is linked to personhood in contemporary legal thought.

Privacy Clashes with the Individual: the *Buivids* Case

We have seen that persons are cast as individuals in privacy law. But occasionally this brings about the conundrum of privacy rights clashing with other needs that individuals might have. There are examples of cases where privacy has not been given protection because another individualist interest has weighed more strongly. One rather interesting judgment is *Buivids* from the ECJ.

[54] See, however, the notable exception from the ECtHR, *Roman Zakharov* v. *Russia* ECHR 2015-VIII 205.

[55] See Bart van der Sloot's virtue ethical approach to privacy protection. He argues that letting go of the focus on individual rights, for instance by allowing *in abstracto* claims and class actions, would enable the law to take into account such privacy breaches that have become the main risk in Big Data and mass surveillance situations. van der Sloot, *Privacy as Virtue*.

This case concerns a preliminary reference request from Latvia about protection of personal data and freedom of expression. The judgment was delivered in 2019, and frames the case as a balancing case. In it, the Court not only defines various rules and concepts of data protection, but considers privacy in relation to other, contradictory rights.

Mr Buivids had posted on YouTube a video filmed by himself. It showed a statement that he made in the context of administrative proceedings involving the imposition of a penalty at a Latvian police station. The Latvian DPA (National Data Protection Agency) had considered the video illegal. The recording showed police officers going about their duties in the police station. Mr Buivids had not informed the police officers that he intended to post the video for all the world to see, which the DPA found to be a violation of national data protection law implementing the Data Protection Directive. Hence, the police officers' privacy was the issue here.

The ECJ considered first whether data protection rules applied at all in this situation but found rather unsurprisingly that recording the video and posting it online was to be regarded as processing, and that the contents of the video included personal data. The Court also found that Mr Buivids was to be regarded as controller of the processing. Continuing the well-established path of interpreting these elements of data protection law, it found that the situation did fall under the scope of the DPD, which was applicable law at the time.[56]

The trickier question was whether the Directive prohibited Mr Buivids from posting the video online. Here, the issue revolved around the question whether Mr Buivids' actions could be seen to fit the description of journalistic purposes, according to Article 9 of the Directive.

The Court focuses on teleology in this case as well. It considers the aims of data protection law. However, it notes that even though the objectives of the Directive are rights protection on the one hand and the free flow of data on the other, those objectives need to be reconciled with the fundamental right to freedom of expression. Article 9 seeks to reconcile two fundamental rights: protection of privacy and freedom of expression. This is, however, according to the ECJ, a task for the Member States.[57] Hence, the Court withdraws from the ultimate task

[56] Case C-345/17, *Buivids*, EU:C:2019:122, para. 47.
[57] Case C-345/17, *Buivids*, EU:C:2019:122, para. 50.

of balancing the rights at stake, and leaves it to the Member State's authorities.

The Court does nevertheless give some guidance on how the balancing should be done. It states, among other things, that protection of the fundamental right to privacy requires that derogations and limitations in relation to protection of data are interpreted as strictly necessary.[58] That way, the judgment emphasises that privacy enjoys very strong protection.

The ECJ refers to the case law of the ECtHR on balancing journalistic freedom and privacy rights. The Strasbourg Court has laid down a number of criteria that must be taken into account in these instances. These include, for instance, contributing to a debate of public interest, the degree of notoriety of the person affected, the subject of the news report, the prior conduct of the person concerned, the content, form and consequences of the publication, and the manner and circumstances in which the information was obtained. Similarly, the possibility for the controller to adopt measures to mitigate the extent of interference with the right to privacy must be taken into account.[59]

The ECJ concluded in *Buivids* that the factual circumstances of the case may constitute processing of personal data solely for journalistic purposes, within the meaning of the Directive, if it is apparent from the video that the sole object of the recording and publication was disclosure of information, opinions or ideas to the public.[60] It seems, therefore, that Mr Buivids' actions can be acceptable, even though the privacy of the police officers was compromised.

Buivids constitutes a rare personal data judgment from the ECJ because of its results. In the Court's balancing, personal data protection does not automatically weigh heaviest. Privacy rights are not given preference, but are rather considered as one value requiring comparison with others.

Buivids is also an unusual case because a private person is the controller, just as in the early case of *Lindqvist*. The essence of personal data law, as we have seen, is usually to protect the individual. The threat comes from companies or governments. Here, one individual's infringement on another individual's privacy – albeit an individual in a governmental role – is under scrutiny.

[58] Case C-345/17, *Buivids*, EU:C:2019:122, para. 64.
[59] Case C-345/17, *Buivids*, EU:C:2019:122, para. 66.
[60] Case C-345/17, *Buivids*, EU:C:2019:122, para. 69.

Even though the Court leaves the final balancing to the Member State, the judgment shows that protection of privacy becomes quite tricky when individual interests apply on both sides of the scale. The usual logic of privacy and personal data law does not quite work because the logic is geared towards protecting individuals. Cracks open on the surface of data protection law.

It might be possible to ameliorate dilemmas like the one caused in *Buivids* by adopting a more nuanced view of privacy protection, one that acknowledges the relational nature of privacy and does not focus so strongly on protecting individual personhood. In the current ideology underlying privacy rights, the individual is the centre around which the law revolves. Ideology is persuasive because it gives meaning to the apparatus – in this case law – that functions according to the ideology.

Even Relational Privacy Can Be Individualistic

The benefits of privacy can be argued from the point of view of an individual seen as a separate entity, or from the point of view of an individual in relation to others. Both views can be individualistic.

Charles Fried argued back in 1968 that privacy is necessarily related to ends and relations of the most fundamental kind: respect, love, friendship and trust: 'Privacy is not merely a good technique for furthering these fundamental relations; rather without privacy they are simply inconceivable. They require a context of privacy or the possibility of privacy for their existence.'[61] Fried goes on to say that a threat to privacy is a threat to the very integrity of the person. This stems from his view of morality, where everyone is entitled to equal basic rights by their status as a person. Privacy is one of those rights.

Following the common liberalist interpretation of Kant, Fried sees the only justifiable qualification of rights stemming from situations where it is necessary to restrict one person's rights for the protection of the rights of others. Persons need to be regarded as ends in themselves and their liberty is the most fundamental value.[62]

This ethical view allows for a variety of values and interests to be pursued as long as they are consistent with an equal right of all persons to similar liberty. Liberty needs to be respected. From this can be derived

[61] Charles Fried, 'Privacy' (1968) 77 *The Yale Law Journal* 474–93 at 477.

[62] Fried, 'Privacy', 478.

the definition of a person. Persons are those who are obliged to observe the constraints of the principle of morality in their dealings with each other.[63]

What is interesting in Fried's liberalist view of privacy is that he notices a significant connection between society and action. Acts derive their meaning partly from their social context, from how many people know about them, and what they know. Privacy gives us control over the context in which we act.[64] It gives us possibilities to shape the meaning of our actions by, for instance, limiting the amount of people who know about them. We get the freedom to share our lives, or not, if we so wish.

The dimension of control became evident in the above discussion of liquid modernity and privacy as an index of individualisation. The less control we have of social and material realities, the more attention is paid to the narratives of our individual lives. In Fried's view, privacy is used precisely as an instrument to control the context in which we act, thus enabling us to manage the meanings that our action is given.

The connection between love and privacy is one example. Fried argues that love and friendship involve mutual respect as well as some degree of intimacy. These kinds of relationships include sharing information about our actions, thoughts, beliefs and emotions. We have the right to choose whom we share these with and to not to share them with just anyone.[65]

Privacy, then, creates 'the moral capital' that we spend in friendship and love.[66] Today, this capital would perhaps be personal data. Either way, the argumentation takes place within an individual-centred view of privacy. Already the choice of examples is indicative. Love and friendship are predominately relationships between individual persons. They do not refer to groups or communities. Privacy is like a gift that an individual may wish to give to another person, and the individual is free to choose to whom to give that gift.

There is no reason why privacy and social values should necessarily be at odds with each other. Often the value of privacy is conceptualised as protection of the individual *and* society. Privacy is deemed important for different forms of social interaction, and therefore for society more

63 Fried, 'Privacy', 479.
64 Fried, 'Privacy', 482.
65 Fried, 'Privacy', 484.
66 Fried, 'Privacy', 484.

generally. When individual privacy is threatened, this also endangers social relationships and practices. It can ultimately endanger the integration of society as well.[67] It is noteworthy, though, that this kind of thinking understands the primary function of privacy to be the protection of individual freedom and autonomy.

[67] Beate Roessler and Dorota Mokrosinska, 'Privacy and Social Interaction' (2013) 39(8) *Philosophy and Social Criticism* 771–91.

3 The Autonomous Person

'There can be no normative order without persons, for what is ordered is the conduct of persons and the treatment they are to receive.'[1] The conceptual links between legal order and the human being understood as an autonomous person are numerous. Lon L. Fuller's view is well known:

> To embark on the enterprise of subjecting human conduct to the governance of rules involves of necessity a commitment to the view that man is, or can become, a responsible agent, capable of understanding and following rules, and answerable for his defaults. Every departure from the principles of the law's inner morality is an affront to man's dignity as a responsible agent.[2]

Fuller argues that the very possibility of legal order is contingent on the agency of the legal subject. The form of social ordering called law is the kind where the agency of law's subjects is upheld.[3] This is one necessary requirement of a legal system: in order for it to command obedience as a legal system, it has to treat its subordinates as persons who are able to act, make choices and commit to certain ways of life.

Fuller's idea is that the moral understanding of the legal person as a rational, autonomous agent who is capable of self-directed activity is necessary for law because the whole logic of law depends on it.[4] Legal rule differs from managerial ordering, for instance, which is not predictable or rule-bound and does not necessarily respect persons as autonomous agents.[5]

1 Neil MacCormick, *Institutions of Law* (Oxford: Oxford University Press, 2007), p. 77.
2 Lon L. Fuller, *The Morality of Law*, revised ed. (New Haven, CT: Yale University Press, 1969), p. 162.
3 Kristen Rundle, *Forms Liberate: Reclaiming the Jurisprudence of Lon L Fuller* (Oxford: Hart Publishing, 2012), p. 82.
4 Rundle, *Forms Liberate*, p. 106.
5 Rundle, *Forms Liberate*, p. 82.

Fuller's account of law is delightfully nuanced, however, because he also sees law as *constitutive of human agency*. The law takes part in making people into autonomous agents. Law as a system of general rules constitutes persons as responsible agents who orient their behaviour towards general rules.[6] The rules may have any kind of content, moral or not, just or unjust, but the necessary condition of persons as autonomous agents still applies. The active legal subject thus occupies a central role in Fuller's anti-positivist view. In order to determine whether a system is a legal system at all, it is necessary to consider how it constructs persons.[7]

However, responsible agency does not have to be understood in an all-or-nothing way. Autonomy and agency are one thing, complete autonomy and fully capable agency another. The rules of law would be pointless if people had not the freedom of will or capacity to adjust their behaviour accordingly. But law does not have to presuppose a completely free and autonomous individual whose hopes, fears and actions are always under control.

The idea of law constituting autonomous persons, not only presupposing them, is found elsewhere in jurisprudence as well. The choices that people make are responses to the normative order, while the person making the choices is also influenced by that very same order. For instance, MacCormick goes so far as to argue that '[i]n the development of moral agency, heteronomy precedes autonomy'.[8] The law and the autonomous person are constituted by one another.

MacCormick notices something intriguing. As construction of the law and the person in law goes back and forth both ways, there can be no completely independent, free or autonomous person. In order to be autonomous selves, we are already permeated by otherness.[9] The question is, then, how does this understanding of personhood fit with contemporary regulation of privacy?

6 Rundle, *Forms Liberate*, pp. 104, 107.

7 Rundle, *Forms Liberate*, p. 118.

8 Neil MacCormick, 'My Philosophy of Law', in L. J. Wintgens (ed.), *The Law in Philosophical Perspectives* (Dordrecht: Springer, 1999), pp. 121–45 at 128.

9 See also Roger Cotterrell's interesting discussion of human dignity and autonomy from a sociological point of view in Roger Cotterrell, 'Justice, Dignity, Torture, Headscarves: Can Durkheim's Sociology Clarify Legal Values?' (2010) 20 *Social & Legal Studies* 1–18.

Privacy Rights Protect Personhood

We have so far established that privacy rights, which are currently dominated by personal data protection, construct the person first and foremost as an individual in control. The next step is to consider what features this individual possesses.

The aim of enhancing individuals' control corresponds with widespread agreement that privacy is valuable because it is an essential component of individual development, self-definition, personality and autonomy.[10] The precise meaning and relationship between all these concepts is far from clear, though.

What is the law protecting when it prohibits the publication of, say, diary entries or recordings of conversations without a person's knowledge or will? What is the value or the aim of granting everybody the right to keep their personal data, as well as their thoughts, feelings, hopes and fears, to themselves?

According to the original legal proponents of privacy, Warren and Brandeis: 'The principle which protects personal writings and all other personal productions, not against theft and physical appropriation, but against publication in any form, is in reality not the principle of private property, but that of an inviolate personality.'[11] Hence, the law protects privacy because of the underlying aim of protecting inviolate personality. Attaching privacy rights to personality has been a prevalent feature of legal conceptions of privacy from the start. Privacy is somehow intertwined with, if not even necessary for, personhood.

What is striking in legal academic literature is the frequency and stability of certain claims. A majority of studies on privacy and personal data regulation refer to this article by Warren and Brandeis from 1890. Its position as a foundational text is generally accepted, and very few accounts of the history of privacy, even European ones, discuss older material.

The importance of this article is one constant feature of privacy scholarship, and another is the overriding agreement that there is no definition of privacy. Several influential writers argue that the meaning of privacy is diffuse, unclear or elusive,[12] thus re-iterating the idea that the exact meaning of privacy cannot be defined.

[10] See e.g. Westin, *Privacy and Freedom*; but also e.g. Buitelaar, 'Privacy: Back to the Roots'.
[11] Warren and Brandeis, 'The Right to Privacy', 205.
[12] E.g. Buitelaar, 'Privacy: Back to the Roots', 182.

Nevertheless, this general acknowledgement of undefinable privacy still results in many academics trying. Daniel Solove, for instance, argues that a single definition of privacy cannot be developed, nor would it be beneficial. He puts forward a taxonomy of privacy, which takes its model from the Wittgensteinian idea of family resemblance. Solove distinguishes between the right to be let alone, limited access to the self, secrecy, control over personal information, protection of one's personality, individuality and dignity, control over one's intimate relationships or aspects of life as various elements of privacy.[13]

Privacy, hence, has many components. All of them point towards an individual, who is a self, whose control over their information and their life needs to be respected. In sum, it is personhood that needs protection.

A remarkable feature of privacy scholarship is that the functions, aims and values of privacy are often defined in naturalistic terms. Westin begins his 400-page classic by analysing the natural state of animals and man, where we can observe that privacy is a commonly found value. He argues that anthropological research has shown that individuals in virtually every society seek privacy at times, and disclosure and companionship at others. Restricting information about oneself and one's emotions is crucial for protecting the individual in social interaction. Needs for privacy and corresponding norms are found in all societies.[14]

That way, privacy is understood to be a natural need for man. Even though the naturalistic fallacy looms large over this reasoning, it is interesting to note that similar views still tend to make their appearance in legal discourses on privacy. It is as if legal norms on privacy and publicity require a firm and solid moral foundation, which is found in the nature of man.

What is forgotten, however, is precisely the constructive features of privacy, especially when it becomes codified and protected by law. Legal regulation not only reflects the values of society, but also influences those values in many ways. Morality, as well as normality, may be just as much a product of the legal system as its basis. It is nowadays impossible to say what comes first, regulation of behaviour or behaviour itself. The

[13] Daniel J. Solove, *Understanding Privacy* (Cambridge, MA: Harvard University Press, 2008). Solove himself advocates taking into account the social values of privacy as well.

[14] Westin, *Privacy and Freedom*, pp. 12–21.

otherness at the heart of the person is, however, seldom acknowledged in privacy law.

The huge debate about privacy and its limits that started in the global arena post-Snowden attracted contributions from people occupying various roles, private and public, commercial and non-commercial. There are cries for more privacy, but also different kinds of privacy, especially the right to be left alone by surveillance apparatus as well as by commercial enterprises. The idea of privacy rights protecting personality, or rather personhood, appears often in this debate.

We find, for instance, an endemic cry for privacy by Michael Lynch in *The New York Times*. Breaches of privacy like government spy programmes are, according to him, a threat to the self. According to Lynch, the connection between loss of privacy and dehumanisation is a well-known fact because privacy is intimately connected to what it means to be an autonomous person. But Lynch goes further than this and argues that if someone else could have access to one's innermost thoughts, dreams and fears, they could start controlling them. Thus, what is at stake is not only one's autonomy, but one's freedom, too. There would be nothing subjective about one any more. One would have become dehumanised.

The tradition of understanding privacy as protecting our innermost selves is strong. However, certain aspects of this fear – that with loss of privacy we could lose ourselves – require further thought. There is something uncanny about a self that has been lost. Is it possible that we are afraid of losing something that we did not have in the first place? The fear would seem to imply that there exists an autonomous selfsame person to be protected and that it could be lost if not well enough protected.

The supposition that our innermost selves are in urgent need of protection supposes that everything *could be* revealed were privacy rights not there to safeguard us. The underlying idea is that everything about the self could be said, shown or expressed. However, as psychoanalytic theory has convincingly shown, much stays hidden all the time.[15]

Lynch concludes with an argument that is by no means unique:

> However we resolve these issues, we would do well to keep the connections between self, personhood and privacy in mind as we chew over the recent revelations about governmental access to Big Data. The underlying issue is not

[15] See e.g. Slavoj Žižek, *The Sublime Object of Ideology* (London: Verso, 1989).

simply a matter of balancing convenience and liberty. To the extent we risk the loss of privacy we risk, in a very real sense, the loss of our very status as subjective, autonomous persons.[16]

Where Warren and Brandeis are concerned with everyone's inviolate personality, Lynch asserts that losing privacy ultimately means loss of our autonomous selves. There is a difference between these two positions, even though it might seem tiny. That is, where the first connects privacy with community, the second does not. Warren and Brandeis have in mind the common law of tort, which includes an element of respect for social life, not only autonomous selves.[17]

Privacy Rights Focus on Protecting Autonomy

The relation between privacy and autonomy is referred to in most legal expositions of privacy, albeit with rather meagre analysis of the complexities of the relation. That autonomy and privacy are connected is seldom expanded upon, but that the connection is there is usually taken for granted.

Either privacy is seen as a social circumstance necessary for individuals to become autonomous beings, or the value of privacy is argued in light of the fact that we are autonomous persons – or both. Westin, for instance, argues that privacy is valuable particularly *because* it protects autonomy. According to him, one of the four main functions that privacy performs for individuals in a democratic society is personal autonomy.[18]

Paul Bernal, on the other hand, argues that privacy rights can be directly deduced from the idea of autonomy: they arise from autonomy and if brought into play they support, protect and help preserve autonomy. His prime concern is privacy as a protector of autonomy rather than privacy per se.[19]

[16] Michael P. Lynch, 'Privacy and the Threat to the Self', *The New York Times*, 22 June 2013, http://opinionator.blogs.nytimes.com/2013/06/22/privacy-and-the-threat-to-the-self/.

[17] See Robert C. Post, 'The Social Foundations of Privacy: Community and Self in the Common Law Tort' 1989) 77 *California Law Review* 957–1010 especially at 959, 963. Post in fact sees in the intrusion tort an example of where the debate between liberals (who stress the aspects of the self that are liberal and autonomous) and communitarians (who emphasise those aspects that are embedded in social norms and values) is transcended, for the tort presides over those social norms that enable an autonomous self to emerge. At 974.

[18] Westin, *Privacy and Freedom*, p. 35.

[19] Paul Bernal, *Internet Privacy Rights: Rights to Protect Autonomy* (Cambridge: Cambridge University Press, 2014), p. 9

Bernal draws on Joseph Raz's definition of autonomy. The autonomous person is somebody who controls, to some degree, their own destiny, fashioning it through successive decisions throughout their lives.[20] According to Bernal, autonomy is the capacity people have to decide upon a good life, as well as rationally pursue it. It also includes the element of one being the author of one's own life. Autonomy is therefore necessarily connected to freedom.[21]

Privacy protects the freedom to choose a life without coercion or manipulation, and to live accordingly. These are echoes of liquid modernity. Rights are meant to protect people's free choices of – and on – (caravan) sites. Privacy and data protection are especially well-suited for the task because of their inbuilt individualistic nature.

We should notice the hesitation in Raz, though. An autonomous person is the author of their own life, but not necessarily the only author. A whiff of otherness comes in here. This is what MacCormick also sees: as persons in law, we are conditioned by otherness.

Julie Cohen is one of the few who has paid attention to the flaws in our current thinking where autonomy is the most important value protected by privacy: 'The problem . . . is not simply that autonomy is constituted over time and by circumstances; it is that including autonomy in the definition of the ultimate good to be achieved invokes a set of presumptions about the separateness of self and society that begs the very question we are trying to answer.'[22] The most common theoretical conception of privacy among legal scholars is thus one where autonomy is not really questioned. This strikes one as odd, considering that mainstream jurisprudence, as we have seen, has acknowledged the otherness at the heart of the legal person for decades.

Considering legislation and case law, on the other hand, we have seen that the person in control is the most obvious person constructed by the law today. This view of personhood corresponds to a majority of privacy law theory. Still, another kind of person also emerges from privacy law. Even though the rules seek to empower individuals and give them control over their data, they also protect vulnerable persons, at least to some degree.

[20] Joseph Raz, *The Morality of Freedom* (Oxford: Oxford University Press, 1986), p. 369 (as cited in Bernal, *Internet Privacy Rights*, p. 24).

[21] Bernal, *Internet Privacy Rights*, pp. 24–5.

[22] Julie Cohen, *Configuring the Networked Self – Law, Code, and the Play of Everyday Practice* (New Haven, CT and London: Yale University Press, 2012), p. 113.

Personal Data Law Protects Vulnerable Persons

In the active person, the law sees a free and rational agent. In the passive, it sees first and foremost a vulnerable being. Both appear frequently in law, although different legal fields tend to uphold more the one than the other. For instance, fundamental rights law, consumer law and many areas of family or social security law revolve around the individual in need of protection. In data protection law, the person in control is intertwined with the vulnerable person.[23]

The passive person emerges especially as a product of the principle of accountability, which runs through the whole Regulation. This means, among other things, that the controller has to implement data protection in its operations and has to be able to show that it has followed the Regulation. The lawful grounds for processing in Article 6 need to be considered by the controller in advance of any processing. And data protection needs to be incorporated into all relevant operations by design and default.[24] Article 25 stipulates, among other things, that the controller has to take appropriate technical and organisational measures to implement data protection principles, such as data minimisation, in an effective manner. These include pseudonymisation. The Regulation, hence, requires protection of privacy regardless of the data subject's active steps towards that end. The burden of proof for compliance lies with controllers and/or processors.

Furthermore, many rules in the Regulation are not waivable. They continue to apply even after a person has consented to data gathering and processing. The Regulation is not meant as just another exercise in clicking 'I agree' to unread and unnegotiable terms.[25] That way, the protection it affords a passive or vulnerable person is effective.

[23] For recent critical analysis of liberalism and agency, see Ratna Kapur, 'In the Aftermath of Critique We Are Not in Epistemic Free Fall: Human Rights, the Subaltern Subject, and Non-Liberal Search for Freedom and Happiness' (2014) 25 *Law & Critique* 2–45.

[24] Reg. (EU) 2016/679, OJ 2016 No. L119, 4 May 2016. Preamble 78 states that 'The protection of the rights and freedoms of natural persons with regard to the processing of personal data require that appropriate technical and organisational measures be taken to ensure that the requirements of this Regulation are met. In order to be able to demonstrate compliance with this Regulation, the controller should adopt internal policies and implement measures which meet in particular the principles of data protection by design and data protection by default.'

[25] See Chris Jay Hoofnagle, Bart van der Sloot and Frederik Zuiderveen Borgesius, 'The European Union General Data Protection Regulation: What It Is and What It Means' (2019) 28 *Information & Communications Technology Law* 65–98 at 68.

All in all the GDPR displays an interesting tension between, on the one hand, the active person whose means of controlling data are enhanced and protected, and, on the other hand, the vulnerable person whose protection does not rely on their own consent, claims or demands.

Fashion Id: the Activity of the Person Is Irrelevant

We have considered several cases where the ECJ has put responsibility on controllers for gathering data in ways that individuals may not even notice. These judgments not only protect a person in control, but also a person who is not.

Another striking example from the ECJ is *Fashion ID*.[26] Here, a German court requested a preliminary ruling on, inter alia, the definition of controllership. The issue concerns Fashion ID, an online retailer that embedded Facebook's 'Like' button on its website. As a result, when a user visits the Fashion ID website, information about that user's IP address and browser string is transferred to Facebook. The transfer occurs regardless of whether the user has clicked 'Like' or whether the user even possesses a Facebook account.

The central question in the case concerns which party should be considered the controller in this scenario, Facebook or Fashion ID. Here, too, the Court concluded that both the online retailer and Facebook can be regarded as controllers and therefore responsible for their part of the processing.

According to Advocate General Bobek, Fashion ID should be seen as a controller for the collection and transmission of users' personal data. However, the company's (joint) responsibility should be limited to those operations for which it effectively determines the means and purposes of processing personal data.[27] When issuing his opinion, the Advocate General referred to the Court's reasoning in *Wirtschaftsakademie* several times. For instance, according to him, the court's statement that joint responsibility did not necessarily imply equal responsibility among the various operators involved in processing personal data suggested the need to limit the liability of a (joint) controller.[28]

[26] Case C-40/17, *Fashion ID GmbH & Co. KG* v. *Verbraucherzentrale NRW e.V., joined parties Facebook Ireland Limited, Landesbeauftragte für Datenschutz und Informationsfreiheit Nordrhein-Westfalen*, EU:C:2019:629.

[27] Case C-40/17, *Fashion ID*, Opinion of AG Bobek, EU:C:2018:1039, para. 142.

[28] Case C-40/17, *Fashion ID*, Opinion of AG Bobek, EU:C:2018:1039, para. 94.

In Fashion ID, the Advocate General also raised the concern that under the new system of joint liability introduced in Article 26 of the GDPR, it might be difficult to envisage how joint responsibility could imply unequal responsibility.[29] To determine the responsibility of controllers, two key elements are decisive: means and purpose. The result is a step-by-step tool for analysing processing situations, thereby resolving the issue of which party or parties should be regarded as controllers and how much responsibility each of them should bear:[30] 'I consider that the liability of the Defendant (Fashion ID) has to be limited to the stage of the data processing in which it is engaged and that it cannot spill over into any potential subsequent stages of data processing, if such processing occurs outside the control and, it would appear, also without the knowledge of the Defendant.'[31] What is interesting in the Advocate General's opinion is that he explicitly calls for balancing of rights and interests when applying the Directive. He argues that in order to assess the legitimacy of data processing, as set out in Article 7(f) of the DPD, the legitimate interests of both joint controllers must be taken into account and balanced against the rights of data subjects.[32] The opinion, hence, continues the Court's practice of using data subjects' rights as the yardstick for legitimacy. However, those rights are not seen as automatically overriding the interests of controllers.

Controllers have the duty to obtain the consent of the people whose data is processed when consent is used as a lawful ground for processing. They are also responsible for respecting all the other data protection rights that the law provides. In this case, it became important to consider which party or parties are controllers in order to know who is required to obtain consent and inform the data subjects of the processing. Fashion ID did not know the exact scope and purpose of the processing done by Facebook. Hence, Fashion ID could not inform data subjects accordingly or obtain their informed consent.

The Court considered that Fashion ID's embedding of the Facebook 'Like' button on its website allows it to optimise the publicity of its goods by making them more visible. The reason why Fashion ID seems to have agreed, at least implicitly, to collection of the personal data of visitors to its website by embedding such a plug-in is to benefit from the commercial advantage of publicity for its goods. Processing is therefore

[29] Case C-40/17, *Fashion ID*, Opinion of AG Bobek, EU:C:2018:1039, para. 96.
[30] Case C-40/17, *Fashion ID*, Opinion of AG Bobek, EU:C:2018:1039, para. 102.
[31] Case C-40/17, *Fashion ID*, Opinion of AG Bobek, EU:C:2018:1039, para. 107.
[32] Case C-40/17, *Fashion ID*, Opinion of AG Bobek, EU:C:2018:1039, paras. 125–7.

done in the economic interests of both Fashion ID and Facebook Ireland. Hence, it can be seen that Fashion ID and Facebook Ireland jointly determine the purposes of collection of personal data.[33]

The Court concluded that the operator of a website such as Fashion ID can be considered a controller by embedding on that website a plug-in causing the browser of a visitor to that website to request content from the provider of that plug-in and, to that end, to transmit to that provider the personal data of the visitor. The liability of such a controller is, however, limited to processing personal data of which it actually determines the purposes and means.[34]

A duty to inform the data subject is incumbent on Fashion ID, but the information that it must provide to the data subject need relate only to processing personal data in respect of which it actually determines the purposes and means. Consent must also be obtained by Fashion ID for this same personal data.[35]

Here, the Court followed closely its argumentation in *Wirtschaftsakademie* when analysing the responsibility of the controller. The activities of data subjects became irrelevant. The case shows that the law protects a person regardless of the fact that they know, or do not know, that their data is being processed. The case is illuminating in this regard. A person did not need to press the 'Like' button, but their data was collected all the same. Respect for their rights was demanded by the Court regardless of the data subject's action.

The case does, however, concern consent and therefore the person in control makes an appearance in this case, too. An important reason for defining controllership is precisely to distinguish which party needs to obtain consent. That way, the case does presuppose a person who can and should control their data, that is, an autonomous person.

However, it is not only the autonomous individual that the law here protects, but a person who may be completely clueless – or careless – or vulnerable, or both. Perhaps the person knows that their data is being processed, perhaps not. The Court did not consider these issues. The important thing was to determine which party is responsible for safeguarding the data subject who visits a website.

[33] Case C-40/17, *Fashion ID*, EU:C:2019:629, para. 81.
[34] Case C-40/17, *Fashion ID*, EU:C:2019:629, para. 85.
[35] Case C-40/17, *Fashion ID*, EU:C:2019:629, para. 106.

Deconstructing the Autonomous Legal Person

What happens to the person in law if we take seriously the idea that they are not simply an autonomous individual, but something much more complex? The standard account of liberalism presupposes the freedom of a self-conscious (and/or rational) agent, who is at liberty to choose the kind of life they want to lead, and is therefore responsible for their actions and omissions. Privacy rights do reflect this view. They are the rights of such persons, but they also protect persons without full knowledge of their actions, too.

An alternative to liberalism is to see a right not as an individual entitlement but as something that is born in relations. These relations make the person and also form the foundation for rights.[36] That way, a community has to be presupposed simultaneously with the person. Let us consider what this alternative logic would entail.

According to Slavoj Žižek, a foundational foreignness or otherness already lies at the heart of the Cartesian subject. Not even the original idea of an ego is therefore free from alterity.[37] Later on, modernity created the subject as a conscious and rational person who decides to enter into a constitutional agreement in order to form a government, or who negotiates the best possible government behind a veil of ignorance. The postmodern subject, on the other hand, is defined by a fundamental helplessness. For the postmodern person, there are no objective truths, no clear value systems and no credible ideologies. Nor is the postmodern person completely intelligible to themselves, or conscious of the motives for their actions. These are the basic types of subjectivity, as they appear in the history of Western thinking. Žižek's own view stands in opposition to all these (simplified) depictions.

Žižek's subject is thoroughly political.[38] Political (and legal) systems create ways of being human, so the subject is never completely their

[36] See Susanna Lindroos-Hovinheimo, 'Excavating Foundations of Legal Personhood: Fichte on Autonomy and Self-Consciousness' (2015) 28 *International Journal for the Semiotics of Law* 687–702.

[37] See e.g. Slavoj Žižek, *The Ticklish Subject: The Absent Centre of Political Ontology* (London: Verso, 2008), pp. 48–52, 68–72; Slavoj Žižek, *Less than Nothing: Hegel and the Shadow of Dialectical Materialism* (London: Verso, 2012), pp. 140–89; and Adrian Johnston, *Žižek's Ontology: A Transcendental Materialist Theory of Subjectivity* (Evanston, IL: Northwestern University Press, 2008), p. 10.

[38] Žižek has been criticised for mixing a psychological analysis of human beings with an examination of social structures and political organisation. He continually steps across the border between the private and the public. This is evidently a conscious move, as it seems that for Žižek there can be no individual without the social. See Adrian Johnston,

own master. The subject is conditioned by something foreign to them. However, the subject has a core that resists the power structures that constitute it. The idea is that in order for the subject to be able to identify with certain ways of being – that is, to become constituted by systems – they should already have something or *be* something. Žižek conceptualises this something as a void or a gap. The fundamental structure of human beings, the structure on which political subjectivity is grounded, is *a nothing* that nevertheless exists.[39]

A person is not completely definable by outside forces because they do contain an autonomous core of sorts. Yet this core is nothing concrete or substantial. The way we are, the lives we want to live, the values we hold dear are all imposed on us by power structures beyond our control.

We are intertwined in many ways. Our opacity to ourselves is foundational in all human relationships. When we understand that we can never know ourselves completely, we realise that we cannot expect anything else from others either. Every relationship is based on certain amounts of ignorance and assumptions, about ourselves and others.

Judith Butler turns upside down the idea that a subject who is opaque to themselves is therefore not fully responsible for their actions. The fact that we are always interrupted by alterity means that we are ethically involved in the lives of others. Butler's understanding of responsibility takes into account the fact that we are not complete, autonomous and self-present persons but that our identities are constructed in different social contexts. This kind of ethics is based on our shared partial blindness about ourselves. The realisation that one is not completely intelligible and that there might always be something for which one cannot give an account might at least induce patience towards others. One would not expect other people to be completely rational at every moment either.[40] Hence, there are ethical implications in seeing human beings as fundamentally void, lacking and unknown to themselves. This conception of personhood can be a foundation for law as well. It acknowledges autonomy but sees it as preceded by heteronomy.

Badiou, Žižek, and Political Transformations: The Cadence of Change (Evanston, IL: Northwestern University Press, 2009), pp. 86–7.

39 Žižek, *The Ticklish Subject*, p. 348.

40 Butler, Judith, 'Giving an Account of Oneself' (2001) 31 *Diacritics* 22–40 at pp. 27, 37; Judith Butler, *Giving an Account of Oneself* (New York: Fordham University Press 2005), pp. 83–92.

Such an understanding of the person brings a new twist to privacy rights. If we are strangers to ourselves, at least to some degree, then we should respect that others are strangers to themselves as well. Communication, for instance, runs the risk of imprecision and misunderstanding, two incomprehensible beings searching for rapport.

Stanley Cavell points at this aspect of the 'other minds' problem – and the aspect that shows how it is not merely a philosophical problem. The difficulty is encountering others. A certain amount of strangeness always prevails. It is hard to know another person. It might even be impossible. There is a real difficulty in how little we can reveal ourselves to another's gaze, or bear that gaze, Cavell says.[41]

At this stage we can sum up the critique against the autonomy doctrine inherent in privacy law: it is based on a myth that persons are selfsame beings in control of themselves. When they turn out to be something else entirely, the legal logic of privacy becomes unclear. Other strategies for protecting individuals are then called for, one of which makes itself apparent in the accountability rules of the GDPR.

Subjective Conceptions of Privacy

I have argued so far that even though the meaning of privacy is often debated, its value is not. This value is intertwined with what I have tentatively characterised as individualism. The way privacy rights are predominately understood in law emphasises the autonomous individual in control.

There are, however, alternative possibilities for conceptualising privacy and personal data protection. For instance, Jill Marshall has developed a view of human rights that tries to strike a balance between individuality and commonality. She argues for an understanding of rights as socially interconnected but still powerful in protecting individuals.

Even though the whole purpose of rights is to protect everyone's dignity and ensure them the possibility to develop their personality freely, this is not supposed to happen in a subjective vacuum. Marshall points out that personality development, even dignity, requires interaction and interconnectedness with other people.[42]

[41] Stanley Cavell, *Conditions Handsome and Unhandsome: The Constitution of Emersonian Perfectionism: The Carus Lectures* (Chicago, IL: University of Chicago Press 1990), p. 90.

[42] Jill Marshall, *Human Rights Law and Personal Identity* (Oxon and New York: Routledge, 2014).

Such a social nature of rights was explicitly noted in the Universal Declaration of Human Rights 1948 (UDHR). According to Article 29, everyone has duties to the community in which alone the free and full development of their personality is possible. The community is here seen as a focal point of rights protection.

Marshall argues that identity and personality can only be formed in contact with others, in a community: 'Identity and personality is formed in large part by the social conditions in which people find themselves, and can contribute to varying degrees to create and change. These social conditions include legally formed policies to develop self-confidence, self-respect and self-esteem.'[43] However, the law does occasionally take a very narrow look at the person, focusing only on their subjective understanding of privacy, thus sidestepping the view of persons as embedded in community. A rather famous case from the European Court of Human Rights – *Peck* v. *United Kingdom* – illustrates the tenuous relation between privacy rights and commonality.[44] The Court ruled in 2003 against the UK, holding that the privacy of the applicant had been violated.

Article 8 of the ECHR says that everyone has the right to respect for their private life. This protection encompasses many things, for instance family life, home and correspondence. According to the Court's case law, protection of private life includes personal freedom. Issues such as autonomy, identity and integrity are repeatedly referred to by the Court.[45]

The objective of Article 8 is to prohibit unwanted intrusions into people's private spaces, be they physical or mental, especially by public authorities. In some situations, this may mean safeguarding against legal intrusions, that is, intrusions through national legislation.

One might say that protection of private life functions as a security break that sets limits on public authorities and power-wielding bodies. It is designed to enable people to live the life they choose, shape their identity freely and become who they are.[46] But there are limits to this freedom. The law is essentially an instrument of social co-ordination

[43] Jill Marshall, 'The Legal Recognition of Personality: Full-Face Veils and Permissible Choices' (2014) 10 *International Journal of Law in Context* 64–80 at 75.

[44] *Peck* v. *United Kingdom* ECHR 2003-I.

[45] See Jill Marshall's excellent research, *Personal Freedom through Human Rights Law?* (Leiden: Martinus Nijhoff, 2009).

[46] See Marshall, *Personal Freedom through Human Rights Law?*, p. 7.

and organisation, which both creates certain kinds of legal persons and discourages other alternative ways of being.[47]

The applicant had been filmed by closed-circuit television (CCTV) cameras in a public place while in the process of committing suicide. Although he did not complain about being filmed, which in fact saved his life, he objected to the subsequent publications and broadcasts of the material. The CCTV footage did not show him actually cutting his wrists but the applicant argued that it concerned a period immediately following his suicide attempt and thus related to a very personal and private matter.

The applicant was in the street, but it was late at night, and he was not taking part in a public demonstration (the main reason for demonstrating is to be seen). He also argued that given his psychological state, he was not there voluntarily at all.

The Court ruled that the broadcasters of the material could have achieved their objectives by masking the applicant's identity. The Court did not accept the government's claim that respecting the applicant's right to privacy would have undermined the important conflicting rights of the press guaranteed by Article 10. Instead, the Court concluded unanimously that there had been a breach of the right to private life.

In this case, I find especially interesting the tenuous relationship between subjective and general conceptions of privacy. What became relevant were the unusual psychological circumstances in which the person was when he happened to be filmed. The place was public, but from his own subjective point of view he was in an especially fragile state. His personal life was somehow extra present in the situation, even though he was in a public place.

From the government's point of view, however, he was just a man in the street. Generally speaking, there was therefore nothing especially private to be protected. The man's freedom was in no way restricted when he was being filmed, or when the footage was shown. Nor was his autonomy intruded on any more than the average person's who happens to be filmed by CCTV cameras.

The Court ruled for the applicant, which shows that it did pay attention to his subjective interpretation of the situation. His own view of privacy and his particular need thereof were deemed important. Here, the problem was not the CCTV filming itself, which serves

[47] See Robert M. Cover, 'Nomos and Narrative' (1983–4) 97 *Harvard Law Review* 4–68.

an acceptable common purpose, but the later broadcasting of the material.

A person's own views of whether and how their privacy has been infringed upon can become relevant in legal argumentation. Hence, we see that even though the law – in this case the ECHR and its praxis – does not expect people to be islands, it does pay attention to their subjective experiences. Persons may develop their personality in a community with others, but the function of privacy rights is primarily to protect persons as individuals.

The law is common and needs to operate with general concepts. This generalisation of personal experience is visible in the case law of the ECtHR as well. Every judgment includes a test of social adequacy. Even in the *Peck* judgment, the Court considered the aims and purposes of broadcasting in comparison to the harms that the applicant suffered. Because the Court is a transnational one and has to operate in dialogue with national legal systems, it also analyses the individual's situation through the lens of public morals or reasonableness within the community, or sometimes states' public policy goals. That way, individuals' grievances are always contextualised and generalised.

What comes out of this analysis is that even though the legal rules that govern privacy rights would be general and meant to apply to many different kinds of cases, in legal practice the definition of privacy can sometimes become subjective.

Such a result is one problematic aspect of the myth of autonomy that privacy law is based upon. If persons are seen as completely autonomous beings whose control of their own data is the focus of privacy law, then it easily follows that these persons themselves need to be the arbiters of the kinds of privacy they require in different situations. However, such a subjective definition of privacy rights for each and every individual is impossible to obtain in a legal order. The law must operate with some rule-bound standards. There is always room for interpretation, to be sure, but the room cannot be filled with individual tastes.

This is the paradox of privacy rights – a paradox that springs from an overly individual-centred view. Such a view emphasises the autonomy of persons, and requires that autonomy be protected but ends up in a dead-end alley where the subjective autonomy of each individual simply cannot be protected. In this view, privacy rights can only fail because it is impossible for them to deliver on a promise based on myth.

Persons Are Formed by Ideology

Among the very few privacy scholars who have considered personhood in less individualist terms is W. L. Weinstein. He notes that there are difficulties in distinguishing where the individual begins and where they end. What is it that counts towards being an individual, and what role does the social context play in making the individual what they are?

Even if people had the freedom to choose different modes of behaviour, they are nevertheless shaped by a process of socialisation. This makes their ability to make completely free choices less obvious.[48] In the USA, this issue is often seen as a debate between liberalism on the one hand and communitarianism or republicanism on the other. Republicanism understands the individual as constituted at least partly by the society in which they live. A person's identity does not pre-exist the community but is constituted by the community.[49]

In the European tradition, a useful reference point for understanding how persons are constituted by their surroundings is provided by Louis Althusser. Indeed, Althusser's description of subject-formation as interpellation carries much explanatory force. His central idea is that it is ideology that creates subjects. In the present context, where we are considering persons constructed by law, the importance of diverse power relations requires some thought. Althusser's thinking leads us in this direction.

Ideology is a complex concept, but for Althusser it refers primarily to the ways in which reality is represented. Ideology is here used in a sense similar to 'worldview'. Althusser notes that ideology concerns an imaginary relationship between individuals and their real conditions of existence.[50] Ideologies do not necessarily correspond to any reality.

Indeed, according to Althusser it is not the real world that ideology represents but, rather, our relation to the real conditions of existence that are represented. This is where we can search for the cause of – or reason for – ideologies. They are a way of giving meaning to our relationship with the real world.

Following Marx, Althusser accepts that it is real material conditions that produce relations between people occupying different positions in society. Ideology does not represent these real conditions but the

48 W. L. Weinstein, 'The Private and the Free: A Conceptual Inquiry' (1971) 13 *NOMOS: Yearbook of the American Society for Political and Legal Philosophy* 27–55.

49 Jed Rubenfeld, 'The Right to Privacy' (1989) 102 *Harvard Law Review* 737–807.

50 See Louis Althusser, *Lenin and Philosophy and Other Essays* (New York: Monthly Review Press, 1971), p. 162.

imaginary relationship of individuals to them.[51] Hence, there can be a difference between real living conditions and the various roles we play in society on the one hand and, on the other hand ideology, which depicts the understanding we share of those roles.

It is noteworthy that ideology is not here seen as a purely negative construct. People need ideologies and will always have them because they have to make sense of their lives and the world they inhabit. Ideologies are indispensable, even though they are imaginary.[52]

How, then, do individuals choose a specific ideology, let us say a religious, legal, ethical or aesthetic one? An individual may believe, for instance, in God, duty or justice. The belief is the individual's own and derives from their own consciousness. Because of that individual's ideology, they act in certain ways and participate in practices of their freely chosen ideological apparatus, for instance the church. If they believe in duty, they will basically try to act accordingly. If they believe in justice, they will submit to the rules of law and may want to defend them if they are threatened.[53] What is interesting here is that a person is (more or less) conscious of their acts and the reasons for them. A person makes free choices.

However, when one takes part in practices organised by institutions like the church or the legal system, then ideas guiding choice of belief tend to disappear. The ideology underlies the practice. This is, however, very seldom reflected on in acts carried out in rituals and habitual behaviour. We behave according to some ideological outlook without usually questioning it.

Because a person's behaviour is habitual and follows the practices and rituals of the institutions that exist in society, they become shaped by ideology. But rather than acting from an ideological conviction of how things are and what the world is, they are in fact acted upon by the ideological apparatus.

Althusser ends up in a position according to which the subject is the constitutive element of ideology. There is no ideology except for concrete subjects and ideology is enabled by concrete subjects. A double

[51] Althusser, *Lenin and Philosophy*, pp. 164–5.

[52] Paul Ricoeur, 'Althusser's Theory of Ideology', in Gregory Elliott (ed.), *Althusser: A Critical Reader* (Oxford: Blackwell, 1994), pp. 44–72 at 56–7.

[53] Althusser, *Lenin and Philosophy*, pp. 166–7. As Paul Ricoeur points out, for Althusser there are ideologies and ideology. For instance, humanism is an ideology and has determinate boundaries. It is a specific anthropological field. Some people belong to it and others do not. Particular ideologies like humanism are not the same as ideology in general, which is a permanent structure. See Ricoeur, 'Althusser's Theory of Ideology', p. 49.

bind appears. Ideology is for the subject; but the category of the subject is constitutive of all ideology. And every subject is necessarily an ideological subject:[54] '[Y]ou and I are *always already* subjects, and as such constantly practice the rituals of ideological recognition, which guarantee for us that we are indeed concrete, individual, distinguishable and (naturally) irreplaceable subjects.'[55]

The attentive reader asks, of course, about Althusser's own perspective. From what position does he himself argue all this? He is not, however, so naïve as to claim that he would be describing ideology from a non-ideological point of view. His difficult task is to acknowledge that he, too, is an ideological subject writing according to the practices of certain ideologies. He speaks about ideology in ideological terms and from within ideology.[56] This difficulty prevails, of course, in all discourses about constitutive power.

Althusser offers a famous example that illustrates how one becomes a subject. All ideology interpellates or *hails* us as subjects. Ideology 'recruits' subjects among us and 'transforms' us into subjects. The process can be imagined in the situation where a police officer shouts 'Hey, you there!' Happening in the street, this will make one turn round and in that instance one will become a subject: 'By this mere one-hundred-and-eighty-degree physical conversion, he becomes a *subject*. Why? Because he has recognized that the hail was "really" addressed to him, and that "it was *really him* who was hailed".'[57] Althusser adds that in the example it seems as though the hailing would take place outside ideology, in the street, that is, on neutral ground. This is not the case. It takes place in ideology. Those who are in ideology tend to think of themselves as outside it. This is one of the most curious but nonetheless rather commonsensical ways in which ideology functions: one of its effects is a denial of the ideological nature of ideology. Ideology never says 'I am ideological' nor does it have an outside.[58] The example of the police officer in the street sounds temporal, but Althusser maintains that individuals are always already interpellated, or hailed.

Althusser recognises that in ordinary use the term 'subject' means both free subjectivity and a subjected being. The individual is interpellated as someone who freely submits to ideology. In many ways the

[54] Althusser, *Lenin and Philosophy*, p. 171.
[55] Althusser, *Lenin and Philosophy*, p. 172.
[56] Althusser, *Lenin and Philosophy*, p. 173.
[57] Althusser, *Lenin and Philosophy*, p. 174.
[58] Althusser, *Lenin and Philosophy*, p. 175.

subject can also remain free even though a subject. Still, being a subject also means that one is interpellated and thus subjected.

The ideological aspects of law are one more reason that make it difficult to think about persons in law as completely free or autonomous. In order for us to be recognised by law as persons, we are already subjected. We are within an ideology, even though that ideology would be one that respects autonomy.

State apparatuses have two aspects. They may be repressive or coercive, like the prison system, or they may be simply ideological, like education or culture. In some cases they are, of course, both like the law. It involves various kinds of power, which shapes us, protects us and punishes us. Law functions as a repressive system, but also as a symbolic system transmitting values, duties and beliefs – that is – ideology.

An interesting detail that Althusser points to is the division between public and private, which for him is a bourgeois concept. The state interferes in both the public and the private. A seemingly private issue, such as family or ethical belief, is not outside the state's influence.[59] This we see in privacy law. Law regulates the private as much as it does the public sphere of life.

Privacy rights are entangled with ideology through and through. There is no way we can think of them as protecting individuals' autonomy or freedom *against* ideology. They are not a safety net where people could withdraw into their freedom, or develop their personality at liberty.

This short analysis of Althusser takes our discussion about privacy rights one step further. Privacy rights are ideological. They operate in a society and for a society. The persons that privacy rights protect are always embedded in various environments with corresponding ideologies.[60] Even though both theory and practice occasionally presuppose a free and autonomous individual as the focus of privacy protection, there is no such person. We are all cast as individuals, as Bauman says, but the casting is done by ideological apparatuses. These do not show the reality as it is. They do not depict the real, they show us an ideological picture of who we are and how we are related to each other.

[59] See Ricoeur, 'Althusser's Theory of Ideology', p. 52.
[60] See also Cover, 'Nomos and Narrative'.

4 The Immune Person

Let us analyse further the operational logic of privacy protection. We have seen that privacy rights are primarily constructed as a means of protecting persons in their capacity as autonomous individuals. The relational and social aspects of personhood are seldom problematised in privacy law, even though clashes between the individual and the common make appearances in case law.

What kind of ideological presuppositions guide the view of the private individual, affecting much of privacy and personal data protection law? In this chapter, I will address that very question. The issue of openness and closure will be our main topic and it will be discussed through the theoretical concept of immunity.

One underlying reason why autonomy stands at the centre of privacy protection is its conceived connection to a democratic society. Personal autonomy is seen as a prerequisite for open and free democratic government.[1] The idea is that personal autonomy and an open society committed to tolerance and pluralism go together.[2] How legal protection of privacy works in accordance with this logic raises questions, though. Is an open society committed to pluralism one that seeks to enhance people's privacy or not? It can easily be argued that an open society would be precisely one that did not elevate privacy to the status of a fundamental right. Openness requires accessibility, transparency and shared information, after all.

[1] Westin, *Privacy and Freedom*, p. 35.

[2] Ruth Gavison, 'Privacy and the Limits of Law' (1980) 89 *The Yale Law Journal* 421–71 at 450.

Privacy As Immunity: An Obstacle to an Open Society?

In law, the concept of immunity has traditionally been linked to the diplomatic immunity of foreign nationals, but in the following, I will consider it in the context of Roberto Esposito's work.

Immunity is connected to particularity in Esposito's view – indeed it is a condition of particularity. Even when referring to a collective, immunity always belongs to someone. It is also antisocial or anti-communal, an exceptional quality that defines whoever is immune as belonging in some way outside the community.[3] This is the traditional way in which immunity has been used as a legal concept, too. Diplomatic immunity refers to existence outside the community. For instance, it grants non-interference and safety from the powers of the sovereign.

In biomedical language, immunity means exemption from, or protection against, an infectious disease. In law, it refers to a position outside and beyond common law as broadly understood.[4] What unites both of these meanings is immunisation as a situation that saves someone from risk. Immunity forms some kind of shield or cover providing safety.

For Esposito, community and immunity are in fundamental opposition. Immunity is the opposite of community:[5] 'Immune is he or she who breaks the circuit of social circulation by placing himself or herself outside it.'[6] The immune person does not participate fully in the common activities of society, but avoids them by closing themselves off from some of them.

Certain features of privacy and personal data protection reflect this pattern of thought. The right to be let alone includes an element of being on one's own, withdrawing into a private space, restricting access, closing oneself off from community and social circulation.

Privacy and personal data protection are examples of rights that belong to individuals but they also protect broader interests, like the right to develop one's political views and, for instance, integrity of voting in public elections. In this sense, privacy law protects collective values. However, in a situation where an individual's right to privacy is set against a collective good, the fundamental elements of the guiding

[3] Roberto Esposito, *Immunitas: The Protection and Negation of Life* (Cambridge: Polity Press, 2013), p. 6.

[4] Roberto Esposito, *Terms of the Political: Community, Immunity, Biopolitics* (New York: Fordham University Press, 2013), p. 58.

[5] Esposito, *Terms of the Political*, p. 58.

[6] Esposito, *Terms of the Political*, p. 59.

ideology of privacy can be teased out. If privacy rights are consistently regarded as stronger than the values of the common good, then this would be another clear indicator of individualist tendencies in the ideological foundation of privacy law. Such an indication is in fact what we find in transparency cases in the Union.

Privacy and transparency are one classic pair of conflicting interests. Examples of case law from the ECJ where data protection and transparency are balanced show that privacy rights tend to weigh more. Important early rulings are *Bavarian Lager* and *ClientEarth*.[7] In both, the privacy-friendly trend of EU law was upheld.

In the *Psara* judgment from 2018,[8] the General Court considered the right to access information against the right to personal data protection. The applicants, a number of individuals including Maria Psara from Greece, wished to access documents relating to expenses of Members of the European Parliament (MEPs). The purpose of the request was to check whether the MEPs' expenses had been appropriate. The Parliament had refused to give the applicants the documents, after which the conflict was brought to the General Court by the applicants.

One interesting issue concerned demarcation between the private and the public spheres. The applicants claimed that the information they wished to receive 'does not fall within the MEPs' private sphere, but rather their public sphere, since the documents requested relate to the performance of their duties as elected representatives'.[9] The applicants argued that disclosure of the documents requested would not undermine protection of privacy and the integrity of the individual, as defined in Article 4(1)(b) of Regulation No 1049/2001,[10] in that, even if they contain personal data, that data does not relate to MEPs' privacy. According to this article, institutions will refuse access to a document where disclosure would undermine the protection of privacy and the integrity of the individual, in particular in accordance with Community legislation regarding the protection of personal data.

[7] Case C-28/08 P, *European Commission* v. *The Bavarian Lager Co. Ltd.* EU:C:2010:378 and Case C-615/13 P, *ClientEarth and Pesticide Action Network Europe (PAN Europe)* v. *European Food Safety Authority*, EU:C:2015:489, para. 50.

[8] Joined Cases T-639/15 to T-666/15 and T-94/16, *Maria Psara and Others* v. *European Parliament*, EU:T:2018:602, paras. 73–4.

[9] Joined Cases T-639/15 to T-666/15 and T-94/16, *Psara*, EU:T:2018:602, para. 42.

[10] Reg. (EC) No 1049/2001 of the European Parliament and of the Council of 30 May 2001 regarding public access to European Parliament, Council and Commission documents, OJ 2001 No. L145, 31 May 2001.

Many issues are noteworthy in the applicants' argumentation. Firstly, they try to detach privacy from personal data. This separation is uncomfortable in EU legal thinking and the argument did not succeed.

Even though it is generally accepted that privacy and personal data protection are not the same right – as most clearly evidenced by their respective regulation in the Charter – it is hard to see how transmission of personal data would not constitute a potential infringement on the privacy of an individual. The other European Court, the ECtHR, however, has upheld this idea with some success and has stated that not all processing of personal data necessarily amounts to an infringement of privacy according to the ECHR.[11] Hence, a separation is conceptually possible within the framework of the Convention, but not really within the legal framework of privacy and data protection in the EU.

Secondly, the *Psara* judgment includes some intriguing formulations pertaining to the distinction between the public and the private spheres. The applicants argued that the MEPs' personal data which the applicants wished to receive did not belong to the MEPs' private sphere but, rather, belonged to their public sphere. However, within the legal framework of personal data protection no reasonable argument can be made about personal data that would be public.

All personal data is personal and, hence, protected as one form of privacy right. If data is not regarded as personal within the definition of personal data, then it does not fall under the protection of the legislation on personal data. In these instances, data is 'non-personal',[12] and can perhaps be called public, but regulation of data protection does not apply to such data. In other words, personal data that would somehow be public – in the sense of belonging to the public sphere – does not make much sense within the legal architecture of the EU.

Let us pause a moment to reflect that the definition of personal data, as explained in previous chapters, is any data by which a person can be identified. The easiest example is a person's name, which is clearly personal data, even if names are perhaps the most public feature of an individual. Hence, data protection is clearly aimed at protecting that

[11] *Magyar Helsinki Bizottság* v. *Hungary*, ECHR:2016, para. 194.

[12] In fact, the EU legislator has started to pay more attention to non-personal data as well. See Regulation (EU) 2018/1807 of the European Parliament and of the Council of 14 November 2018 on a framework for the free flow of non-personal data in the European Union.

which is personal in the sense of one's own, not towards what is private as opposed to public.

In *Psara*, the Court says just this. It reasons that the distinction, advocated by the applicants according to whether MEPs are in the private or in the public sphere, is to confuse between what is meant by personal data and what is regarded as relating to private life. The Court also says that the concepts of personal data and of data relating to private life are not to be confused.[13]

The Court emphasises that the fact that persons' names are listed on the Parliament's internet site does not mean that that data can no longer be characterised as personal.[14] Personal data is personal regardless of its being publicly available. Hence, personal data remains personal even when made public.

In *Psara*, the Court decided to override the request to access documents because of privacy concerns. The balancing of the two values is by no means easy because both are protected in primary and secondary law of the Union.

The Court does not give clear reasons why privacy rights should win over transparency of government in the case. Access to documents is noted by the Court as an element that promotes closer union among the peoples of Europe. The Court also mentions that this would be a Union in which decisions are taken as openly as possible and as closely as possible to the citizen. The right of public access to documents is connected with the democratic nature of the EU institutions.[15] Hence, transparency is linked to democracy but still does not weigh stronger than privacy.

The Court refers to its previous case law where it has held that derogations from protection of personal data must be interpreted strictly. This is the leading argument that in the end tips the scale in favour of data protection. As in the ground-breaking *Bavarian Lager* case, the Court says that when the situation has to do with access to information containing personal data, that data may be transferred only if its addressee shows that transfer is necessary and if there is no reason to believe that that transfer could prejudice the legitimate interests of the person concerned.

[13] Joined Cases T-639/15 to T-666/15 and T-94/16, *Psara*, EU:T:2018:602, para. 50. The Court refers here and in several other sections to its previous *ClientEarth* judgment (Case C-615/13 P, *ClientEarth*, EU:C:2015:489, para. 32).

[14] Joined Cases T-639/15 to T-666/15 and T-94/16, *Psara*, EU:T:2018:602, para. 52.

[15] Joined Cases T-639/15 to T-666/15 and T-94/16, *Psara*, EU:T:2018:602, para. 64.

Whoever requests a transfer of documents must first establish that it is necessary. If it is demonstrated to be necessary, the institution concerned has to determine whether there is reason to assume that the transfer might prejudice the legitimate interests of the person concerned.[16] In *Psara*, the Court found that the applicants had stated various objectives pursued by their requests for access to documents, namely to enable the public to verify the appropriateness of expenses claimed by MEPs in the exercise of their mandate and to guarantee the public right to information and transparency. However, these reasons were so broad and general in wording that the Court did not see them as establishing a need for the transfer of the personal data.[17]

The Court held that the wish to foster public debate is sufficient to show a need for transfer of personal data. The Court also stated that no automatic priority can be conferred on the objective of transparency over the right to protection of personal data.[18] However, what the Court does not say is how, in the end, priority is then conferred on data protection over transparency.

In transparency versus privacy cases, courts have to balance the rights against each other no matter how hard it may be. These cases concern Union institutions and the courts cannot leave the balancing to the Member States' courts, which occasionally happens in preliminary reference rulings.[19] Therefore, these cases show rather clearly the strong position that privacy rights enjoy in the EU.

It becomes clear in *Psara* that when privacy is balanced against a common good, privacy tends to win. This trend does not have unambiguous backup from legislation because both privacy and transparency are protected and the rules are open enough to enable competing interpretations.[20]

Why privacy should get the upper hand is not explicitly explained in the ruling. One possible reason is that data protection is conceptualised

[16] Joined Cases T-639/15 to T-666/15 and T-94/16, *Psara*, EU:T:2018:602, para. 71.

[17] Joined Cases T-639/15 to T-666/15 and T-94/16, *Psara*, EU:T:2018:602, paras. 73–4.

[18] Joined Cases T-639/15 to T-666/15 and T-94/16, *Psara*, EU:T:2018:602, paras. 90–1.

[19] Transparency is not harmonised in the way that data protection is. The legal framework for transparency is, at the moment of writing, still a framework that concerns EU institutions and does not as such apply to the Member States. Therefore, these cases are ones in which the courts resemble a federal court. The type of claim is different from preliminary reference cases. This is clear in *Psara*, where the applicants seek annulment of EU law under Article 263 TFEU.

[20] For further discussion, see e.g. D. Wyatt, 'The Anaemic Existence of the Overriding Public Interest in Disclosure in the EU's Access to Documents Regime' (2020) 21 *German Law Journal* 686–701.

as a fundamental right and as such has a very strong status. The common good of transparency is a value that is more open, as well as more easily negotiated. For instance, there is no doctrine about the *essence* of the common good that must always be protected, such as there is with fundamental rights.

In these cases that concern transparency, the logic of closing off and shutting out can be discerned. The individual is protected by the law even against competing common values. Privacy rights become a form of immunity protection that grants non-interference and safety from the gaze of others.

Transparency includes the logic of opening and sharing. By its very nature, the idea of transparency is to make things visible.[21] According to Advocate General Eleanor Sharpston, the purpose of transparency is to further openness in a democratic society. Granting wide access in order to inform the public and create democratic debate enables citizens to exercise effective supervision over how public authorities make use of their power. According to her, when greater transparency means more openness and more democratic accountability, greater transparency is to be applauded.[22] Privacy rights work in the opposite direction. They restrict the opening and the sharing and introduce instead the need to close off and shut out.

Following Esposito, we can say that even though privacy rights would also be linked to collective interests, they always belong to someone. They are in this sense anti-communal. As the discussion above shows, their function is to construct persons as immune individuals who can stay outside the common gaze.

Immunisation: Means for Withdrawal

The transparency-versus-privacy cases include a rather straightforward opposition between openness and closure. But there is more to the logic of immunisation.[23] Esposito's understanding of immunity traces its significance from its biological origins in vaccination. Using law as

[21] See Ida Koivisto for an interesting analysis of transparency. Ida Koivisto, 'The anatomy of transparency: the concept and its multifarious implications' Working Paper EUI MWP 2016/09, 1–29.

[22] See also Joined Cases C-92/09 and C-93/09, *Volker und Markus Schecke and Hartmut Eifert* v. *Land Hessen, joined party Bundesanstalt für Landwirtschaft und Ernährung*, Opinion of AG Sharpston, EU:C:2010:353, paras. 69–70.

[23] Esposito takes inspiration from Derrida's analysis of *pharmakon*. See Jacques Derrida, *Dissemination* (Chicago, IL: University of Chicago Press, 1981).

a defence mechanism means a certain kind of immunisation. For privacy rights, this entails that the private is protected as something that is good for everybody, perhaps even a common good, but protection of that good requires that the community be disrupted. In this way, closing individuals outside the logic of community is a way in which the community defends itself.

In the Jehovah's Witnesses' case, for instance, the Court had to consider two different values: the right of a religious community to organise its activities as it saw fit, and data protection. The Court decided that only data protection was relevant in the circumstances but it is not hard to imagine a scenario where the community's interests would have needed protection as well. This case has an element of community versus individuality at the heart of it, even though the Court does not pay it much heed.

Esposito argues that the immunitary *dispositif* has spread from biomedicine and law to all sectors and discourses of our lives. This has happened to the extent that immunity has become a major feature, both real and symbolic, of contemporary existence. Moving from the medical field to the sociocultural, we now find immunitary logic everywhere.[24]

Esposito's thesis is that when the idea of immunity is carried past a certain threshold, it becomes a risk in itself. Instead of protecting life, it starts undermining it. The *meaning* of our collective existence gets lost. The flow of meanings and those encounters with others that a community consists of disappear. Community is conditioned on openness, whereas immunity is the activity of shutting out and closing in.[25] The same logic is inherent in privacy rights protection. It closes off the flow of meanings when it focuses only on the protection of autonomous persons. Forgetting the way every one of us is embedded in society, it disrupts collective existence.

Privacy can then be understood as analogous to immunisation: the right allows the subject to withdraw and resist intrusion. The right to privacy functions as an individualisation mechanism, where the law draws boundaries for subjects' personal spheres. It defines what is personal and what is not, what is general or public and what is not, what is secret and what is not. Privacy is an instrument of the community by which it defines the limits of community.

[24] Esposito, *Terms of the Political*, p. 59.

[25] Esposito, *Terms of the Political*, pp. 60–1.

Drawing on both Esposito's and Bauman's critical frameworks, it can be argued that the focus of data protection is too narrow to protect the sharing of data, that is, communication. This is due to the fact that the individualising undertones of privacy have become so strong.

Not all forms of privacy rights necessarily share this trait. Some of the older forms of privacy protection can more easily function so as to protect meanings that are shared, transmitted and developed together with others. Such an understanding of privacy would necessarily correspond to a different conception of the person. Instead of just focusing on the autonomous individual, the person would then appear predominately as a relational being embedded in community.

Openness and Closure: the Right to Be Forgotten

The famous *Google Spain* case is a good example of a judgment that shows immunitary logic at play. The judgment is a preliminary ruling given in 2014 by the ECJ on request of the Spanish National High Court. It is a Grand Chamber judgment.

The facts of the case are roughly as follows. Mr González's real estate had been auctioned and this had been reported in 1998 by the Spanish newspaper *La Vanguardia*. The complaint by Mr González was that when an internet user entered his name in the Google search engine he would obtain links to two pages of the newspaper on which the auction was mentioned. On these pages the real-estate auction was connected with proceedings for the recovery of social security debts. The information had subsequently been digitalised and made available on *La Vanguardia*'s web pages.

Mr González first contacted the publisher of the newspaper and requested that the announcements be removed from the paper's web pages. The publisher refused to do so, referring to the fact that the original publication of the announcements had been effected by order of the Spanish Ministry of Labour and Social Affairs.

In 2010, Mr González contacted Google Spain SL and requested that reference to the newspaper announcements be removed from the results to searches for his name. Google Spain forwarded his request to Google Inc., taking the view that Google Inc. was the company actually providing the internet search service. Finally, the dispute ended up in the High Court, which decided to stay the proceedings and refer certain questions to the ECJ for a preliminary ruling.

The questions posed to the ECJ concerned several important issues in EU data protection law, for instance the definition of 'data controller' as specified in Article 2 of the Data Protection Directive.[26] Additionally, the issue of the territorial scope of EU law was controversial because Google Inc. is the parent company of the Google group and has its seat in the United States.[27] However, most interesting in our context is the question of whether individuals have a right to be forgotten in EU law.

One question posed by the referring court specifically concerned the right to be forgotten. The national court framed the question thus:

> must it be considered that the rights to erasure and blocking of data . . . extend to enabling the data subject to address himself to search engines in order to prevent indexing of the information relating to him personally, published on third parties' web pages, invoking his wish that such information should not be known to internet users when he considers that it might be prejudicial to him or he wishes it to be consigned to oblivion, even though the information in question has been lawfully published by third parties?[28]

The national court wondered whether it is in accordance with the DPD that Mr González can address himself to a search engine in order to prevent information on the auction of his estate from popping up in searches. Mr González wanted the information to be 'consigned to oblivion', even though the information had been lawfully published by *La Vanguardia*.

The ECJ ruled that a search engine can indeed be obliged to remove information relating to a person even when the web pages are not erased and even when publication of the information on the pages is lawful in itself. Thus the Court confirmed the right to be forgotten.

The Court's ruling and Advocate General Jääskinen's opinion on the case represent opposite views on how to balance individuals' right to privacy and the right of the general public to obtain information. The Advocate General places weight on the nature of information that the web pages contained. The information on Mr González was not false. The Advocate General interprets Article 12(b) of the Directive to state that the right to erase or rectify data arises only if the search engine were to process inaccurate or incomplete data.[29] He does not see that

[26] Directive 95/46/EC, OJ 1995 No. L281, 23 November 1995, p. 38.

[27] See the first *Schrems* case where territoriality of data protection is taken to a whole new level of importance. Case C-362/14, *Maximillian Schrems* v. *Data Protection Commissioner*, EU:C:2015:650. This ruling will be discussed further on.

[28] Case C-131/12, *Google Spain and Google*, EU:C:2014:317, para. 20.

[29] Case C-131/12, *Google Spain and Google*, Opinion of AG Jääskinen, EU:C:2013:424, para. 105.

the Directive would include a general right to be forgotten in the sense that a person would have a right to limit or stop the dissemination of personal data whenever they find dissemination harmful or in contradiction to their interests.

The Advocate General emphasises that when data is being processed without the consent of the data subject, then the interests of processing must be compared with the interests of the data subject. The subjective opinions of the data subject should not be taken into account here because they are not 'compelling legitimate grounds', which Article 14(a) mentions as a presupposition for a data subject's right to object.[30] The Court disagrees on this, which is one of the main reasons for it to construct a right to be forgotten.

The Advocate General argues in his opinion that even though the operator of the search engine might be held responsible for personal data published on web pages, the data subject still would not have an absolute right to be forgotten that they could invoke against the operator. The Advocate General maintains that there is no general right to be forgotten in EU law. The data subject's right to protection of their private life must be balanced with other fundamental rights, especially freedom of expression and freedom of information.[31]

According to the Advocate General, the right to private life does not override the right of the public to have access to information. Indeed, he maintains that the right to search for information on the Internet by using search engines is one of the most important ways for the public to get information in our contemporary information society. He warns against the dangers that would threaten the freedom of information if search engines did not display, for instance, data concerning a person's business or political activities in situations when the data was accurate. It would lead to search engines giving 'bowdlerised' versions of information, not truthful ones.[32] In addition to the public's right to have access to information, the Advocate General also underlines a search engine service provider's freedom to conduct business and its freedom of expression.

[30] Case C-131/12, *Google Spain and Google*, Opinion of AG Jääskinen, EU:C:2013:424, para. 108.

[31] Case C-131/12, *Google Spain and Google*, Opinion of AG Jääskinen, EU:C:2013:424, paras. 126–33. Even though the right to be forgotten is now regulated in a new way in Article 17 of the GDPR, it is still not an absolute right, as seen in the wording of the Article.

[32] Case C-131/12, *Google Spain and Google*, Opinion of AG Jääskinen, EU:C:2013:424, para. 131.

The Advocate General's opinion concludes that the case presents a particularly complex and difficult constellation of fundamental rights. It does not, however, allow for reinforcement of data subjects' legal protection, nor does it offer reason to construct a general right to be forgotten.[33] Any generalised right to be forgotten cannot be invoked against search engine service providers on the basis of the Directive even when it is interpreted in harmony with the Charter.[34]

The Advocate General draws his conclusion after considering other fundamental rights and freedoms and subsequently balancing them. He does not, however, undertake a nuanced analysis of what a right to be forgotten would actually entail, even in theory. Still, his views on the case present an alternative to current data protection thinking. Firstly, he does balance data protection with other rights, most importantly here the public's right to information. He is also sceptical of seeing data protection as an overriding right. We can see that since publication of this opinion, legal development in the EU has progressed towards a more privacy-intensive view. Important steps in that direction were taken by the Court in *Google Spain*.

The Court disagreed with the Advocate General on several points. In its judgment, the Court emphasises that the Directive seeks to ensure a high level of protection of the fundamental rights and freedoms of natural persons, in particular their right to privacy.[35] Hence, the Court immediately focuses its reasoning around individuals' rights as the main issue involved in the case.

The Court refers to its previous judgments, where it is – according to the Court – evident that personal data protection is increasingly permeated by strong fundamental rights arguments.[36] Furthermore, the Court notes that interference with individuals' privacy rights cannot be justified merely by the economic interest of a search engine operator.

As for the legitimate interest of internet users to have access to information, a fair balance should be sought between that general interest and the data subject's fundamental rights under Articles 7 and 8 of the Charter. This balance may depend, for instance, on the

[33] Case C-131/12, *Google Spain and Google*, Opinion of AG Jääskinen, EU:C:2013:424, para. 133.

[34] Case C-131/12, *Google Spain and Google*, Opinion of AG Jääskinen, EU:C:2013:424, para. 136.

[35] Case C-131/12, *Google Spain and Google*, EU:C:2014:317, para. 66.

[36] Case C-131/12, *Google Spain and Google*, EU:C:2014:317, paras. 68–79.

role played by the data subject in public life.[37] The Court concludes, however, that the individual's right to protection of personal data overrides, *as a rule*, not only the economic interest of the operator of the search engine, but also the interest of the general public in finding information upon a search relating to the individual's name.

The Court's conclusions in 2014 set the direction in which EU data protection law – and privacy law more generally – would develop in the coming years. This is why the judgment has become so important: it is one of the first to clearly state that the individual's right does – and should – override other, more general interests, even though those interests would also be protected as rights.[38]

Later Approaches to the Right to Be Forgotten

The right to be forgotten saga did not end with *Google Spain*. The most significant judgment to date that interprets *Google Spain* is *GC and Others*, which came to the ECJ from France.[39] In this case, Advocate General Szpunar noted that: 'reconciling the right to privacy and to the protection of personal data with the right to information and to freedom of expression in the internet era is one of the main challenges of our time'.[40] This Advocate General also calls for balancing of privacy against other rights. He is not shy of including a bit of critique of the Court's *Google Spain* judgment in his opinion. He argues that it would have been helpful if the Court had expressly mentioned the fundamental right to freedom of expression in its judgment. That would have revealed more clearly that it is not solely a question of weighing up Articles 7 and 8 of the Charter, on the one hand, and freedom of information, on the other, but that freedom of expression must also be taken into account.[41]

The *GC and Others* case concerned not only personal data, but also sensitive data, that is, special categories of data under Article 9 of the

[37] Case C-131/12, *Google Spain and Google*, EU:C:2014:317, para. 81.

[38] A slightly similar case is *Manni*, where judgment was given 9 March 2017. It, too, has to do with public availability of personal data. Case C-398/15, *Camera di Commercio, Industria, Artigianato e Agricoltura di Lecce* v. *Salvatore Manni*, EU:C:2017:197. An example where the common or the social is clearly valued is *Zakharov* from the ECtHR. *Roman Zakharov* v. *Russia* ECHR 2015-VIII.

[39] Case C-507/17, *Google LLC, successor in law to Google Inc.* v. *Commission nationale de l'informatique et des libertés (CNIL)*, EU:C:2019:772; and Case C-136/17, *GC and Others* v. *Commission nationale de l'informatique et des libertés (CNIL)*, EU:C:2019:773.

[40] Case C-136/17, *GC and Others*, Opinion of AG Szpunar, EU:C:2019:14, para. 1.

[41] Case C-136/17, *GC and Others*, Opinion of AG Szpunar, EU:C:2019:14, paras. 67–8.

GDPR. When it comes to this data, the Advocate General argues that there is no room for a balancing exercise. Provided that it is established that sensitive data has been processed, a request for de-referencing should be granted.[42]

Advocate General Szpunar argues, however, that there generally needs to be a balancing of the right to information because privacy is not an absolute right. He refers to the case law of the ECtHR, among other things, to support this argument. The Internet plays an important role in enhancing public access to news and facilitating the dissemination of information. He points out that the right of the public to receive and impart information made available on the Internet is protected by Article 11 of the Charter and a search engine plays a pivotal role in such dissemination of information.[43] Article 9 of the DPD, according to which *GC and Others* was to be decided, included explicit reference to freedom of expression as well as to freedom of the media.

In its judgment, the Court did take a step back and consider the different rights involved in the situation. This case became a balancing case. The Court does weigh the freedom of information of internet users against the right to privacy.

The Court concludes that the operator of a search engine is in principle required to accede to requests for de-referencing links to web pages containing special categories of personal data.[44] This is the main rule. However, the operator may refuse to fulfil a request if it establishes that processing the data is covered by the exception in Article 8(2)(e) of the DPD, that is, the processing relates to data that is manifestly made public by the data subject or is necessary for the establishment, exercise or defence of legal claims. In the end, the Court argues that it is the job of Google as the search engine operator to undertake a careful analysis of the different rights at stake and act accordingly. The operator must ascertain, on the basis of all the relevant factors in the particular case and taking into account the seriousness of interference with the data subject's fundamental rights to privacy and protection of personal data laid down in Articles 7 and 8 of the Charter, whether it is strictly necessary to show the subject's name to protect the freedom of information of internet users.[45]

[42] Case C-136/17, *GC and Others*, Opinion of AG Szpunar, EU:C:2019:14, para. 69.
[43] Case C-136/17, *GC and Others*, Opinion of AG Szpunar, EU:C:2019:14, paras. 41–2.
[44] Case C-136/17, *GC and Others*, EU:C:2019:773, para. 69.
[45] Case C-136/17, *GC and Others*, EU:C:2019:773, para. 68.

A third Google case, *Google* v. *CNIL*, also dealt with the right to be forgotten. In this case, where judgment was also delivered in 2019, the Court's reasoning again shows a rather moderate approach. The Court here emphasises the need for a fair balance between privacy and other interests. When considering Google's responsibility to de-reference personal data, freedom of information has to be taken into account as well.[46]

The issue was whether Google has an obligation under EU law to apply the right to be forgotten globally. The Court said 'no'. It held that a search engine operator, who grants a request for de-referencing by a data subject, is not obliged to carry out de-referencing on all versions of its search engine.[47] Also in this case, the Court's reasoning sets limits to the right to be forgotten. A search engine operator who grants a request for de-referencing is only required to do so on the versions of that search engine corresponding to all the Member States, but not globally. This is a logical outcome, which corresponds to the limits of the reach of EU law. The Internet may be global and it may not know any borders, but the law still does.

Summing up these three cases concerning the right to be forgotten, we notice that the Advocate Generals' calls for balancing collective rights against privacy have been heard, at least to some extent. The individual-centred reasoning of *Google Spain* has been ameliorated. This development may represent an alternative to the immunitary logic that has been visible in privacy law for some time. Individualised rights have tended to override common and collective interests. Why is this problematic? Because it threatens community. But the recent cases show that there seem to be possibilities of thinking differently, even in law. We shall now start looking for alternative theoretical frameworks that would be less individualising than the main paradigm has been.

Searching for Possibilities of Re-thinking: Impersonal Law

Esposito's work on the concept of the third person is compelling because it provides a genuine attempt to think of law in a new way. His main idea is that the person is the problem. The law's dependence on the category of the person is a hindrance for our thought.

[46] Case C-507/17, *Google* v. *CNIL*, EU:C:2019:772, para. 72.
[47] Case C-507/17, *Google* v. *CNIL*, EU:C:2019:772, para. 64.

The centrality of the concept of the person leads to many of the failures that we associate with the law, that is, its impotence in protecting those who need it the most. We can see, for instance, that the right to life is not really guaranteed, even though there is a strong tendency to tie together personhood and fundamental rights. According to Esposito, the language of the law must be changed into the impersonal if problems of justice are to be solved.

If there is one unquestioned assumption in contemporary individualistic debate, it is indeed the value awarded to the category of the person.[48] Esposito notes that the person is the concept by which correct discourse is legitimated in every discipline, be that philosophy, theology or law.[49] It is a given, some kind of axiom, and does not seem to require any proof. Personhood is seldom the object of discussion or disagreement, nor is its value questioned.[50]

Ultimately, Esposito's worry is with society, that is, with politics and democracy.[51] True democracy is no longer possible. What we have nowadays is something else and that something else is built on a particular understanding of human beings. The life of individuals and populations has become fundamental to all the most important political decisions today.[52] Political conflicts and debates circulate around individuals.

Esposito claims that this focus means a move away from democracy. The ideological underpinnings, the concepts and the very logic of democratic rule simply do not fit the biopolitical thinking of today.

48 Esposito argues that no other term, leaving aside democracy, enjoys such success as 'person' does today. Roberto Esposito, 'The Dispositif of the Person' (2012) 8 *Law, Culture and the Humanities* 17–30 at 17–18.

49 Esposito's discussion of the category of the person is highly complex. He, of course, recognises that there is no unified meaning of the term but it does produce certain effects that can be explained, although perhaps not exhaustively.

50 Roberto Esposito, *Third Person: Politics of Life and Philosophy of the Impersonal* (Cambridge: Polity Press, 2012), p. 1.

51 It can be argued that Esposito's interest in law is secondary to the other issues that he studies, namely sovereignty, politics and globalisation, to name a few. He has, however, studied juridical problems, too. See on the importance of Esposito's work for legal thought e.g. Adalgiso Amendola, 'The Law of the Living: Material for Hypothesizing the Biojuridical' (2012) 8 *Law, Culture and the Humanities* 102–18.

52 Esposito has discussed the issues of life and the politicisation of biology in many of his works. We can see that his thinking is associated with that of Foucault, Agamben and Deleuze, among others. See a general introduction to this e.g. Timothy Campbell, '"Bios", Immunity, Life: The Thought of Roberto Esposito' (2006) 36 *Diacritics* 2–22; and Roberto Esposito, 'Totalitarianism or Biopolitics? Concerning a Philosophical Interpretation of the Twentieth Century' (2008) 34 *Critical Inquiry* 633–44 at 642–3.

Democracy concerns a totality of *equal* subjects, not individual bodies. It is inapplicable to something like a unique individual, understood in their particularity.[53]

Esposito suggests that we need to depersonalise political thought. This might open up the possibility of equality. Depersonalisation involves a certain kind of disembodied subjectivity, that is, subjectivity that is not completely fixated on unique and individual bodies.

Democracy in the traditional sense is no longer a realistic alternative. There might nevertheless be a possibility to imagine another kind of democracy, democratic biopolitics or biopolitical democracy perhaps.[54]

Esposito's normative arguments should not be exaggerated. Politics is always in some sense biopolitics, so biopolitics is not something bad that we should try to move away from altogether. It might be the case that we can develop an affirmative biopolitics but Esposito does not indicate an easy path on which to tread towards it.[55] The critical force of Esposito's thought consists of attempts to reveal the ways in which biopolitics functions and to re-think biopolitical operations in contemporary societies.

Justice through the Impersonal?

Esposito draws on Simone Weil in his argument about justice presupposing impersonality. The person is dependent on society and rights are dependent on force. Rights are necessarily connected with force, or otherwise not granted at all. What is more, a right can only protect a particular category of people. Those who do not fit the category are left out. To think that the same privileges would apply to everyone is absurd because privilege, by definition, is not equal. Rights, in themselves, necessarily include the idea of discrimination:

> This is a truism that has characterized the legal form since its origins: even when the law is general or a generalization is called for, it always remains essentially particular, or even personal, because it concerns a legal person. The dimensions of this person may vary, from the discrete entity of a single individual to the institutional magnitude of a state, but the way it deals with all

[53] See Esposito, 'Totalitarianism or Biopolitics?', 643–4.

[54] See Esposito, 'Totalitarianism or Biopolitics?', 643–4.

[55] See e.g. Timothy Campbell and Federico Luisetti, 'On Contemporary French and Italian Political Philosophy: An Interview with Roberto Esposito' (2010) 75 *Minnesota Review* 109–18 at 111, 114. See also Roberto Esposito, Jean-Luc Nancy and Timothy Campbell, 'Dialogue on the Philosophy to Come' (2010) 75 *Minnesota Review* 71–88 at 85–6.

> other legal persons does not: always and forever through comparison, negotiation, and contention. What this implies . . . is its opposition in principle to the concept of community. Laws are always partial, never for every one. . . . It is logically impossible to extend a right to all without emptying it of meaning as a right.[56]

Rights belong only to persons, whereas justice pertains to the impersonal, the anonymous.

The impersonal is not the opposite of the person, but that which stands before or after the personal subject. The impersonal is that element of personhood which 'stops the immune mechanism that introduces the "I" into the simultaneously inclusive and exclusive circle of the "we"'.[57] The impersonal is thus not something outside the person, something completely alien to personhood, but that part of the person that includes an element of generality, anonymity and commonness.

Weil opens up an avenue of thought that enables us to perceive the person in a profoundly novel way. Through the impersonal, we can finally think about human beings as such. Weil does not describe the non-person in much detail, but Esposito develops the idea further by comparing the first two personal pronouns with the third. The *third person*, he or she, is categorically different from I and you. When I speak, I am occupying the position of the subject in relation to you. You assume the role of a listener. These positions are reversed during a conversation, where the roles of speaker and listener continuously change. But only one can occupy the role of the 'I' at any moment and the 'I' is the only subject. Thus the role of the subject is passed back and forth in the exchange. The 'I' is the subject who always desubjectifies the other person (you).[58]

If this is the case, then what is a third person? The third person is what escapes this movement of subjectification.[59] The third person is never

[56] Esposito, *Immunitas*, p. 24.

[57] Esposito, *Third Person*, p. 102.

[58] Esposito, *Third Person*, pp. 104–6. One interesting aspect of Esposito's thought is his disagreement with Levinas, which cannot be discussed in detail here. Esposito argues that Levinas is trapped inside the language of the person and this leads his thinking into impasses that prevent him from giving adequate answers to the question of justice. The language of the person must be changed into the impersonal if problems of justice are to be solved. Esposito, *Third Person*, p. 125. On Levinas and law, see Susanna Lindroos-Hovinheimo, *Justice and the Ethics of Legal Interpretation* (Oxon and New York: Routledge, 2012).

[59] Esposito, *Third Person*, pp. 104–6.

the name of a subject. The role of the third person is that of a non-personal person or non-person. He or she *is* somebody. That somebody is anybody but does not occupy the position of a speaker or actor. He or she is never the unique subject who utters something to somebody in a particular dialogue but an anonymous *whoever*. The third person is not an individual person at all.

The third person is a difficult idea for privacy law where legal thinking tends to revolve around unique individuals. Esposito's argument is that we are too committed to the category of personhood and this commitment is a hindrance for justice.

But law does not need to see the person only as an individual. Law can operate with different kinds of persons. The category of the legal person, as we have seen, is general and vague, and more of an empty placeholder. It flexes and bends according to the ideologies of law. Understanding the legal person in a less individualistic way moves us towards an idea of justice that opens up to generality, commonality and community. It would be a different kind of ideology from the one we live in today.

5 The Person at Liberty

The roots of liberalism can be traced to the seventeenth century, where we find the origins of a modern way of valuing the rights of the individual. Locke is perhaps the most important philosopher in this trajectory. His theories shaped the way we understand rights, as well as the individual.

Thomas Hobbes may be a surprising figure to include in this discussion because his political philosophy can hardly be called liberalist. However, his theory takes individualism as a theoretical presupposition, even if his conclusions are not liberalist. Hobbes' philosophy rests on deducting political rights and obligations from the interest and will of dissociated individuals.[1]

The individualist ideas developed by both Hobbes and Locke are important because they lived on in later struggles for a liberal state. They were influential throughout the eighteenth and nineteenth centuries. For instance, Bentham built his utilitarianism on certain Hobbesian ideas,[2] which still have an impact on our thinking today.

Links between the person and rights can be conceptualised in many different ways. I shall now consider C. B. MacPherson's analysis of the possessive character of seventeenth-century individualism, which holds that the individual is primarily the owner of their own person or capacities and owes nothing to society for them.[3] An individual is *in possession* of their own self.

In possessive individualism, and the liberalism that derives from it, freedom is defined as freedom from dependence on the will of others.

[1] C. B. MacPherson, *The Political Theory of Possessive Individualism: Hobbes to Locke* (Oxford: Clarendon Press, 1962), p. 2.

[2] MacPherson, *The Political Theory*, p. 2.

[3] MacPherson, *The Political Theory*, p. 3.

Freedom is a function of possession because an individual is free if the owner of their person and capacities.[4]

With such presuppositions, it is easy to see that the definition of society becomes a collection of free individuals who are all proprietors of their own selves, their person and their capacities. They also own all that they have acquired by using these capacities. This is the starting point that leads to the relation of exchange between individuals becoming the defining feature of society.[5] A late-modern version of such a society is the liquid modern one characterised by Bauman's caravan site metaphor. The relations between people are relations between atomised individuals.

There are interesting details in early possessive individualism that deserve further thought in connection to privacy rights. For Hobbes, the human is defined as a competitive being, whose primary aim is to gain power over others. MacPherson argues that the society model that best corresponds to Hobbes' political theory is a possessive market society. The state of nature that Hobbes describes is not exactly a state of natural humans as such. It is rather a description of the human as a civilised being, a being whose basic characteristics Hobbes observed in his own society. And what he saw is continual competition between individuals on all levels.[6]

In a market society, everyone is a possessor of something, at least their capacity to work. Competition determines what everyone gets. Such a society requires legal rules for protection, which we also find in Hobbes' theory. Society is secured, contracts are protected and market exchange can be enforced by law. A strong sovereign that keeps the peace does all of this. Therefore, state regulation is needed primarily to ensure a functioning market.[7]

Similar basic ideas traverse European privacy rights. They, too, are shaped by individualism, which occasionally takes a possessive form. One reason is surely that there is now a market in data, which sets the scene for relations of exchange between individuals, on the one hand, and companies or governments on the other. The idea of ownership fits this situation well. The market puts a price on everything while everybody is a possessor of marketable commodities.[8] Nowadays, it is not

[4] MacPherson, *The Political Theory*, pp. 3, 263.

[5] MacPherson, *The Political Theory*, pp. 3, 263.

[6] MacPherson, *The Political Theory*, pp. 22, 53–62.

[7] MacPherson, *The Political Theory*, pp. 22, 53–62.

[8] See Käll on how difficult it has become to make a distinction between persons and things, that is, persons and their property. Jannice Käll, *Converging Human and Digital*

perhaps only our labour that we primarily possess, but our personal data. This development corresponds to the conception of individuals as being first and foremost owners of themselves, their personality and their data.

In MacPherson's reading of Hobbes, the need for privacy rights becomes apparent. Human beings are naturally inclined to be invasive towards one another and, hence, a sovereign is necessary to keep the peace. In a possessive market society, humans need a sovereign and can logically support one because a sovereign enables them to get certain possessions from each other but without destroying each other. A sovereign's function is to keep these invasions within certain bounds, thus ensuring the continuing functioning of the market. Hence, humans have an interest in being ruled by the sovereign. Too far-reaching invasions into other people's lives, possessions, capacities and persons cannot be tolerated. The protection of privacy rights can be seen as a natural development of this idea. We need immunity from one another and privacy rights are one instrument that provides just that.

Liberalism and the libertarianism developed later by, for instance, Robert Nozick, takes our freedom as humans to be paramount. Freedom comes, however, most often combined with ownership, as for instance in Locke's theory. The individual has property in their own person. It is this property, in the sense of a right to enjoy and use one's capacities and to exclude others from them, which makes human beings what they are.[9] Our essence is freedom, but it is first and foremost a freedom to enjoy personal property.

Importantly, in possessive individualism this property is something for which the individual owes nothing to society. In Locke's thinking, the idea is especially evident. An individual has a property in their own person and no one has a greater right to that property. When mixing labour with nature, the result also becomes one's own. Because property is derived from natural rights, humans owe no debt to society for what they own.[10]

Let us consider how the logic of privacy law works from this point of view. In data protection, we do not think about personal data as the private property of an individual, but as something that individuals

Bodies. Posthumanism, Property, Law (Gothenburg: University of Gothenburg, 2017), pp. 215–30.

9 MacPherson, *The Political Theory*, p. 142.

10 MacPherson, *The Political Theory*, pp. 214–21.

possess. I can share my data with others for instance by consenting to it being processed, and I can also take it back by withdrawing consent or asking for it to be erased. But the data will still be my personal data, even if I sell it. This is a crucial feature of data protection law, and privacy protection more generally. Even if I let my picture be taken and spread through various media, I do not give up my privacy rights. Some features of the picture always stay in my control. In this sense, my data is my possession.

Other possessive individualist ideas also occur in data protection law. Data is occasionally conceptualised almost as a part of ourselves, an instance of our personality, which we have the right to control completely. The *Google Spain* case illustrates such a view, where personality is seen as if it were a personal possession, which can be detached from society, separated completely from other data. This kind of possession belongs completely to an individual who owes nothing to anyone else. Data protection in this ruling resembles a right to exclude others. Such a view corresponds with an atomistic understanding of people.

The later *Google* judgments from the ECJ take a more nuanced view, emphasising that persons and their data are embedded in society and entangled with other people. The regulation of them is necessarily intertwined with questions of the common good of everyone.

Durkheim's Impersonal Individualism

Émile Durkheim's classic sociological theory is valuable because it can be set as a contrast to the form of individualism that is prevalent in the EU today. He offers an alternative version in his analysis of modernity. It entails an individualism that is not focused on the self as understood in an atomistic manner.

Durkheim's studies on solidarity and individualism provide lucid arguments for unpicking the relation between the individual and society. In addition, because of Durkheim's interest in law, his studies are especially useful for the purposes of legal analysis. The theory may be old – he started developing it in his doctoral thesis, *The Division of Labour in Society*, published in 1893 – but it provides a model for studying law in society that is still pertinent today.

Durkheim sets out to explain the emerging industrial society. He is perplexed by the question: What holds modern societies together? It would seem at the outset that the industrial society – and the increasingly urban ways of life that go with it – dissolves many of the ties that have bound people together. How, then, can a modern society function as a unit with at least some, if not complete, cohesion between people?

Durkheim famously formulated his answer by explaining the division of labour to be the source of mutual ties between individuals. The emerging industrial form of production replaced the earlier artisanal mode of production. In this older form of labour, the same producers would complete the whole product. Compared to artisanal products, products in the new industrial form were seldom produced by an individual manufacturer. They were created by the co-ordinated labour of a large number of persons. Each of these persons would perform specialised tasks and they would require special skills or expertise. According to Durkheim, this diversification of work coincided with differentiation in several areas of society. These include, for instance, science and government, as well as law.[11] An increasing number of legal fields started emerging, each with their own rules. Each field of law also started to require specialised knowledge.

Pre-modern societies were essentially held together by sameness: common values, norms and shared beliefs. Modern industrial societies were characterised by difference. Mutual interdependence of different units and a developed division of labour held them together. Durkheim holds that this kind of organic solidarity is the only type of solidarity possible in complex modern societies. And in Durkheim's view, some form of solidarity – that is, some kind of stable social bonding – is necessary for societies to function.

Durkheim's work draws out the relations between social conditions and the different kinds of subjectivity that emerge in them. Modernity is the era of the individual. The division of labour and the corresponding specialisation and differentiation in society created people who are in many ways different from one another. Not everybody leads the same kind of life. Not everybody does the same kind of work. And not everybody necessarily has the same values as everyone else.

However, it is useful to note here that Durkheim saw individuals in modern societies more as societal creations than existential givens. Individuals may form a society, but society shapes individuals.[12]

[11] See Lewis Coser, *Introduction in Durkheim: The Division of Labour in Society* (Basingstoke: Palgrave, 1984), pp. ix–xxiv.

[12] See Coser, *Introduction in Durkheim*, p. xv.

A society is nothing without individuals, for sure. Nevertheless, each individual is more a product of a society than its author.[13]

Indeed Durkheim goes so far as to say that society 'does not find ready-made in individual consciousness the bases on which it rests; it makes them for itself'.[14] A clear affinity with Foucauldian ideas of subject production can be discerned here.

Older forms of society were held together by mechanical solidarity created by shared beliefs and values. Modern societies create bonds between people in other ways. Durkheim argues that it may seem that the ties which emerge from the division of labour in modern societies are weaker but this is not the case. In societies where solidarity through similarities is the only or almost the only tie that binds people, the breaks to these ties are most frequent. In these older societies, a lot of social rules were communicated and upheld by coercion. Modern societies include several different kinds of rules upheld by various means and often without a central controlling agency. The ties that bind people together and to an ordered society derive from mutual need and co-dependence.[15]

One does not need to agree with Durkheim on the accuracy of his historical analysis in order to appreciate his explanation of the special features of modern, industrialised societies. What he argues is that the cult of the individual is a feature emblematic of modernity. In drawing out the societal implications of individualism and in explaining the most complex connections between individualism and modern societies, Durkheim's theory is very helpful. As befits a sociologist, he considers society as primary and individuals – with their psychological traits, religious beliefs and other personal features – as secondary. His analysis of individualism is therefore not person-centred in its methodological approach.

Indeed, this view of individualism has an impersonal feature that makes it distinct from late-modern versions. Because individualism does not entail an atomistic attitude, it can function as a unifying social value. In contrast also to the older theorists Hobbes and Locke, for Durkheim the individual is created in society and dependent on it: 'Collective life did not arise from individual life; on the contrary, it is the latter that emerged from the former. On this condition alone can we

[13] Émile Durkheim, *The Division of Labour in Society*, W. D. Halls and Lewis Coser trs., introduction by Lewis Coser (Basingstoke: Macmillan, 1984), p. 288.

[14] Durkheim, *The Division of Labour*, p. 287.

[15] Durkheim, *The Division of Labour*, pp. 101–4.

explain how the personal individuality of social units was able to form and grow without causing society to disintegrate.'[16] This explains how the power of the social world affects an individual's experience. Morality, for instance, is created by society and forms an expression of social conditions. All rights and freedoms are also produced by society. They are not inherently given, as liberal theory or various forms of Kantianism would have it.[17] Rights are bestowed on the individual by the state, and the state acts as an agent for society as a whole.

Hence, Durkheim uses the term 'individualism' in a highly specific sense. He does not adopt it as a methodological approach to social theory but understands it rather as a morality developed through the growth of the differentiated division of labour. In his earliest writings he does use the term to refer to any social philosophy that grants individuals some kind of superiority or primacy over society. But he later came to use the term more precisely to mean the 'cult of the individual', the moral individualism created by society. Thus individualism is meant to answer the question of what the moral foundation of modern solidarity is.[18]

Moral individualism requires respect for the individual. The state must organise and ensure protection of individuals. But the state gets its authority to do so from the collective consciousness. Protection of rights in this view is one of the elements of good governance because by protecting rights, the state can protect the people.

The impersonal nature of individualism lies in the strong emphasis on the social: modern conditions of social complexity create interdependence, which makes individualism objective or, at least, intersubjective. Modern societies also allow for individual personalities to grow more complex. Where traditional societies presuppose uniformity, a kind of universal human, modern society demands specialisation and thereby greater self-autonomy. However, it is significant that this development does not drive people apart but increases the strength of the reciprocal ties between them.[19] In this sense, the picture drawn here is different from Esposito's, or indeed Bauman's. In their theories, we can see that our late-modern society does not correspond to the

[16] Durkheim, *The Division of Labour*, p. 221.

[17] Durkheim, *The Division of Labour*, pp. 73–7.

[18] See Anthony Giddens, 'The "Individual" in the Writings of Émile Durkheim' (1971) 12 *European Journal of Sociology / Archives Européennes de Sociologie / Europäisches Archiv für Soziologie* 210–28.

[19] See Giddens, 'The "Individual"', pp. 210–28.

impersonal individualism of early modernity any more. Immunisation emphasises the divisions between people and the protective walls raised between them. Liquid modernity, on the other hand, paints a picture of a much more egocentric person than Durkheim's.

In Durkheim's view, even though modern society created more specialised individuals, specialisation functioned as a unifying principle in society and as a foundation for morality. The solidarity produced was not only the solidarity of economic exchange, but something that created between humans a whole system of rights and duties joining them together.[20]

A historical look at privacy supports the idea that there has been a shift towards more individual-centred understandings. In David Vincent's study of the development of privacy in Britain from 1300 onwards, no clear trend emerges. In fact, Vincent argues that there is no unambiguous narrative of privacy to be found through the centuries. However, he does notice that in modern times an individualistic understanding of privacy has gained traction. There is a lot more emphasis on the isolated, self-sufficient citizen that protects their personal archive from outside intrusions. The emblematic text where this kind of privacy is expressed is, according to Vincent too, Warren and Brandeis' article from 1890. Such a private figure who has a right to be left alone is hard to find in earlier European sources.[21]

However, this does not mean that no privacy – or no wish for privacy – existed from the fourteenth century onwards. Even in medieval society, there were times when individuals, families or other groups of people claimed the right to withdraw to a space of their own. Still, privacy was a scarce commodity, for instance in crowded cities such as London, where the infrastructure and the ways of life simply did not allow for people to spend much time by themselves.[22]

For the legal development of privacy rights, it has been important from early on to distinguish between public and private spaces. In particular, the demarcation between the inside and the outside of a home, however overcrowded it might have been, was relevant in early case law.

Vincent argues that the legal defence of privacy, hence, developed in tandem with defence of occupancy of property. For instance, the

[20] Durkheim, *The Division of Labour*, pp. 334–40.
[21] Vincent, *Privacy: A Short History*, p. 2.
[22] Vincent, *Privacy: A Short History*, pp. 2–5.

concept of trespass is known in early-fourteenth-century legal cases.[23] Privacy has developed in pace with technology throughout its history. Print and other new forms of communication involved possibilities for withdrawal, anonymity and isolation. In addition, the development of urban society afforded new ways for privacy. Larger crowds in public spaces made it impossible for people to know everyone. Face-to-face communication outside the home gradually decreased in large cities.[24]

An interesting feature in the development of privacy through the ages is that the management of information within and beyond the walls of the household has been constantly important.[25] People have sought intimacy for many reasons and by many means. This has not, however, always meant individual isolation. The aim of privacy has been the enjoyment and free development of social life. Privacy for various relationships, such as friendship and family life, has been equally important – or even more so – than individuals' rights to be left alone.

We see that alternative understandings of individualism and privacy are possible. The way privacy law constructs persons is not the only way possible. Individualism does not have to be egocentric and privacy does not have to be immunological.

The Person As an Economic Agent in the EU

Moving towards present-day analysis, we can trace some elements of possessive individualism in the EU as well. One of the original forms of legal personhood in the Union has been the free-moving economic agent. In personal data regulation, that person is reflected in rights such as data portability. The free movement of people from one EU country to another is also supported in the privacy setting. People are meant to be able to do their internet shopping in any Member State, as well as to live, work and enjoy themselves on social media within the EU, while feeling that their personal data is safe. This links data protection rather clearly with economic liberty.

Hence, in addition to protecting fundamental rights, data protection rules include an attempt to facilitate the person's enjoyment of their free movement rights. Trust in a fair and inviting market is created by regulating the free flow of data. Trust, in this sense, has economic

[23] Vincent, *Privacy: A Short History*, pp. 2–3.
[24] Vincent, *Privacy: A Short History*, pp. 27, 53, 66.
[25] Vincent, *Privacy: A Short History*, pp. 9, 39, 93–7.

undertones. The aim is to uphold and strengthen the economic interests of the European market as well as to foster data-driven innovation within the Union.[26]

Some argue that a new form of individualism has developed in Europe - one which is at odds with other conceptions of justice.[27] J. H. H. Weiler elaborates on this concern:

> the profound commitment to the individual and his or her rights, relentlessly (and in many respects laudably) placing the individual in the centre of political attention, has contributed to the emergence of ... self-centered individuals. Social mobilization in Europe is strongest when the direct interest of the individual is at stake, and at its weakest when it requires tending to the needs of the other, as the recent Euro crisis, immigrant crisis and other such instances will readily attest.[28]

Sometimes the political effort to salvage the European project is directed into the promise of justice through rights. This can backfire if it ends up developing an ever more individualised society. We see this in discourses on privacy and personal data protection. These discourses set the debate about justice in certain - usually individual-centred - ways, and these ways tend to discard other possibilities.

Alexander Somek is one of the scholars who has expressed concern that the Union is undermining national welfare states without re-building any equivalent system of social protection. On the other hand, the Union also creates opportunities where previously there were none. Both workers and students are given more access to the social benefits of any Member State where they happen lawfully to reside. In fact, the Union has attempted – and succeeded since the mid-1980s – to balance the project of free market building with social goals. It has developed its own policies as well as assisting Member States in reforming their old ones. According to this point of view, the EU is strongly committed to social justice

[26] Further legal advancements towards such ends are visible, for instance in the European Data Strategy, which the Commission announced in 2020. See https://ec.europa.eu/info/strategy/priorities-2019-2024/europe-fit-digital-age/european-data-strategy_en.

[27] See e.g. Stavros Tsakyrakis, 'Disproportionate Individualism', in Dimitry Kochenov, Gráinne de Búrca and Andrew Williams (eds.), *Europe's Justice Deficit* (Oxford: Hart Publishing, 2015), pp. 235–46 at 236.

[28] J. H. H. Weiler, 'Deciphering the Political and Legal DNA of European Integration: An Exploratory Essay', in Julie Dickson and Pavlos Eleftheriadis (eds.), *Philosophical Foundations of European Union Law* (Oxford: Oxford University Press, 2012), pp. 137–58 at 158.

and inclusion. It combines economic values with solidarity in a powerful way.[29]

Somek argues, though, that European social policy is instrumentalist in the sense that it subordinates the social to economic policy. The former is often treated as if it were only an extension of the latter. Somek's view is rather bleak as he pronounces that the main interest of the Union is the optimal investment of human capital into productive pursuits. This attitude is especially visible in the two major fields of EU social policy: employment and social insurance.[30]

Somek expresses the often-heard worry that the integration process results in a gradual weakening of social policy. Integration has been based on faith in achieving both social and economic objectives simultaneously. There seems to be nothing outside or alternative to the market economy, whereby European social policy is rooted in a hope that the tension between capital and labour will somehow magically disappear, possibly through harmonisation. Because of these strong economic and political commitments, it becomes impossible for the European citizen to perceive the EU as a project of emancipation, where relations of dependence and hierarchy, exploitation and inequality could be overcome.[31]

Here, individualism and solidarity become opposing values. The connection between the two is, however, rather complex. Quite a few voices have been heard in recent years demanding more solidarity in the EU. In fact, solidarity has a long history as a value of the Union, at least on paper. As long ago as 1951, the Preamble of the Treaty of Paris recognised solidarity as a goal to be achieved through integration. Again, in the Maastricht Treaty solidarity is set as a central aim of European co-operation. In the Lisbon Treaty solidarity is defined as a value that binds together Member States as well their citizens. Officially, then, it seems that solidarity appears in the EU as a unifying factor that integrates, both on the level of states and on the level of citizens.

In European academic debates, solidarity is often pitched against liberalism. There is uneasiness at the liberalising effects of European integration, which is seen to reinforce the impact of globalisation and

[29] Alexander Somek, 'Integration without Emancipation: Reflections on "Social Europe"', in Bjarne Melkevik (ed.), *Standing Tall: Hommages à Csaba Varga* (Budapest: Pázmány Press, 2012), pp. 419–36.

[30] Somek, 'Integration without Emancipation', p. 426.

[31] Somek, 'Integration without Emancipation', pp. 425–32.

weaken the possibilities of maintaining the welfare state model of government. A consistent trend has therefore been attempts by the EU to balance the internal market agenda with social values. Additionally, the ECJ has developed jurisprudence where it refers to principles of solidarity when trying to balance market interests and social protection objectives.[32]

Solidarity, or rather lack thereof, can be connected to other problems plaguing the EU, especially the lack of a social contract or legitimacy of government. Andrea Sangiovanni frames the discussion of solidarity in the EU as a search for international but regional justice. Justice is here to be understood primarily in a John Rawls-inspired way as distributive justice, which emerges through social co-operation.

Sangiovanni outlines three possible approaches, all of which he refutes. The first version, statist solidarity, entails social obligations at the domestic level, but denies obligations of solidarity or justice beyond the nation state. Post-national solidarity means that the EU should be recognised as a pan-European welfare state. This version can be attributed to Habermas. The third alternative form of solidarity is, according to Sangiovanni, solidarity as fraternity. Here emphasis is put on the link between trust and nationality or, alternatively, on the link between collective agency and nationality. The idea is that distributive justice cannot be achieved without some basis in the sense of fellow-being or mutual trust.[33]

Solidarity as fraternity may seem appealing because it starts off with a description of the bonds between people that arguably form the very essence of solidarity. However, the demands of solidarity as fraternity are often made in a liberal nationalist framework building on the idea of shared identity, which is unfeasible in the EU setting. In addition, this version of solidarity risks sounding like an exclusionary mechanism with echoes from other nationalist discourses. Emphasis on shared identity might also reflect a preference for sameness, shared values, beliefs and ways of life, that is, the mechanical solidarity described by Durkheim as a basic glue keeping together pre-modern societies of a low level of differentiation. If nothing else, then, this version of solidarity is old-fashioned and fits badly with the modern (or postmodern) complex societies of today.

[32] See Andrea Sangiovanni, 'Solidarity in the European Union: Problems and Prospects', in Julie Dickson and Palvos Eleftheriadis (eds.), *Philosophical Foundations of European Union Law* (Oxford: Oxford University Press, 2012), pp. 384–411 at 385–6.

[33] Sangiovanni, 'Solidarity in the European Union', pp. 387–409.

Sangiovanni is not happy with any of the three forms of solidarity. He sees the most plausible account of European solidarity as one that begins with the special nature of European social, political, legal and economic co-operation. It is necessary to focus on the character of public goods that the EU generates. In doing so, we can think of solidarity arising from the fact that we take part in the maintenance and reproduction of these public goods, which include social justice.[34]

Sangiovanni's rather pragmatic solution to the solidarity problem focuses on what the EU can deliver. Perhaps solidarity can be founded on public goods transformed through reciprocity into some version of common good. But what is lacking in this solidarity debate is a way to conceptualise the common in a meaningful way. For this purpose, I shall turn to Jean-Luc Nancy towards the end of the book.

Deutsche Post: Functioning Administration Overrides Data Protection

Balancing data protection and common values has become increasingly urgent because the privacy paradigm at work in EU law is in opposition to several other rights and freedoms. In *Deutsche Post*, the ECJ considered whether functioning administration can override privacy concerns.[35]

The judgment is a preliminary ruling that the ECJ gave in January 2019 on a request from the Finanzgericht Düsseldorf (Düsseldorf Finance Court). The parties in the national proceedings are Deutsche Post AG, a German postal services company, and the Hauptzollamt Köln, which is the Principal Customs Office in Cologne.

The legal disagreement concerns the personal data of individuals, which Deutsche Post was asked to submit to the authorities. The company opposed the customs authority's order to send personal data about its employees to the customs office. The main argument put forward was that the request for personal data by the authorities was excessive. The customs office, on the other hand, argued that it was acting in accordance with EU legislation in asking for the information. EU rules obliged the authorities to inspect undertakings such as Deutsche Post.

[34] Sangiovanni, 'Solidarity in the European Union', p. 410.

[35] Case C-496/17, *Deutsche Post AG* v. *Hauptzollamt Köln*, EU:C:2019:26. The discussion of this case draws upon a case note published as Susanna Lindroos-Hovinheimo, 'Data Protection Does Not Always Override Authorities' Need to Obtain Data' (2019) 4 *European Data Protection Law Review* 568–72.

The important question from the point of view of privacy law was the nature and extent of personal data that has to be submitted for inspection for a company to qualify for the status of an 'authorised economic operator' (AEO) according to the Union Customs Code.[36] According to the Code, an economic operator established in the customs territory of the Union may apply for AEO status. This status affords the operator certain benefits.

In order to be granted AEO status, the operator must meet certain criteria, which include the absence of any serious infringement or repeated infringements of customs legislation and taxation rules, including no record of serious criminal offences relating to the economic activity of the applicant. The issue to be resolved in the case was *what personal data can and should be submitted to the authorities* so that AEO status can be granted.

The most interesting feature of the judgment from a data protection perspective is that the Court had to test the strength of data protection rules while also interpreting their exact meaning. The rules needed to be balanced against other rules that require data to be collected and processed. In this case, the other rules happened to concern the customs union, and, hence, belong to the historical core of European integration.

The ECJ found that, in this case, data protection did not override other interests. The authorities had a legitimate reason to collect data such as tax identification data about a number of Deutsche Post's employees, regardless of the fact that some of them had objected to it.

The argumentation in the ruling is concise and to the point. The Court here interprets the DPD[37] as well as the GDPR[38] in a sound and sober manner, not making data protection a trump that would override all other interests. The analysis of data protection – especially its value in relation to other values – is done in a way that does not make data privacy an absolute right.

This case became a balancing case. In reasoning its decision, the Court takes into account the aims and purposes of both data protection rules and customs rules. Because of this, the judgment provides some clarification of data protection rules, but its usefulness for privacy and data

[36] Reg. (EU) No 952/2013 of the European Parliament and of the Council of 9 October 2013 laying down the Union Customs Code, OJ 2013 No. L269, 10 October 2013, 'the Customs Code'.

[37] Dir. 95/46/EC, OJ 1995 No. L281, 23 November 1995.

[38] Reg. (EU) 2016/679, OJ 2016 No. L119, 4 May 2016.

protection lawyers lies especially in the way data protection is explicitly compared with other interests.

The facts of the case were as follows. The Hauptzollamt requested that Deutsche Post reply to a self-evaluation questionnaire. It asked the company to identify in detail the members of its advisory and supervisory boards, its principal managers and the persons in charge of managing customs matters or those responsible for dealing with such matters. Deutsche Post was requested to send, among other information, the tax identification numbers of all these persons and the details of the tax offices responsible for their taxation.

Deutsche Post challenged the obligation and claimed that numerous individuals were affected by the request, and some of them did not agree to transmission of their data. The company argued that the situation of its wage-earning employees with respect to income tax was not relevant to an assessment of whether serious or repeated infringements of customs legislation or of tax rules, or serious criminal offences, had been committed in the context of its economic activity.

According to Deutsche Post, the collection of tax identification numbers was neither necessary nor appropriate for the purpose of determining its reliability in terms of customs law. The company also argued that verification of the tax situation of all the individuals affected was disproportionate in relation to the purpose of the authorities.

The Hauptzollamt, on the other hand, considered that transmission of the data was necessary to ensure unmistakeable identification of the persons concerned and that the group of individuals affected was compatible with EU customs legislation.

In addition to the issues of appropriateness and proportionality, the referring court also considered whether it was completely necessary for the authorities to have access to the personal data of Deutsche Post's employees and members of its supervisory board. According to the referring court, the personal data of wage-earning employees has no direct link with assessment of the company's reliability in terms of customs law and has no connection with its economic activity. The question also arose as to whether transmission of the data constituted lawful processing.

Delving into the material consideration of the case, the ECJ started by analysing the relevant customs rules. The rules state that the criterion laid down in Article 39(a) of the Customs Code is fulfilled where, over the preceding three years, none of the persons specified has committed a serious infringement or repeated infringements of customs legislation or taxation rules or has had a record of serious criminal offences relating to their economic activity. The persons are the AEO applicant, the person in charge of the applicant or exercising control over its management, and the employee in charge of the applicant's customs matters. According to the Court, the provisions indicate that the list is exhaustive.

Therefore, according to the Court, the rules may not be interpreted as concerning natural persons other than those who are in charge of the applicant who exercise control over its management or who are in charge of the applicant's customs matters. Accordingly, the rules do not affect the members of the advisory boards or supervisory boards of legal persons, divisional heads other than those in charge of the applicant's customs matters, accounting managers and persons whose duties involve dealing with customs matters.

Within an undertaking's organisation, a number of natural persons may be in charge of or have control over its management. Consequently, the Court held that the natural persons affected are all those who, within the applicant's organisation, are in charge of it or who exercise control over its management, as well as those who are in charge of its customs matters.[39] Interestingly, here the Court adopted an expansive interpretation of the list of persons, even though it considered the list itself to be exhaustive.

The Court argued that the customs authorities should be permitted access to data that enables them to establish that none of the persons specified have committed any serious infringements or repeated infringements of customs legislation and taxation rules or have any record of serious criminal offences relating to their economic activity.

However, the Court stressed that, if the authorities process personal data, they have to respect EU legislation on data protection. The legislation entails that respect for the right to private life concerns any information relating to a natural person who is identified or identifiable.[40] It is clear that tax data, such as tax identification numbers, constitutes 'personal data' within the meaning of both the DPD and the GDPR.

The Court pointed out that personal data must be collected for specified, explicit and legitimate purposes and must be adequate, relevant

[39] Case C-496/17, *Deutsche Post AG*, EU:C:2019:26, para. 50.

[40] Here the ECJ referred to its judgments of 9 November 2010 in Joined Cases C-92/09 and C-93/09, *Volker und Markus Schecke and Eifert* EU:C:2010:662, para. 52; and of 17 October 2013 in Case C-291/12, *Michael Schwarz* v. *Stadt Bochum*, EU:C:2013:670, para. 26.

and not excessive in relation to those purposes. As the lawful ground of processing, the Court understandably identified necessity to comply with a legal obligation.[41]

In the situation at hand, the tax identification numbers of natural persons were initially collected by their employer. Their subsequent collection by the customs authorities was, according to the ECJ, clearly necessary to comply with a legal obligation incumbent on those authorities. Hence, the data was processed for specified, explicit and legitimate purposes. According to the ECJ, this was also true of collecting the details of the tax offices, since the aim there was also to enable the customs authorities to respond to an AEO application.

In contrast to the referring court, the ECJ held that the data collected by the customs authorities was adequate, relevant and not excessive in relation to the purposes for which that data was collected. The customs authorities granting AEO status to an operator means that certain customs legislation control functions are delegated to that operator. Consequently, before that status is granted, those authorities need to be able to obtain information on the reliability of the applicant. Therefore, collection of the data constitutes an adequate and relevant measure.

Moreover, the Court noted that personal data collected by the authorities appeared limited to what was necessary and did not reveal to the customs authorities sensitive information on personal circumstances, such as marital status or religious affiliation, or the income of the persons concerned.

The ECJ stressed that the authorities must make sure that the applicant complies with customs legislation. For this purpose, it is important to ascertain that certain persons who have authority in the organisation have not committed infringements, whether or not those infringements have any connection to the economic activity of the applicant. Only by doing so are the authorities able to determine if AEO status should be granted or not. However, the authorities are obviously not allowed to collect any and all personal data. They may collect only such data that enables them to obtain information on serious or repeated infringements of customs legislation or of tax rules or on serious criminal offences committed by those natural persons and related to their economic activity.

[41] Art. 7(c) DPD and Art. 6(1)(c) GDPR.

On these grounds, the Court concluded that the customs authorities may require an applicant for AEO status to send to them the personal data that enables the authorities to obtain information on serious or repeated infringements of customs legislation or of taxation rules or on serious criminal offences.

In this judgment, protection of individuals' personal data was not deemed more valuable than a functioning administration. In this regard, the case belongs to a minority of data protection decisions by the ECJ that have a connection to administration. As we have seen in, for instance, *Psara*, data protection has often been the more important value in the eyes of the Court - more important than, for instance, transparency in administration.[42] Herein lies the added value of the Court's reasoning in *Deutsche Post*. It now takes a more measured approach to privacy than in some of its earlier praxis.

In its weighing of interests, the ECJ considered here whether it was really necessary to collect all the data that the tax authorities wanted. The Court notes that it was, because only by doing so could the tax authorities be sure that the applicant could be granted AEO status. The decisive limit was that the data was related to the natural persons' economic activity. It did not have to be connected to the economic activity of the company.

An alternative reading of the judgment is, however, also possible. It can be argued that the judgment does not form a very big diversion in the ECJ's tendency to afford individuals strong protection when personal data is concerned. Even though individuals' interests did not override the authorities' need to obtain data and the company's interest in being granted AEO status, the persons whose data was processed were perhaps not understood primarily *as individuals* in the context of this case. They occupied professional roles, and their data was collected and processed because of this.[43] Perhaps in this case, the Court understood the personal data of the people concerned in a depersonalised manner.

Occasionally people are seen by the law in more – and occasionally in less – individualised ways. In this case, the people whose data was collected and processed were perhaps not considered by the Court to be in such a vulnerable position as in some other cases. Their data was

[42] See also e.g. Case C-28/08 P, *The Bavarian Lager* [2010] ECR I-6055; Case C-615/13 P, *ClientEarth*, EU:C:2015:489.

[43] See for comparison the *Buivids* case. There, too, the role of the persons whose data was processed was relevant. Case C-345/17, *Buivids*, EU:C:2019:122.

not processed by a company to make profit but to fulfil a lawful obligation. There is a power structure at play here, too, but it is not the same as in cases where multinational companies such as Google or Facebook are doing the processing.

It seems that the Court considers some data to be more personal than others, even though the legislation does not make any distinction as such, except for health data and similar special categories of personal data.[44] In its reasoning, the Court stressed that the authorities are allowed to collect only data related to the economic activities of persons.

The economic activities of persons are perhaps not as personal as some other information might be.[45] Developing this idea further, it can be argued that the Court took a step away from personal protection of individuals but could do so only through depersonalising the data first. Data protection did not weigh heaviest in this judgment because the data was not that personal. A similar logic appears in *Buivids*, which we discussed earlier. The personal data of the police officers at the station may not have been as personal, in the eyes of the Court, as for instance the personal data collected by Facebook in, say, *Wirtschaftsakademie*. Read in this way, *Deutsche Post* or *Buivids* do not depart from the individual-centred paradigm that permeates data protection law.

Surveillance Capitalism and Related Individualisation

Even though the EU promises more liberty for the free-moving person with rights, this economic agent may not be as free as it might seem. The ideology is one where freedom to move, consume, work and invest in all the different Member States brings about possibilities. The reality may be another. It is impossible for us to delve into a thorough critique

[44] However, if the tax identification number is considered a national identification number, the situation becomes more complex. Art. 87 GDPR establishes *the possibility* for Member States to determine the conditions under which national identification numbers can be processed. On this point, the GDPR differs in wording from the DPD. According to Art. 8(7) DPD, 'Member States shall determine the conditions under which a national identification number or any other identifier of general application may be processed.' In this ruling, the ECJ implies that the setting of rules by a Member State may no longer be mandatory. The author wishes to thank Tijmen Wisman for making this excellent point.

[45] Even though it is clear that our economic activities can reveal a lot about ourselves. Indeed, the issue in *Google Spain* also concerned data about economic activities.

of the capitalist features of the Union, but we do need to consider the ways in which capitalism, individualism and privacy come together.

There is much discussion on the way persons are being exploited as faceless giants – especially commercial ones like the social media companies – collect our data. Shoshana Zuboff has developed a sophisticated analysis of the dangers of data-driven economics in *The Age of Surveillance Capitalism*. Her work is pertinent and powerful. It does, however, hold on to the same individualist presuppositions that traverse possessive liberalism and become visible in various aspects of privacy law.

She starts with a discussion of individualism that comes very close to Bauman's. We basically live in a contradiction. In accordance with prevailing individualism, we have a need to exercise control over our lives, but that control is not within our grasp. The problem is that we want a fulfilling life but in order to get the resources for it, we are forced to battle economic and political situations. And both of these areas, economics and politics, see us merely as ciphers.[46] We are constantly being used as fodder in the workings of capitalism.

Zuboff calls for greater recognition of individuals. According to her narrative, it is problematic that we as persons have become invisible. Our unique personhood is neither acknowledged nor respected by those in power.

Zuboff, however, does not see that the problems pertaining to the current form of capitalism, that is, surveillance capitalism, are simply problems of privacy. They go beyond that. Nothing less than individual sovereignty is at stake, including our right to the future tense, she says. The extreme asymmetries of power and knowledge that surveillance capitalism entails are an imminent threat to many of our rights. Our lives are rendered as data that enables new forms of social control in the service of the interest of others.[47]

Zuboff has interesting things to say about privacy. It is not the case that privacy is under threat, nor that more privacy would be the means to resist this new form of capitalism. More complex developments are taking place:

> Surveillance capitalism lays claim to . . . decision rights. The typical complaint is that privacy is eroded, but that is misleading. In the larger societal pattern, privacy is not eroded but redistributed, as decision rights over privacy are

[46] Shoshana Zuboff, *The Age of Surveillance Capitalism – The Fight for a Human Future at the New Frontier of Power* (London: Profile Books 2019), pp. 44–6.

[47] Zuboff, *The Age of Surveillance Capitalism*, pp. 54–5.

claimed for surveillance capital. Instead of people having the rights to decide how and what they will disclose, these rights are concentrated within the domain of surveillance capitalism. Google discovered this necessary element of the new logic of accumulation: it must assert the rights to take the information upon which its success depends.[48]

We need to understand how surveillance capitalism works and fight it. But the fight needs to be about capitalism, not privacy.[49]

Technological capitalists gather data about us in order to sell advertising. They also gather data to change our behaviour to suit their purposes. Advertising and behaviour modification are the means by which surveillance capitalists accrue their surplus. Surveillance capitalism modifies human action secretly and for profit, thus exiling us from our own behaviour.[50]

What is special in the new form of capitalism that Zuboff describes is not only that the tech giants have a monopoly in their respective fields. They differ from traditional capitalists in the sense that they do not themselves sell any goods. They are merely marketplaces that sell advertising.

The profit that these companies get is dependent on the advertising that they sell. They gather data to maximise that profit, and one part of the process is to modify people's behaviour in order to sell goods. This advertising is in fact manipulation. Being situated between consumers and producers of goods and services, the surveillance capitalists can effectively exploit both. They are in a position where they alone determine the price of the marketplace, that is, how much each actor has to pay to get their advertising on the site.

It is interesting to note that this idea about behavioural modification brings to the fore a rather dynamic view of personhood. Surveillance capitalists can modify behaviour to extract profit from it precisely because the individual is not set in stone but an embedded being. Encounters with others in and through various media have an effect on who we are and what we want. Focusing only on the protection of autonomous selfsame individuals, these dynamic features of personhood can easily be overlooked.

Does privacy protection need to take for granted that a person is somehow given in advance and that the law protects this autonomous

[48] Zuboff, *The Age of Surveillance Capitalism*, p. 90.
[49] Zuboff, *The Age of Surveillance Capitalism*, p. 194.
[50] Zuboff, *The Age of Surveillance Capitalism*, p. 309.

individual? What the behavioural modification tendencies of current capitalism show so well, after all, is that a person is not a fixture but continuously dependent on their conditions. For this reason alone, some the presuppositions of individualised privacy need to be re-thought.

Holding on to the idea of the autonomous individual as the person of privacy rights does not necessarily help in combating current capitalist logic. Privacy rights can do little to prevent our personhood from being tangled up in our surroundings. Our embeddedness affects us in both benevolent and less benevolent ways. We are a part of society and society is part of us. The links between us are formed by various media, some of which are undoubtedly making money in the process.

We can conclude by noticing how the individualism emblematic of liquid modernity has certain economic features. These are reflected in the person that privacy rights produce. An economic agent is the product of ideology, whose correspondence to reality is fragile. Such an economic agent is not really a person in control but a person at the mercy of market forces.

Privacy rights, especially data protection, strive at keeping the individual safe from economic exploitation, while similarly protecting their status as an autonomous economic agent. However, some of the possessive individualist assumptions that the economic agent is built upon may hinder the development of more just societies. What is lacking is the solidarity element, the idea that we are fundamentally in it together, and our lives are not only our own affair.

Discussion of surveillance capitalism is most effectively had in the plural. *Our* data forms the raw material of the capitalists. *We* are being exploited in new ways. Privacy rights may be one tool in the fight against this capitalism, but the fight is ours, as is privacy. It is not the case that unique individuals are being exploited, but large groups of people. The issue is common, and so are the threats. The person of privacy protection should be anyone of us, not me.

A critique of individualism such as the one developed on the pages of this book leads naturally to questions about alternatives. What is the other option? The last chapters of the book will take up this challenge.

6 The Political Person

Let us take stock. So far, I have argued that the dominant view of the person constructed by privacy law is a person in control. This is mostly caused by the important role that data protection plays today. In data protection law, as we have seen, protected data is always data about an individual. There are many rules about how such data can be collected, stored, processed and removed but one significant aim of them is to empower people, which shows in the emphasis on control. This approach chosen by the legislator and upheld by case law demonstrates that the person is predominately understood as an autonomous individual.

This brings about several problems, both theoretical and practical. Firstly, a focus on individuals and their control does not apply easily in Big Data scenarios, nor in situations where more people than one would require protection. Secondly, an individualist starting point can lead to the paradox of privacy, where a person's subjective understandings of privacy clash with the necessarily general nature of law. Thirdly, views that are too individualised can contribute to the development where the common good cannot be upheld against individuals' rights. Transparency of government and the rights of freedom of speech and freedom of information are examples that we have discussed in this context.

As for theoretical perspectives discussed so far, Bauman's analysis of late-modern society explains the broader societal context in which privacy as an individual entitlement becomes intelligible. Liberalist theories explain the roots of this kind of individualism. Durkheim, on the other hand, shows us that individualism does not have to be egoistic or atomistic. Esposito's illuminating analysis of immunisation fits the current trends in privacy law and warns us of the potential dangers to society that can result from over-emphasising individuals' rights to be left alone.

There are alternatives, of which the idea of the third person is one. Durkheim offers another view that, even though individualist as well, takes into account that people are always embedded in society. The person in society, the political person, is our topic in this chapter. Is there a way in which the person protected by privacy rights can be a political person too, not only an individual in charge of their own affairs? This chapter analyses Rancière's understanding of political subjectivity in search for more alternatives.[1]

It is clear from the outset, however, that Rancière does not merge well with mainstream jurisprudence, if indeed the two can interact at all.[2] Why, then, should his ideas be of interest to our investigation? I propose that we can gain from him a new way of thinking. A Rancièrean understanding of subjectivity has its own specific features.

I will focus on the connections between equality and political personhood. For Rancière, equality is a presupposed principle, not only an aim. Everybody is equal to begin with. Therefore, anybody and whoever can be a political subject. The uniqueness of individuals is not the crucial factor in this theory.

Before going into the complexities of the philosophy, we need to pay attention to Rancière's overall project and methodology. He is adamant that his aim is not to engage in political philosophy at all. He is not drafting a theory of politics, not even a philosophy of the political.[3] His method consists of reading others. He analyses historical progresses and situations, debates and narratives. Even though he occasionally does draw general conclusions from some of his examples, and we can undoubtedly classify several of his texts as theoretical, he emphasises

[1] Parts of this chapter are based upon the article Susanna Lindroos-Hovinheimo, 'Ranciere and the Legal Subject – Coming to Terms with Non-Existence', in Mónical López Lerma and Julen Etxabe (eds.), *Rancière and Law* (Oxon and New York: Routledge, 2018), pp. 73–91.

[2] The relationship between Rancière and the mainstream is contentious at best in terms of political theory, or philosophy, too. Perhaps one of the best attempts to situate him is to see him in 'a position of mainstream marginality in contemporary thought' Christopher Watkin, 'Rancière Now: Current Perspectives on Jacques Rancière (Review)' (2014) 68 *French Studies: A Quarterly Review* 418.

[3] In 'From Politics to Aesthetics?', published in 2005, he refers to the research he has done previously, for instance in his doctoral dissertation La nuit des prolétaires [Proletarian nights] as 'historical' and 'political'. He also says that he is no more a political philosopher than he is a philosopher of art Jacques Rancière, 'From Politics to Aesthetics?' (2005) 28 *Paragraph* 13–25 at 13 and 18.

in several writings that he is not engaged in a theory, nor is he making deductions from a theoretical framework to the understanding of politics, art or literature.[4]

For Rancière, there can be no 'theory' that explains things separate from 'practice' founded on the lessons of theory. Speaking about himself (interestingly enough in the third person) he says: '"It might be" is a formulation consistent with Rancière's peculiar practice of "theory". As I mentioned earlier, even when he writes "theses on politics", he does not say what politics is but what it might be. He does not build a theory starting from the ontological principle of politics to deduce its consequences.'[5] His task, as he sees it, is to move from particular examples to tentative models for how things might be. The 'might be' is the end of the process, not the beginning. By analysing occurrences that seem paradoxical, he constructs, for instance, a view of what the term 'democracy' might mean, how equality can be understood, and what the intricate collaborations between disruption and order could be. He uses expressions such as 'the dramaturgy of politics',[6] 'a moving map of a moving landscape'[7] or 'topography'[8] to refer to what he is trying to achieve.

The subject is an important theme for Rancière, but he regards it as a difficult topic to approach theoretically. In a short text called 'Work, Identity, Subject' he calls the question of the subject 'monstrous':

> Who plays the part of the subject who incarnates, represents or symbolizes work: that is the way in which, in the end, the 'question of work' has presented itself for me. It is also the way in which I have been able to address that monstrous question that has always terrorized me in the same measure as my contemporaries made it paramount: the 'theory of the subject'. This explains why I have only ever addressed it but from the side, through a specific aspect; namely, the relationship between subject and identity.[9]

[4] Jacques Rancière, 'A Few Remarks on the Method of Jacques Rancière' (2009) 15 *Parallax* 114–23 at 114–17.

[5] Rancière, 'A Few Remarks on the Method', 119.

[6] Rancière, 'A Few Remarks on the Method', 119, 120.

[7] Rancière, 'A Few Remarks on the Method', 120.

[8] Jacques Rancière, 'The Janus-Face of Politicized Art: Jacques Rancière in Interview with Gabriel Rockhill', in Jacques Rancière, *The Politics of Aesthetics: The Distribution of the Sensible* (New York: Continuum, 2006), pp. 50–2.

[9] Jacques Rancière, 'Work, Identity, Subject', in Jean-Philippe Deranty and Alison Ross (eds.), *Jacques Rancière and the Contemporary Scene: The Philosophy of Radical Equality* (New York: Continuum, 2012), pp. 205–16 at 206.

So Rancière is not after a new theory of the subject. The 'question of the subject' is too difficult, too all-encompassing. It can only be approached in a roundabout way. He addresses only one specific aspect, namely the questionable relationship between subject and identity. That way he engages in critiques of identity.

Some of Rancière's influences derive from Althusser, which is rather evident,[10] but some from Sartre - perhaps less evident but highly interesting. Rancière is concerned with identitarian fixations, that is, fixing identities, an idea that brings to mind a Sartrean notion of freedom.[11] Sartre rejects fixed identities and makes a distinction between doing things and making oneself. This, says Rancière, was the framework for his own first readings of Marx.[12]

Rancière's interest is in explaining how alienation is related to an understanding of the subject as expelled from itself and attached to an alien identity.[13] Having done a lot of research on workers, Rancière notices that not even a worker's identity is fixed. Workers have a capacity, or perhaps we should call it freedom, to contest the alien identities that are given to them. The 'process of subjectivization is a process of disidentification or declassification'.[14]

A political subject can come into existence through denial of identity. This is the main idea in Rancièrean subjectivity: '[A] subject is an outsider or, more, an in-between. Proletarians was the name given to

[10] Rancière was Althusser's student at Ecole Normale Supérieure in the 1960s but his thought later developed in directions that differ considerably from his teacher's. Traces from Althusserian ideas can still be found in Ranciere's works. See his remarks on Althusser in Jacques Rancière and David Panagia, 'Dissenting Words: A Conversation with Jacques Rancière' (2000) 30 *Diacritics* 113–26 at 113–16; and Jacques Rancière, *Dissensus: On Politics and Aesthetics*, Steven Corcoran ed. and trs. (New York: Continuum, 2010), pp. 37–40. For discussions of the two philosophers' similarities and differences see e.g. Steven Corcoran, 'Editor's Introduction', in Jacques Rancière, *Dissensus: On Politics and Aesthetics* (New York: Continuum, 2010), pp. 1–24; and Andrew Parker, 'Editor's Introduction: Mimesis and the Division of Labor', in Jacques Rancière, *The Philosopher and His Poor* (Durham, NC: Duke University Press, 2003), pp. ix–xx. For a discussion of the Althusserian legal subject see e.g. Roberto Buonamano, 'The Legal Subject in Althusser's Political Theory' (2014) 25 *Law & Critique* 231–48.

[11] Their starting points are similar because for Sartre freedom can be understood as indeterminate being-for-itself, a way of being that is not necessarily defined by the roles we are made to play or the identities that are given to us. Everybody defines themselves, instead of being defined by the ways in which they are subjected Peter Hallward, 'Staging Equality: On Rancière's Theatrocracy' (2006) 37 *New Left Review* 109–29 at 110.

[12] Rancière, 'Work, Identity, Subject', p. 207.

[13] Rancière, 'Work, Identity, Subject', p. 207.

[14] Jacques Rancière, 'Politics, Identification, and Subjectivization' (1992), 61 *October* 58–64 at 61.

people who are together inasmuch as they are between: between several names, statuses, and identities; between humanity and inhumanity, citizenship and its denial; between the status of a man of tools and the status of a speaking and thinking being.'[15] Politics opens up space for disagreements about existence and non-existence, being and non-being, subjects and objects. It causes splits and ruptures in ontological divisions and definitions.[16]

Rancière is interested in human beings first and foremost in the political sense. And according to him, a political subject cannot be easily defined. Subjectivity is a *process*, not for instance a state or an attribute: 'Political subjectivity ... refers to an enunciative and demonstrative capacity to re-configure the relation between the visible and the sayable, the relation between words and bodies: namely, what I refer to as "the partition of the sensible".'[17] The idea underlying this open subjectivity is Rancière's conception of equality.

Equality As a Presupposition

Equality enjoys a central – even *the* central – place in Rancière's thought. He describes it as a principle. It has no world of its own, he says.[18] It is nothing in the world in the sense of being fixed, defined or laid down. It is a presupposition, not a goal to be attained. Equality is something that Rancière takes for granted: we are all equal whether that ever shows or is realised or not.

In the text 'The Community of Equals' we find an example of how Rancière understands inequality. An unequal relationship is, for instance, one in which one person explains something to another. I explain something to you assuming that without this explanation you would not understand. Here I assume the role of the one with more knowledge. Explanation establishes a specific bond between people, a bond that upholds inequality. Any hierarchical constructions where people assume roles according to their status serve to disguise the fact that ultimately everyone is equally valuable.[19]

15 Rancière, 'Politics, Identification, and Subjectivization', 61.
16 See Bram Ieven, 'Heteroreductives: Rancière's Disagreement with Ontology' (2009) 15 *Parallax* 50–62 at 50–1.
17 Rancière and Panagia, 'Dissenting Words', 115.
18 Rancière, *Dissensus*, p. 213.
19 Jacques Rancière, 'The Community of Equals', in Jacques Rancière, *On the Shores of Politics*, Liz Heron trs. (London: Verso, 1995), pp. 63–91 at 84.

Actual equality can be advanced on two conditions. It has to be *assumed*, taken for granted and endlessly re-affirmed. But a community of equals can never achieve the form of a social institution. For instance, statutory means can only get us so far in achieving equality in practice. The thought seems to be that as soon as we feel comfortable in our institutions providing for equal measures and protecting our equal interests, we risk losing equality. Institutionalised equality is not equality properly so called.[20]

Equality is a principle or axiom that needs to be assumed and re-affirmed continuously. Still, it can never be fulfilled. There will not come a time when we can announce that we finally live in an equal society. Equality as a principle is, hence, always at work but never achieved.[21]

What is unique in Rancière's thought is that he does not see equality as something that happens *to* people. Traditional political theories often understand equality as received from the state or some other institution with power. Rancière's view is different. We do not *receive* equality, nor is it given to us from a source outside ourselves. It is not granted to us as a right. It cannot be handed to us, we have to grab it. Equality is *done*. It is created by us, not for us. This feature of his thinking is sometimes called his radical anti-liberalism. Todd May argues that Rancière's understanding of politics is the inverse of traditional liberal political theory. Equality comes from the people. It is a presupposition out of which they can act in the political sphere.[22] 'What is at issue in politics is the equality of those who seek to participate.'[23] Political action makes the equality of everyone visible and audible.

Equality is a concept whose precise reference cannot be defined. All it says is that everybody is equal. It is a given, a principle prior to the practical field of politics. Its application, however, is undetermined, so it can operate in various ways, mainly disrupting pre-existing divisions of power or definitions of status and identity. '[T]he egalitarian axiom defines the practices, the modes of expression and manifestation that are themselves always determined by a particular state of inequality and by the potential for equality.'[24] Equality is always possible in

[20] Rancière, 'The Community of Equals', p. 84.

[21] Rancière, 'The Community of Equals', pp. 82–4.

[22] Todd May, 'Wrong, Disagreement, Subjectification', in Jean-Philippe Deranty (ed.), *Jacques Rancière: Key Concepts* (Durham: Acumen, 2010), pp. 69–79 at 72.

[23] May, 'Wrong, Disagreement, Subjectification', p. 75.

[24] Jacques Rancière et al., 'Jacques Rancière: Literature, Politics, Aesthetics: Approaches to Democratic Disagreement' (2000) 29 *SubStance* 3–24 at 6.

principle, a potential waiting to be fulfilled. The presupposition of equality has positive world-altering potential. There are moments when equals declare themselves as such, no matter what the actual conditions in society might suggest. It is in these situations that political acts take place.

Political Speech

Politics is not a field or a place 'out there'. It can always happen here. It takes place when we put into motion the definitions and categories that are in force. There is, properly speaking, no political subject, because politics is precisely the act of putting into question our definitions of political subjects.

Rancière is not primarily interested in revolutions if we understand them as singular upheavals or ruptures. He says that he is not a thinker of the event but 'rather of emancipation as something with its own tradition, with a history that isn't just made up of great striking deeds, but also of the ongoing effort to create forms of the common different from the ones on offer from the state'.[25] A world-altering act can be tiny. It does not have to happen on a barricade.

Philosophy is one example of revolutionary action. According to Rancière, the 'critical practice of philosophy is an inseparably egalitarian, or anarchistic practice, since it considers arguments, narratives, testimonies, investigations and metaphors all as the equal inventions of a common capacity in a common language. Engaging in critique of the instituted divisions, then, paves the way for renewing our interrogations into what we are able to think and to do'.[26] Philosophy can open up possibilities for new ways of thinking and acting. That way philosophy can take part in changing the world. But do you have to be a philosopher to change the world? Certainly not. Anybody can question the given order of things. And the political subject is born *in this questioning*.

Understood in this way, politics may be rare but this does not mean that it only happens in exceptional moments with times of apathy in between. Politics is rare because it does not happen naturally or automatically merely because there are always relations of power. Politics is

[25] Jacques Rancière, 'Democracies against Democracy: An Interview with Eric Hazan', in Agamben et al. (eds.), *Democracy in What State?* (New York: Chichester, 2011), pp. 76–81 at 80–1.

[26] Rancière, *Dissensus*, p. 218.

an affirmation of equality. We can observe it whenever the power of *anybody* emerges.

That everybody is equal means that anybody can be exchanged for an 'other'. Equality includes the idea of substitutability. We are all equally worthy and our roles in society could in principle be reversed at any time. Places and roles are continuously being re-negotiated and re-configured. Political acts can show that there is no difference between the one and the other. This display of substitutability is a display of equality.

According to Rancière, politics is 'almost everywhere and in every time interlocked, if not confused, with police'.[27] Politics and order are intertwined. It is difficult to notice and analyse political acts for this very reason. Dissensus tends to be entangled with consensus and it is by studying situations, usually after they have taken place, that we can distinguish between them.

Speech can be political. But it is not language itself that is political; it is the act of speaking or writing, especially in the sense that it questions the distinction between legitimate and illegitimate speakers.[28] Categories such as 'worker' or 'immigrant' can be re-arranged by taking a talking subject's position. What is required is to put into circulation words that do things or sometimes just to use words in ways that are contested by those who claim to speak correctly. The capacity to speak gives us the possibility to disagree and disrupt the hierarchical order.

According to Rancière, in order to become a political subject, one has to stage a scene. For politics to happen, we must invent a scene upon which words may be audible, objects may be visible and individuals may be recognised.[29] Presupposed equality makes this staging and re-staging possible. It enables constitutive re-thinking.[30]

Political acts disrupt what is visible and audible. They interfere with the partition of the sensible. The aesthetic dimension of politics means the 'staging of a dissensus – of a conflict of sensory worlds – by subjects who act as if they were the people, which is made of the uncountable count of the anyone'.[31] Subjectivation means enactment of equality,

[27] Jacques Rancière, 'A Few Remarks on the Method', 118.

[28] Rancière and Panagia, 'Dissenting Words', 114; Rancière, *Dissensus*, pp. 152–3; Rancière et al., 'Jacques Rancière: Literature, Politics, Aesthetics', 7–8, 12.

[29] Rancière and Panagia, 'Dissenting Words', 116.

[30] Rancière and Panagia, 'Dissenting Words', 120.

[31] Jacques Rancière, 'The Aesthetic Dimension: Aesthetics, Politics, Knowledge' (2009) 36 *Critical Inquiry* 1–19 at 11.

and it is an emancipative process.[32] Presupposed equality is actualised. This can happen in different ways.

Subjectivation entails not only a simple assertion of identity. It is always at the same time denial of an identity given by somebody else, by the prevailing order. Where policy and order are about right names, names that put people in their places and dictate their social roles, politics is about 'wrong' names.[33] So politics is about naming, but not about right names, rather, *other* names. *Demos* or 'the people' is a helpful concept to be applied here. The demos consists of people who are not identified with anybody; they are the masses.

Law and Order

Politics, as we have seen, is closely tied to the principle of equality. Political acts enact equality. This usually requires disruption of the prevailing order of things. Law, however, is the guardian of order. Is law, then, necessarily an antipode to politics? Such a conclusion sounds strange to critical legal scholars, who generally understand law as intertwined with politics. Indeed, for them it is difficult to see how law could exist if devoid of politics.

To become a subject whose equality is recognised, one needs to demonstrate dissensus *to somebody*. Is there a way that the law could function as that scene of such dissensus? In order to use the legal system as a forum, a speaker must adhere to the pregiven hierarchical order of the society and accept the norms that govern it, at least to some extent. In this sense, legal acts cannot be political in a radical way.

Nevertheless, if legal acts interfere in the composition of the political landscape by defining concepts and categories, influencing attitudes and re-configuring power relations, then they can be political. The argument is not that law enables political action but rather that it can in some instances – most specifically in some *cases* – contribute with a platform from which the status quo can be questioned. Law can work as a medium through which questioning can become audible.[34]

[32] See Jacques Rancière, *Disagreement: Politics and Philosophy*, Julie Rose trs. (Minneapolis, MN: University of Minnesota Press, 1999), p. 62.

[33] Rancière, 'Politics, Identification, and Subjectivization', 62.

[34] Interestingly, some of Rancière's own examples of when a re-configuration of the partition of the sensible has taken place are juridical or at least have close affinity with some form of law. See also Lindroos-Hovinheimo, *Justice and the Ethics of Legal Interpretation*, pp. 153–5.

It is difficult to see the legal system purely as a servant of the status quo because the system itself is a multifaceted, complex mess always including elements that may be interpreted as pointing in several different and even mutually exclusionary decisions. There is definitely room for struggle inside the law.

Rancière himself maintains that dissensus is often entangled with consensus and politics with order. The two cannot be conceptually separated. This idea sits well with the self-understanding of a critical lawyer, who sees their task as usurpation of legal principles and concepts. Law is a tool to be used, not simply a pre-dictated order. No legal rule or principle applies itself, which leaves room for interpretation and disagreement. That is exactly what many lawyers are trained to do: to disagree. Their craft consists in using legal concepts as instruments for strategic purposes, thus taking advantage of the leeway of language while simultaneously causing meanings to fluctuate.

Can claims about privacy rights be political acts? Traditionally, they have protected the confidentiality of our letters, emails and phone conversations and, hence, upheld anonymity and the right to be *anyone*. Could they still be understood as the rights of the equal third person?

Let us recall the right to be forgotten, and consider it this time through a Rancièrean lens. *Google Spain*[35] is one interesting case for this. Does it represent a political act where the subject as equal is born?

The case raises a number of questions concerning personhood. A critical reading may begin by asking what kind of agency Mr González's actions presuppose on the one hand and produce on the other. He makes a rights claim, which is ultimately a political and legal speech act. The fact that we have a ruling, in which his speech is taken seriously, attests to his status as a somebody who has the possibility to make themselves heard.

Mr González struggled for the right to have information about him removed from the Internet. His acts can be understood as a search for individual self-determination. He asks for withdrawal.

Google Spain can certainly be understood as a scene where something was staged. A new right was fought for and won. This right entails confirmation of a person's meaningful existence in law by a meaningful non-existence in the Internet.

It also illustrates some of the limits of how legal rights can be used in political struggles. Mr González's performative utterances seem to

[35] Case C-131/12, *Google Spain and Google*, EU:C:2014:317.

point to resistance. His acts are a demonstration of his capacity to reconfigure the world that he inhabits. This is a case where a certain kind of equality is affirmed. The equality between a person and a large multinational service provider is not a trivial thing. It can have meaningful consequences for many.

Schrems I As a Political Act

The first *Schrems* case presents a slightly different scenario from *Google Spain*. Here, a general claim is made, and neither the applicant's nor the Court's purpose is, in the end, to protect an individual's right. The judgment becomes focused on broader issues.

The case deals with two regimes of knowledge colliding. On the one hand, there is the security paradigm, which seeks to allow information to be controlled by various institutions and government bodies. On the other, there is the privacy paradigm, which resists such usage of information.

This case, *Schrems* v. *Data Protection Commissioner*,[36] is the first of a number of cases that Maximillian Schrems has driven to the EU Court. In this one, he fights for his privacy rights against multinational companies, data protection officials and partly against the Commission as well. Later, he has continued the fight and is now a noteworthy privacy activist.

The case concerned a preliminary reference request from Ireland. The request was made in proceedings between Mr Schrems and the Data Protection Commissioner. The latter had refused to investigate a complaint made by Mr Schrems regarding the fact that Facebook Ireland Ltd transfers the personal data of its users to the United States and keeps it on servers there. Mr Schrems was concerned that these large amounts of data were transferred from the EU to the USA and that the data was available to surveillance programmes such as PRISM in the USA. Moreover, EU data subjects did not have any right to obtain access, rectification or erasure of data, or any administrative or judicial redress with regard to the collection and processing of their personal data by US surveillance programmes.

The Commission had adopted Decision 2000/520 on the basis of Article 25(6) of the Data Protection Directive. According to this Safe Harbour Decision, an adequate level of protection for the transfer of

[36] Case C-362/14, *Schrems*, EU:C:2015:650.

data from the EU to the USA would be attained if organisations comply with the safe harbour privacy principles set out in the decision. However, there was still the worry – which the Commission had also recognised later on – that EU subjects' data protection rights were severely threatened by large-scale access by intelligence agencies in the USA by Safe Harbour-certified companies.

Maximillian Schrems is Austrian but the main proceedings took place in Ireland because anyone residing in the Union who wishes to use Facebook is required to agree to a contract with Facebook Ireland. In 2013, Mr Schrems made a complaint to the Irish Data Protection Commissioner by which he asked the Commissioner to prohibit Facebook Ireland from transferring personal data to the United States. Mr Schrems argued that the law and practice in force in the USA did not ensure adequate protection of his personal data against surveillance activities by the public authorities. He referred to the revelations made by Edward Snowden concerning the activities of the United States intelligence services, in particular those of the National Security Agency (NSA).

The Commissioner held that he was not required to investigate the matters raised by Mr Schrems and rejected the complaint as unfounded. The Commissioner considered that there was no evidence that Mr Schrems' personal data had been accessed by the NSA. He added that the allegations raised by Mr Schrems in his complaint could not be profitably put forward since any question of the adequacy of data protection in the USA had to be determined in accordance with the Safe Harbour Decision. The Commission had found in that decision that the United States ensured an adequate level of protection.

After the Commissioner's refusal, Mr Schrems brought an action before the High Court of Ireland challenging the decision. The High Court referred certain questions to the ECJ for a preliminary ruling.

The ECJ gave its Grand Chamber ruling on the case in October 2015. As for the national authorities' duties, the Grand Chamber found in accordance with its settled case law that only the Court itself has jurisdiction to declare that an EU act, such as a Commission decision, is invalid. The national courts are entitled to consider the validity of an EU act but they are not endowed with the power to declare such an act invalid themselves.[37] This technical detail has caused some debate in EU scholarship, but it is not the focal interest for us here. On the other

[37] Case C-362/14, *Schrems*, EU:C:2015:650, paras. 61–2.

hand, the substantive issue – whether the transfer of data should be allowed – is pertinent for us.

Mr Schrems essentially claimed that United States law and practice do not ensure an adequate level of data protection. The ECJ argued, when considering this claim, that protection of personal data is important for the fundamental right to respect for private life. It also noted that when personal data is transferred to a third country that fails to ensure an adequate level of protection, then it is a large number of persons whose fundamental rights are liable to be infringed.[38]

The Court noted that interference with the fundamental rights guaranteed by Articles 7 and 8 of the Charter must be based on clear and precise rules on the scope and application of the measure. There must also be safeguards in place, so that persons whose data is processed have sufficient guarantees about their data being effectively protected against abuse and against unlawful access and use. Moreover, the need for such safeguards is all the greater where personal data is subjected to automatic processing and where there is a significant risk of unlawful access to that data.

As in *Digital Rights Ireland*,[39] here too the Court emphasised that derogations and limitations in the protection of personal data can apply only in so far as strictly necessary. In the eyes of the Court, legislation is not limited to what is strictly necessary where it authorises, on a generalised basis, storage of all the personal data of everyone whose data has been transferred from the European Union to the United States without any differentiation, limitation or exception. In particular, legislation permitting the public authorities to have access on a generalised basis to the content of electronic communications compromises the essence of the fundamental right to respect for private life.[40] Hence, the Court held that the large amounts of data transferred in the manner that Facebook does can in itself amount to a violation of privacy.

The Court considered the Safe Harbour Decision. It stated that legislation that does not provide any possibility for an individual to pursue legal remedies in order to have access to data relating to them, or to obtain rectification or erasure of such data, does not respect the essence

[38] Case C-362/14, *Schrems*, EU:C:2015:650, para. 78.
[39] Joined Cases C-293/12 and C-594/12, *Digital Rights Ireland*, EU:C:2014:238.
[40] Case C-362/14, *Schrems*, EU:C:2015:650, paras. 91–4.

of the fundamental right to effective judicial protection. This right is stipulated in Article 47 of the Charter.[41]

As a conclusion, the Court held that the Commission's Safe Harbour Decision failed to comply with the requirements laid down in the DPD read in the light of the Charter. The Safe Harbour Decision was therefore deemed invalid. There remained no need to examine the content of the safe harbour principles themselves.

In the end, by going through these technical steps, the judgment upheld Mr Schrems' claims. Data protection won the day, but not only for Mr Schrems himself. The judgment established a broader result. The power imbalance of the security establishment and the large number of people who use Facebook was scrutinised and found to be unjust. Here, European law sided with the anonymous anybody, that is, all the people that use or will use Facebook, so that their data would stay protected. Even though the case concerns Mr Schrems' data, the argumentation of the Court does not emphasise protection of him as an individual, nor is it centred around him as a person. More general goals are involved.

We can therefore read *Schrems* more easily as a political act than, say, *Google Spain*. Mr Schrems is not fighting only for his own rights, but the rights of the many. A general claim is made and it is accepted by the Court. As such, the case shows political action being enabled by privacy law.

The situation in *Schrems* is clearly very different from that of *Google Spain*. The *Schrems* case does not concern any clear constellation of rights against rights. In *Google Spain*, an individual's rights are pitched against the rights of the public to obtain information, as well as the rights of Google to continue with their business. In this scenario, the individual's rights are deemed more important. The *Schrems* case, on the other hand, illustrates a situation where argumentation through privacy rights is done in the interest of common values, not simply protection of a unique, autonomous individual. Privacy is here something shared, something that concerns everyone and anyone, not primarily the right of one individual.

This is what politics is about, according to Rancière. It is not disagreement about my right or your right. Nor is it about the fight for power per se. It is about action that achieves the emancipation of anyone. This is not identity politics. It does not strive to achieve better conditions for

[41] Case C-362/14, *Schrems*, EU:C:2015:650, para. 95.

one group of people. In order to be politics, according to this kind of thinking, it needs to be disagreement in the name of anybody.

Occasionally, privacy law does display this kind of political person emerging in the cases. Often, however, the anonymous anybody is lost in reasoning that concentrates on the rights and freedoms of individuals.

Equality and the Digital Poorhouse

Let us continue with the political person of privacy rights, considering more specifically the kinds of equality that these rights may bring about. The value of privacy lies not only in the way it can protect us from the capitalist greed of private actors. Privacy's importance has historically been tied to the ways in which it can protect us from public power. This was at stake in *Schrems* as well.

The debate about public power in the data-driven economy has lasted for a long time but was recently taken up by Virginia Eubanks, who analysed welfare systems in the USA. She argues that automated systems that collect and control vast amounts of data are creating a permanent class among the poor. The most invasive and the most punitive technological systems are aimed at the underprivileged. They contribute to the existence of the poor as a class and collaborate in hiding this class from view: 'Like earlier technological innovations in poverty management, digital tracking and automated decision-making hide poverty from the professional middle-class public and give the nation the ethical distance it needs to make inhuman choices: who gets food and who starves, who has housing and who remains homeless, and which families are broken up by the state.'[42] Most countries no longer have actual poorhouses. Eubanks' analysis shows, however, that automated decision-making systems encage and entrap today's poor in ways that resemble the poorhouses of the past. She uses the term 'digital poorhouse' to describe this phenomenon where technological tools deter people from accessing public services, police their labour, spending and parenting, try to predict their behaviour and punish those who do not comply. These technologies divide people into categories depending on, for instance, who are the 'deserving poor' and who the 'undeserving poor'.[43]

[42] Virginia Eubanks, *Automating Inequality: How High-Tech Tools Profile, Police, and Punish the Poor* (New York: St. Martin's Press, 2018), p. 13.

[43] Eubanks, *Automating Inequality*, p. 16.

America has seen successful civil rights movements, which have fought for welfare rights such as public accommodation. The welfare rights movement has also sought legal means to combat discrimination and exclusion. Various Supreme Court cases are regarded as victories in the battle for welfare rights for the poor.[44] In this sense, law and legal activism have had an impact for the better. There have been backlashes, though. Even though legal rights have been fought for and won, especially during recessions, there is increasing pressure on the welfare system to cut down on its spending.

Eubanks traces the beginnings of the digital poorhouse partly to the 1973 recession when a taxpayer revolt challenged the idea that the poor should have all the rights that are promised in the constitution. In order to contain public assistance spending but simultaneously bound by legal rules against discrimination, new technologies for more efficient distribution of money were commissioned. What happened was that effective walls were built between the poor and their legal rights. The digital poorhouse was born.[45]

A fascinating aspect about computers from the 1970s to the algorithms of today is that both are easily understood as neutral instruments. The early computers were used to increase scrutiny and surveillance of welfare recipients, and in large part this is what algorithms do as well. They both need to be programmed, though, and with that all alleged neutrality is gone. What can be done with the data mining tools of today is to combine data from diverse sources. The data in different state and local registers is collected and combined, which allows for red-flagging anything that looks like suspicious behaviour. Some programs are also tracking tools programmed to seek fraud and corruption in welfare systems. But programs can be biased, too, and most importantly: their logic is often punitive.[46]

Eubanks rejects the argument that the technological tools aimed at poor and working-class people would increase security, transparency and stimulate innovative solutions. On the contrary, she claims that the data analytics of today is 'simply an expansion and continuation of moralistic and punitive poverty management strategies that have been with us since the 1820s'.[47]

44 Eubanks, *Automating Inequality*, p. 31.
45 Eubanks, *Automating Inequality*, p. 33.
46 See Eubanks, *Automating Inequality*, p. 37.
47 Eubanks, *Automating Inequality*, p. 37.

How can we resist the digital poorhouse, or other discriminatory mechanics? One possibility is to drive for change by using existing successful legal tools, whatever they may be. Privacy rights are one obvious choice for such contestation. If legal acts interfere in the drafting of the political landscape by defining concepts and categories, influencing attitudes and re-configuring power relations, then they can be political and they can push for change. For this to happen, the assumption of the equality of everyone has to be at the heart of the discussion.

Data protection offers one instrument by which some of the exploitative results of technological government can be fought. The GDPR does include elements to this effect, including stringent rules on automated decision-making and profiling. They are meant as an answer to the injustices caused by algorithmic governance that escape legal control, due process requirements or other legal safeguards.

Hence, a contemporary instrument by which to fight unequal treatment is provided by privacy rights, especially in instances where they prevent discrimination. These rights can, for their part, hinder the creation of underprivileged and excluded persons. Injustices are often caused by people being fixed by social structures, class, race and market relationships. Privacy rights can counteract this by working as tools for political action.

That way, privacy rights, when derived from the axiom of equality, can become an instrument for dissent. They can enable political acts, through which we can struggle against the identities assigned to us. In this sense, they are a means to achieve something akin to Rancièrean political subjectivation: with the help of rights claims we can disagree with the ways in which we are cast. By arguing about and with rights, we can resists the names we are given. The emancipatory potential of privacy law lies in these instances of resistance.

7 The Person in the Community

In the previous chapter, we started discussing conceptions of the person that would be less individualist. A political person, whose equality is taken for granted, is one aspect of the private person, even though not perhaps the one most commonly encountered. We have seen, however, that privacy rights can be used as instruments for emancipation. They provide tools for resistance and they can be utilised to fight injustices. In these instances, they are not exclusively tied to the individual but linked to more common goals.

The question that arises, however, is whether we lose something valuable with a move away from individualism. The risk is that focus on the third person – or in Rancièrean parlance an anonymous anybody – fails to capture the worth of individuals altogether. Politics is based on radical equality where everyone may be substituted by someone else. However, to completely deny the value of individuals goes against most ethical intuitions. It could even imply totalitarianism. Moreover, such radical equality would be an unusual, if not downright odd, foundation for privacy protection.

Jean-Luc Nancy's philosophy offers a fruitful way of thinking about personhood as intertwined with community, but still holding on to the worth of individuals. We will look for possibilities for privacy rights to be less individual-centred by following Nancy's ideas.[1]

This chapter focuses on community. But what is a community? According to Nancy, it does not include a common being or participation in a shared unit. In this philosophy, a common set of values or

[1] The discussion in this chapter draws on Susanna Lindroos-Hovinheimo, 'There Is No Europe – On Subjectivity and Community in the EU' (2017) 18 *German Law Journal* 1229–46.

a common identity is not a prerequisite for community.[2] Accordingly, no specific definition of the common good can be seen as the ideal by which to evaluate or criticise law. The content of the common good, in order to stay common, must include indeterminacy and openness towards the future.

Nancy: Singular Plurality

What makes Nancy's philosophy so compelling is the amount and depth of thought he devotes to defining community and to the question of the relationship between singularity and community. He does not prioritise singularity or community, nor does he make any easy distinction between the two. He also cannot be understood as a representative of any political programme. Rather, his philosophical project, which resembles Derrida's deconstructive endeavours, consists of attempts to think through the complex relations between community and singularity.

Before delving into questions of community, however, it is helpful to take a look at Nancy's overall project, which is based on a rather ingenious ontology. It lays the foundation for his political thinking and therefore merits some examination.

Nancy's theory of singular plurality develops Heidegger's critique of the subject.[3] Following Heidegger, he investigates being, but he finds a founding plurality in the kernel of *Dasein*. Being is, above anything else, being-in-common. We are *with* and this being-with is not accidental. Ontology has to be understood as primarily plural. That way, plurality is not secondary in relation to singularity because being is in essence plural. This leads Nancy to state that a single being would be a contradiction in terms. A being that would be its own foundation and origin cannot be.[4]

Being is singularly plural and plurally singular, but not in the sense that these would be attributes of being. For Nancy, the essence of being is singular–plural. This is the constitution of being as reflected in every single, substantial essence of being. For existing beings – people, animals and things – this means that whatever exists co-exists. The

[2] Philip Armstrong, Jason E. Smith and Jean-Luc Nancy, 'Politics and Beyond: An Interview with Jean-Luc Nancy' (2015) 43 *Diacritics* 90–108 at 90 and 94.

[3] See Andrew Norris, 'Jean-Luc Nancy and the Myth of the Common' (2000) 7 *Constellations* 272–95 at 274–5.

[4] Jean-Luc Nancy, *Being Singular Plural* (Stanford, CA: Stanford University Press, 2000), p. 12.

implication of existing is the sharing of the world. Understandably, Nancy argues that there can never be any real philosophical solipsism, just as there can never be a theory 'of the subject' understood as a closed-off singular being.[5]

Because he conceptualises being as being-with, Nancy recognises the foundational importance of the term 'with'. If being is being-with, then the 'with' comes to constitute being. 'With' is not simply an addition to some prior being, or a predicament of being, or a definition of certain beings. 'With' lies at the heart of being. This implies a reversal of the order of philosophical exposition compared to quite a few philosophers. For Nancy, the 'with' does not come second to being, as it does for instance in Heidegger's analysis of *Dasein* and *Mitsein*.[6]

Because there is always an element of plurality in being, according to Nancy, he needs to explain how anything could be singular at all. He does this by explaining that the very idea of a singular being implies singularisation from others. A singular being is one that can be distinguished from other singularities. For Nancy, the singular, or a 'one', means primarily 'each one', that is, a being amongst others.[7] This leads to the conclusion that there can be nothing singular without there being other singulars. And if there can never be one singularity without there being others, then being is always both singular and plural. This is the very nature of being, and the foundation on which Nancy's thinking rests. Being cannot be anything but singular *and* plural.

The singular cannot really be understood as a subject like, say, the relation of a self to itself.[8] Rather similar to Derrida's *différance*, singularity is neither me nor you, but that which is distinguished when the two are seen as distinct. It is the cut that differentiates between beings. Hence the importance of the term 'being-with', which refers to singulars singularly together. But it is important to note here that singulars do not form a sum nor are they incorporated into a common being.[9] Singulars, like individual human beings, can never be defined completely without reference to others, but neither do they form a totality that erases their singularity.

[5] Nancy, *Being Singular Plural*, pp. 28–9.

[6] Nancy, *Being Singular Plural*, pp. 30–1; and Frédéric Neyrat, 'No/Us: The Nietzschean Democracy of Jean-Luc Nancy' (2015) 43 *Diacritics* 66–87 at 73.

[7] Nancy, *Being Singular Plural*, p. 33.

[8] See Jean-Luc Nancy, *The Inoperative Community*, Peter Connor ed., foreword by Christopher Fynsk (Minneapolis, MN: University of Minnesota Press, 1991), pp. 26–7.

[9] Nancy, *Being Singular Plural*, pp. 32–3.

This kind of ontology brings with it some methodological problems. It is obviously very difficult for Nancy himself to communicate his theory, because there is no position for him to be outside the theory. A point of view outside being-together is impossible. There is no perspective exterior to being-with from where one could announce what exists. Nancy suggests that the way for a being to speak itself is by saying 'we are'.[10] This problematic theme of how to speak (and write) about being troubles Nancy throughout *Being Singular Plural*. The work struggles to communicate being, to communicate something to others, when the focus of the communication is the being with others itself.

What is important for our enquiry is that, according to this kind of ontology, the question of being and the question of the meaning of being, become questions of being-with. Being is never either singular or plural but always being-together-with-others. On the level of human life, this means simply that we are always with others. And indeed, not only with other human beings: also animals, things, ideas and machines share the world with us.[11] We are each singular, but our being in the world implies being singular together.

An illuminating way of expressing the core idea of singular plurality is the definition of *the one* that Nancy gives. The one is always more than one, not because it would somehow divide itself, but because it equals more than one. One cannot be counted without counting more than one.[12] There is nothing that could be only one because that could never be counted at all. Counting one already implies others from which to count. Otherwise, there could be no singularity at all, only a great mass of totality.

Nancy consistently stresses that neither singularity nor plurality can be given primary status. The social or communitarian dimension is not something added onto the singular being. One often hears such views: first there is the subject, then the group. In a number of theories, the rights-bearing subject comes first, then social relationships. Nancy's argument entails, however, that co-existence is not additional.[13] It is the way things are and have to be, a necessary feature of existence.

10 Nancy, *Being Singular Plural*, p. 33.

11 See e.g. Graham Harman, 'On Interface: Nancy's Weights and Masses', in Peter Gratton and Marie-Eve Morin (eds.), *Jean-Luc Nancy and Plural Thinking: Expositions of World, Ontology, Politics, and Sense* (Albany, NY: State University of New York Press, 2012), p. 95.

12 Nancy, *Being Singular Plural*, p. 39.

13 Nancy, *The Inoperative Community*, p. 28.

Nancy gives examples of areas that are represented as singular practices, even though they could be and should be understood differently. Two of them are particularly illuminating: psychoanalysis and the economy. Psychoanalysis deals with relations, but paradoxically holds on to a strange individualised form. The same is true of the economy, which in its essence means co-action, relations and exchange. However, the unequal co-ordinary nature of the economy often vanishes from discussion. Both in psychoanalysis and the economy, each of which have become global and now exert substantial influence on thinking and ways of living, atomisation has followed.[14] The founding condition of 'with' has become indiscernible.

Even though Nancy does not give preference to either singularity or plurality, when discussing society he does make an interesting observation. He argues that being can only be understood by starting from being-with-one-another. The question of social being must therefore *constitute* the ontological question of being.[15] Because of such commitments, Nancy's ontology is not completely void of normative content.

Community, Not Common Essence

In *The Inoperative Community*, Nancy ponders the connections between the community and politics. Politics certainly has to do with community and being in common, not merely with questions of order and administration. Following this line of thought, politics is not simply a sphere of power relations, even though it is that as well. Relations of force and struggle are important to notice, but, more than anything, what is at stake in politics is community.[16]

Occasionally in Europe, politics morphs into transnational executive government guided by the appearance of necessity, a pertinent example being the financial crisis.[17] Effective problem-solving becomes the focus, and issues of community are moved aside.[18] In these instances, considerations of community tend to give way to the logics of the market.

[14] Nancy, *Being Singular Plural*, p. 45; and Nancy, *The Inoperative Community*, p. 75.

[15] Nancy, *Being Singular Plural*, p. 57.

[16] Nancy, *The Inoperative Community*, p. xxxvii.

[17] Alexander Somek, *Individualism: An Essay on the Authority of the European Union* (Oxford: Oxford University Press, 2008), pp. 22–3.

[18] See Gareth Davies, 'Social Legitimacy and Purposive Power: The End, The Means and the Consent of the People', in Dimitry Kochenov, Gráinne de Búrca and Andrew Williams (eds.), *Europe's Justice Deficit* (Oxford: Hart Publishing, 2015), pp. 259–74.

Another trend in the Union is the strong emphasis put on rights. This is a further reason why attention is sometimes drawn away from community. When rights are legislated upon and put into practice, the political nature of the issue can fade from view.

Nancy's thinking does not provide ready-made tools with which to solve balancing acts between different values. But his theory does give well-grounded reasons for considering community itself as something valuable that should be at the centre of politics. He provides an elegant attempt to articulate an ideal understanding of community that is grounded on a specific and well-theorised ontology: 'we are brought into the world, each and every one of us, according to a dimension of "in-common" that is in no way "added unto" the dimension of "being-self", but that is rather co-originary and coextensive with it'.[19] It is important to stress that, according to Nancy, we should not be seeking the essence of community. Thinking of community through a unifying essence, like nationality, religion or language, can lead to the closure of the political. It assigns to community a common being. Nancy's community is something different, namely, existence in common but without common substance. To be in common is not to be fused into one united substance or social body. On the contrary, being in common means not having such a substantial common identity but *sharing this lack of identity*.[20] Could such a view be fruitful when considering the EU? The appearance of a European polity – a political demos – understood as including some common identity is nowhere in sight. But community should not be built on common identity. Community, in order to be community, is fundamentally lacking.

The myth of Narcissus illustrates the point: to gaze purely and only at oneself without any interference by otherness is impossible. Having access to what is properly oneself requires exposure to others. This means that my face is always turned towards an other and faced by him or her. Such is the starting point, and also the reason for politics. Because we are always already in contact with others who are different from us, space for the political is opened up.[21]

The challenge for politics is to operationalise a community without substance and without identity in the EU. Lack of essence is what makes community. A community cannot have a fulfilled and unified identity.

[19] Nancy, *The Inoperative Community*, p. xxxvii.
[20] Nancy, *The Inoperative Community*, pp. xxxvii–xxxviii.
[21] Nancy, *The Inoperative Community*, pp. xxxvii–xxxviii.

If it becomes a single thing – a body, mind, fatherland – it necessarily ceases to be *in-common*.

However, the opposite fate is also possible and this too endangers community. An individualised society is equally in fear of losing community. It becomes the reduction of the political to management and to power, and to the management of power. Thus the tricky question is how to think of community in between these two negations of being-in-common. What kind of politics does not stem from the will to unify? And, on the other hand, what kind of politics allows people to exist singularly together?

It is not easy to transfer Nancy's philosophy to the level of everyday politics or the law. This problem will be discussed in more detail below. Suffice to say for now that, for Nancy, community is one thing, politics another. Politics refers to action. Political questions require answers and a society has to be organised. That way, there has to be closure and therefore also law. Community, on the other hand, includes openness that stays open.

Community Is Grounded in Freedom

We have previously discussed the liberalist roots of individualism. In Anglo-American debates, opposition to liberalism has traditionally been framed in communitarian terms. Even though the counter-arguments that communitarians pose to liberalism are at times highly perceptive, there are nevertheless nuances in communitarianism that open it up for critique.

As Amitai Etzioni explains, many communitarians are preoccupied with:

> the social preconditions that enable individuals to maintain their psychological integrity, civility, and ability to reason. When community (social webs carrying moral values) breaks down, the individual's psychological integrity is endangered, and a vacuum is generated which invites the state to expand its role and power; when community is properly cultivated, by contrast, the kind of citizen liberals take for granted flourishes. In this sense, liberal treatises, and above all their elaboration of individual rights, presume a communitarian foundation.[22]

[22] Amitai Etzioni (ed.), *New Communitarian Thinking: Persons, Virtues, Institutions, and Communities* (Charlottesville, VA: University Press of Virginia, 1995), p. 16.

Communitarians see the individual always as a contextual being. There can be no individual without community because community shapes individuals into the individuals that they are.

There are obvious similarities with the ideas discussed above, especially Durkheim, Foucault and Rancière. Basically, communitarianism posits that individuals are members of communities rather than freestanding.

However, Nancy's thinking is special because he goes further than this. His conception of singular plurality does not exactly amount to communitarianism because his philosophy blurs the boundary between the individual and the community altogether. Both are determined by each other without there being any clear line, even in theory, that could be drawn between them.

A community is grounded in freedom and a sharing of relations, not in people relating to each other as autonomous individuals.[23] Because being includes being-with, logically there cannot really be any autonomous persons:

> Freedom cannot be presented as the autonomy of a subjectivity in charge of itself and of its decisions, evolving freely and in perfect independence from every obstacle. What would such an independence mean, if not the impossibility in principle of entering into the slightest relation – and therefore of exercising the slightest freedom?[24]

To define the independence of the person is not what Nancy is after, but freedom is an important concept nevertheless. Singular being, being just this once, is possible because freedom grants it the space to take place. Hence, freedom precedes singularity. Freedom is that which spaces and singularises.[25] It is perhaps best understood as the circumstance that makes persons singular.

It becomes evident that in this thinking, the person requires reconceptualisation. The person cannot be understood simply as a selfsame ego. Being-in-common defines personhood. And persons are both singular and plural. They are linked in both profound and

[23] See e.g. B. C. Hutchens, 'Archi-Ethics, Justice, and the Suspension of History in the Writing of Jean-Luc Nancy', in Peter Gratton and Marie-Eve Morin (eds.), *Jean-Luc Nancy and Plural Thinking: Expositions of World, Ontology, Politics, and Sense* (Albany, NY: State University of New York Press, 2012), pp. 129–42.

[24] Jean-Luc Nancy, *The Experience of Freedom*, Bridget MacDonald trs., foreword by Peter Fenves (Stanford, CA: Stanford University Press, 1993), p. 66.

[25] Nancy, *The Experience of Freedom*, p. 78.

superficial ways. They even share that which divides them the most, their birth and their death:

> [My] birth and my death are present to me and are my own only through the births and deaths of others, for whom in turn their births and deaths are neither present nor their own. We share what divides us: the freedom of an incalculable and improbable *coming* to presence of being, which only brings us into presence as the *ones* of the *others*. This is the coming to presence of *our* freedom, the common experience of the exposure in which the community is founded.[26]

Persons' exposure to the incalculability of their birth and their death is the common thing that they share. And then again this fundamental issue is not something shared at all, because my birth and my death are not really my own. I am not present at either of these events and I only experience them through my relations with others.

For Nancy, freedom is neither a right nor an end towards which people should strive. Freedom is more like a fact. It is the original state that precedes singularity and sharing. Freedom cannot be given or guaranteed by the law, but is expressed in the groundlessness of existence. Such groundlessness is in Nancy's theory the opening for justice.[27] This kind of justice is not a theory or a measuring rod, but the unending questioning of justice.

The core of Nancy's ethics forms an anti-Kantian understanding of the person. Where Kant sees the subject constituting itself as its own, autonomous sovereign, Nancy rejects the idea of subjects as autonomous controllers of themselves. A subject is not given to itself and therefore such a self-present agent cannot be the foundation for ethics. For Nancy, the self may be understood as a relation, as an opening or as difference.[28] For the self to identify itself there needs to be an other.

That is one way in which this ontology can be developed into ethics: existence is an exigency, which requires us to become what we ontologically already are. The structure of the argument is then that ontology itself includes an ethical element. This would mean that on the level of existence, a demand is already present.[29]

26 Nancy, *The Experience of Freedom*, p. 95.

27 Hutchens, 'Archi-Ethics, Justice, and the Suspension of History', 139.

28 Marie-Eve Morin, '"We Must Become What We Are": Jean-Luc Nancy's Ontology as Ethos and Praxis', in Sanja Dejanovic (ed.), *Nancy and the Political* (Edinburgh: Edinburgh University Press, 2015), pp. 21–42 at 21.

29 See Morin, 'We Must Become What We Are'; see also Nancy, *The Inoperative Community*, p. 15.

However, the ethical importance of being-with does not stay on this abstract level. It transcends to the more active plane of behaviour. The ontological demand requires a decision for the world. It implies a requirement to inhabit the world in a certain way. We should live in a way that makes the world not a totalised essence, but a plurality of singularities co-existing. No essence or principle summing up the world or its meaning can or should be sought. To inhabit the world requires one to stand within a world that has no firm ground.[30] That way, the world is created. The world has no meaning as such and when we share this lack of meaning, we create a world.

Such a normative challenge is by no means unambiguous. Of course, Nancy has views on politics and justice that can be interpreted in a straightforward manner: A community cannot be a totality with an identity, nor should politics aim at such. That would be totalitarianism. But neither is it atomic and detached. Still, Nancy does not always lend his thoughts to such simple interpretation.

In the *Truth of Democracy*, he clarifies the distinction between ontology and the political. It becomes clear in this text that an analysis of existence does not automatically spill over into politics informing a normative stance. It is important that existence is understood as undefined and open, and thus politics should not colonise ontology by stating what the sense of existence is, or by defining the meaning of (a good) life. Existence is without essence and without definable sense, and staying open to such a view is the requirement that Nancy places upon politics.[31]

He thus demands of politics an openness to creation(s) of the world, that is, space for different worlds to come into being and various things to exist:

> *To create the world* means: immediately, without delay, reopening each possible struggle for a world, that is, for what must form the contrary of a global injustice ... But this means to conduct this struggle precisely in the name of the fact that this *world* is coming out of nothing, that there is nothing before it and that it is without models, without principle and without given end.[32]

[30] Morin, 'We Must Become What We Are'.

[31] Jean-Luc Nancy, *The Truth of Democracy*, Pascale-Anne Brault and Michael Naas trs. (New York: Fordham University Press, 2010), pp. 17–18, 26–8, 34.

[32] Jean-Luc Nancy, *The Creation of the World or Globalization*, François Raffoul and David Pettigrew trs. (Albany, NY: State University of New York Press, 2007), pp. 54–5.

To create a world means to choose a world, one among innumerable alternatives. This most serious ethical and political challenge permeates Nancy's thinking: the world is not given, we must make it. Such is the categorical imperative in this theory: to stand in the open, in the senselessness of the world. It is not a command to occupy the place of God, but to keep that place open, but nevertheless occupy the world. There is no truth about the world, no sense of the world and no world, until we inhabit it by creating it. A world is always to be made and re-made.[33]

Can There Be a European Community?

For Nancy, capitalism threatens to turn singularities into flat commensurable beings. One aim of politics, then, is to contest equivalence.[34] This is a task for the EU as well. As Daniel Augenstein argues, the Union is still ultimately an organisation centred on economic logic, not politics:

> [W]hatever is deficient about EU political justice is not a problem of political *unity*. By conferring rights on individuals as a matter of European law, the ECJ posits the peoples of Europe as citizens of the European Union. Concurrently, by calling upon this citizenry to cooperate in the functioning of the European Union, the Court derives the authority of EU law from a people of Europe. Rather, what is problematic is the EU's *political* unity; that is, recovering the politics of European market integration from behind the veil of the statist separation between the national-as-political and the European-as-economic.[35]

According to Augenstein, the economic cart has been put before the horse. The Union claims to represent the people of Europe and to act in our name, which poses the problem of ownership over the polity.[36] It raises questions of how we can endorse the policies that are presented as ours, even though management of economic necessities in fact drives them.[37]

[33] See Jean-Luc Nancy, 'From the Imperative to Law', in B. C. Hutchens (ed.), *Jean-Luc Nancy: Justice, Legality and World* (New York: Continuum, 2012), pp. 11–18.

[34] Neyrat, 'No/Us: The Nietzschean Democracy', 77–9.

[35] Daniel Augenstein, 'We the People: EU Justice as Politics', in Dimitry Kochenov, Gráinne De Búrca and Andrew Williams (eds.), *Europe's Justice Deficit* (Oxford: Hart Publishing, 2015), p. 159.

[36] Augenstein, 'We the People', p. 159.

[37] Alexander Somek demands social justice: 'monetary union appears to have resulted in the rise of a collective Bonapartism that benefits bankers and harms low earners in the Union'. Alexander Somek, 'The Preoccupation with Rights and the Embrace of

A truly pluralistic Union in the sense of singular plurality would be a community where members are different from each other. They would share the difference, not necessarily anything else, and be in relation to one another this way.[38] Such a community would not be defined by nationality, as most Member States still are, or left to the mercy of economic policies, as the Union still occasionally is.

There may already be potential for such a pluralistic relationship between the community and its members in the Union. As Loïc Azoulai argues, there is something profoundly anarchical about EU law's understanding of the person. It includes the aspiration of self-realisation. Such an aspiration finds its form as the opportunity to choose different territories, lifestyles and regulatory systems combined with the capacity to leave one's own country and to question the prevalence of the bonds of nationality.[39] Understood in this way, Union law – especially EU citizenship – may display a logic resembling singular plurality.

The need to temper nationalist interests can easily lead to community-building that pursues a common European identity. The risk is then that the Union itself becomes constructed as something that has an identity. If Nancy's theory has anything to teach, it is that there is no Europe. To be a community, the Union needs to accept its absent identity and not aim at producing some common European essence.

There is reason to be worried about the normative fetishisation of being-in-common, especially when it develops into a myth of communion like the bond of love among the members of the community. Balibar asks a pertinent question, however: Does not such a myth haunt every communal construction, even when no totalitarian politics is attached to it that would want to produce the community on the basis of the myth?[40] Is not all community threatened by the myth of 'us'?

Inclusion: A Critique', in Dimitry Kochenov, Gráinne de Búrca and Andrew Williams (eds.), *Europe's Justice Deficit* (Oxford: Hart Publishing, 2015), pp. 295–309 at 309.

38 See Andrew Norris, 'Jean-Luc Nancy on the Political after Heidegger and Schmitt', in Peter Gratton and Marie-Eve Morin (eds.), *Jean-Luc Nancy and Plural Thinking: Expositions of World, Ontology, Politics, and Sense* (Albany, NY: State University of New York Press, 2012), pp. 143–58.

39 Loïc Azoulai, 'The European Individual as Part of Collective Entities (Market, Family, Society)', in Loïc Azoulai, Ségolène Barbou des Places and Etienne Pataut (eds.), *Constructing the Person in EU Law: Rights, Roles, Identities* (Oxford: Hart Publishing, 2016), pp. 203–24.

40 Étienne Balibar, *We, the People of Europe?: Reflections on Transnational Citizenship* (Princeton, NJ: Princeton University Press, 2003), p. 69.

This is an important question for this book as well. If we could move from individualist privacy protection towards something that takes for granted people's embeddedness in community, is there a risk that we conceptualise that community in certain value-laden ways? And how do we distinguish what kind of embeddedness is worth protecting by law?

As Étienne Balibar reads him, Nancy responds to this problem by distinguishing between communication and communion. Communion may be based on the myth of us, but communication is not. Communication is not simply the transfer of information from one person to another, but a separation of persons that makes transfer possible.[41] Because of the separation, a non-violent 'us' becomes impossible. Communication involves exposure to others and does not reduce singularities into a common whole. This is the whole point of community: it consists of singular beings that are in common but not totalisable.[42]

The idea is similar to Esposito's third person. It includes a way of focusing less on individuals, me and you, thereby lifting a more inclusive, egalitarian person to the fore. This does not, however, mean that the value of singular persons would be completely denied.

This chapter has sought alternatives to the individualist tendencies in EU privacy law. The framework for this enquiry has been singular plurality. According to the picture drawn, being-in-common defines the person, which means that persons are not primarily autonomous, selfsame agents. A person can be a singular person only together with others, in a community, and community can only exist if its members' singular plurality is respected.

Community is conceptually stretched between atomism and unity. The European integration process is threatened both by tendencies towards atomism and unification, as evidenced by separatist Member States, economically driven agendas and nationalist identity politics.

The kind of community where singularities would stay singular, and singularly valuable, is one where we exist together but without common substance. To be in common in a European community would not mean fusion into a social body, nor would it mean individualistic atomism.

[41] See on this understanding of communication also Norris, 'Jean-Luc Nancy on the Political after Heidegger and Schmitt', p. 147.

[42] Balibar, *We, the People of Europe?*, pp. 70–1.

Community in the singular–plural requires us to inhabit the world in a way that can really form a community: not as one, but as a plurality of co-existing singularities. No essence or leading principle can or should be sought, but a world has to be formed nevertheless. Co-habitation is the key, that is, existence together with others in a way that values singularity without everything being made equally valuable. Interactions between independent individuals do not form a community. Nor does a collection of private selves, whose immunity is protected by the law.

The Benefits of Thinking in the Singular–Plural

Through singular plurality, we have developed a normative framework within which to reflect on the various productions of legal personhood in the regulation of privacy in the EU. The framework includes many elements, of which ethical ones are perhaps most important.

The usefulness of thinking in the singular–plural is manifold. Firstly, it is grounded in an ontology that is both reasonable and intuitively appealing. We see here an explanation of how a person is never only one. Whenever there is existence, it implies co-existence. We always co-habit a world, we are always in a world and we are always together with others. Because of this, it is clear that a person is never simply an individual. There can be no individual that would not already be exposed to alterity from the very foundations of their existence.

The specific benefit of Nancy's theory, compared to other alternatives that might also be communitarian-minded, is that his philosophy enables thinking about the paradoxes of personhood. He allows for things to be simultaneously both-and. Tensions and aporias do not need to be forcefully solved. Beings can be singular, even though they are plural. Community can consist of a lack of commonality. In many philosophical theories, such contradictory conclusions are not tolerated but Nancy gives inspiration for thought that has no necessary compulsion to resolve every contradiction. Things in the world (and in law) may present themselves in many forms, some of which may seem contradictory, yet nevertheless ring true.

The most important reason to read Nancy in the privacy context is his understanding of community's value. If it is true, as this book has tried to show, that both privacy regulation and case law display individualistic tendencies, then there needs to be an alternative against which these tendencies can be shown and, if possible, evaluated.

Nancy's understanding of community fits this purpose well because it does not negate the value of unique singularities. Quite the contrary. The political theory that emerges from his writings is one where uniqueness is respected against all kinds of totalising pressures. Nevertheless, there are limits to how atomistic the law should be because community has an inherent value as well.

However, the limits of this analysis should not be neglected. Nancy, Rancière or Esposito do not solve questions of how privacy should be regulated. They do not specifically discuss law to any significant degree, and privacy rights even less. Their thinking works best as an inspiration for legal theory, albeit an eye-opening one. What would privacy regulation look like if we take these theoretical foundations seriously?

Singular–Plural Privacy?

I have argued that individualist assumptions affect privacy rights in many ways. These assumptions are seldom coherent or well-explicated in legal practice, nor are they always acknowledged in legislative processes. They can nevertheless shape the law, even though this happens in a complex and occasionally ambivalent manner.

I argue that the political person is someone who takes political action. Shaped by their surroundings, they nevertheless make choices. The political in the political person is derived from presupposed equality, which is their defining feature. Through their action, a political person can become visible in law as well. Privacy rights enable political action when they strive for equality. In these instances, the community is valued, not only the single individual.

Drawing on Nancy, we can understand community and individuality as co-existing. Any community will be composed of singular existences, and this singularity needs to be respected. Privacy rights can be a means to do this. In case law, we have seen that they occasionally have this capacity as well.

As Nippert-Eng argues in her sociological study of privacy in the USA, privacy is a large collection of concepts, ideological goals and practical matters. It amounts to aspirations to live together both as a member of social units and as an individual. The tension between being a member and being a unique self lies at the heart of modern life. It is present in every relationship that we have. The need for privacy is a desire to connect *and* disconnect.[43] Following these lines of thought, an understanding of privacy as protecting singular plurality comes naturally.

Nevertheless, Nancy's main suggestion that being is always plural does not fit easily with the primary aspirations of the EU legislator in privacy and personal data protection. The law seeks to protect the individual from intrusions, to guarantee the right to be let alone. Are there, then, in current European law already openings for understanding persons in more community-enhancing ways?

We have seen that the current emphasis on strong protection of personal data in the EU occasionally directs focus away from more traditional forms of privacy. This is primarily due to the technological developments of data processing, which requires new forms of protection. But the trend was also evident in *Jehovan todistajat*, which does not concern Big Data, social media or the Internet at all. With the shift of emphasis away from the right to private life towards protection of personal data, privacy law has changed. The defining features of data protection point strongly towards individualism. Personal data refers by definition only to identified or identifiable individuals, whereas protection of private life can conceptually include protection of a more general anybody. For instance, protection of the home as a private space is not dependent on an analysis of which individuals are located within that space.

The more traditional forms of privacy, such as protection of the household or protection of correspondence, are also sensitive to the plurality in human existence. None of them is solely aimed at protecting an autonomous individual. They protect us by taking into account the relational aspects of life. For instance, protection of correspondence includes both the sender and the receiver. This right is flexible and not tied to a singular individual. It is perhaps the best example of singular plurality working in privacy law: it protects communication.

Data protection is clearly more individualist in its working logic. However, as we have seen in some of the case law, courts do occasionally take into account the more relational aspects of life. For instance, in the *Nowak* judgment, the ECJ did open a path towards considering the personal data of groups. Clearly, the same information may relate to a number of individuals and may be personal data for each of them. That way, it is not helpful to always start an analysis of data protection by

[43] Christena Nippert-Eng, *Islands of Privacy* (Chicago, IL: The University of Chicago Press, 2020), p. 6.

identifying one individual. Data is shared and exchanged all the time because we live together and interact with each other.

This is why possessive individualism is such a difficult foundation for privacy protection. Our data is seldom only ours. Most often it is something that we share and pass on to others, as in the case of social media posts. Or it is created in other forms of communication, when we talk to each other about ourselves and listen to others talk about themselves. Or it is created by the way we move with others or away from them, as in the case of location data.

This is what the Court hints at in *Nowak* as well. As we recall, some of the data at issue was linked to the candidate, but also included information about the examiner.[44] It is an obvious fact that the same data can constitute the personal data of many people. A singular–plural view of personal data can perhaps be extracted from this simple observation.

In *Bărbulescu* from the ECtHR, we saw privacy being conceptualised in an inventive way. The case concerned private communication in the workplace. Even though the Court focused on the applicant's right to privacy and did not consider that other peoples' privacy was infringed upon as well, the Court nevertheless maintained that there exists such a thing as *private social life*. Such a concept can come rather close to a singular–plural view. Even though the exact meaning of private social life is not quite clear in the Court's argumentation, it cannot be the possession of any one individual, nor a right to be let alone, but must include the relational aspects of human life.

When the person of privacy law is detached from a rigidly selfsame autonomous individual, new avenues for thought are opened up in data protection law, too. Privacy rights can protect the things we share knowingly as well as the things we share unknowingly. These rights protect the narratives that we tell about ourselves, but also – especially when defined as personal data protection – all the other signs that can be read about us even when our intention is not to communicate them.

Location data automatically collected by the devices we carry, IP addresses or genome data are examples of personal data that we do not formulate ourselves or usually share with others in the form of communication. Nevertheless, as the ECJ has stressed, such data can reveal a lot about a person. In these instances, privacy is not about self-management at all, nor about protecting autonomous subjects in

[44] Case C-434/16, *Nowak*, EU:C:2017:994, paras. 44–5.

control. Rather, data protection can entail the protection of things we do not know about ourselves, unconscious or accidental things, the random signs that we leave of our existence, as well as purposeful communication.

Various instances in case law point towards openings that can develop privacy into more singular–plural forms. They show that such tendencies are already bubbling away as alternative ways to understand privacy itself. They can create a different kind of person from the one we have seen constructed in the earlier chapters: one that would not only be an individual, but a person embedded in society. Their existence would be that of being-with, where their ties to others would be protected just as much as their singularity.

These are some examples of how singular plurality can work in privacy protection. We can also consider, in passing, the broader jurisprudential issues that are involved. It is clear that plurality is by no means a logic foreign to law. Legal systems are complex conglomerates of norms, which bend, shift and multiply continually. Their applicability is meant to be plural. Any rules apply to more cases than one. As such, the logic of the law is permeated by recurrence, repetition and generality. The conception of unique singularity is, one could say, rather rare in modern law.

A legal system is plural also in the sense of being common, a system that generalises us and that takes for granted that we are many. Law is shared.[45] It governs us as people, groups, families, citizens and other pluralities. There are always many persons for law, and persons are always generalised according to some common signifier.[46] In other words, the person of the law is plural.

Nancy's thinking shows how even personal matters, such as bodies, opinions, ethnicity, sexual identification, information about ourselves that we might want to keep to ourselves, need to be conceptualised as singular–plural. Singularities are unique. In privacy and personal data protection, this singularity is protected in the plural.

[45] See also Helen Nissenbaum's account of privacy, which conceptualises law in slightly similar ways. She maintains that contextual integrity is the framework that should be used when analysing whether privacy has been breached or not. According to her, the social contexts in which we live our lives should be the starting point for preserving and protecting privacy. Helen Nissenbaum, *Privacy in Context: Technology, Policy and the Integrity of Social Life* (Stanford, CA: Stanford University Press, 2010).

[46] Here I follow Levinas in considering ethics as something that concerns primarily the one's relationship with the other and law as something that concerns the realm of the third. See Lindroos-Hovinheimo, *Justice and the Ethics of Legal Interpretation*.

That way, a non-binary split separates the public and the private, which appears when the singular–plural nature of personhood is taken seriously. Such a view opens up ways of thinking about the legal right to privacy not as completely cut off from the political, and, hence, not inherently individual-centred, but always intertwined with community. Privacy can be rendered politically potent when it is operationalised in struggles for equality.

Returning to the Productions of Law

It has been my purpose to show how the person is constructed in privacy law but I have also analysed that person in a critical manner. However, the aim has not been to reveal the correct picture behind the illusion, but to show that illusions also have effects.

Hence, the critique of individualism has not been put forward from a position outside the law, nor following any pre-posited ethical value. Through the case analyses, I have tried to highlight problems, both conceptual and practical, with the constructions of personhood in privacy law.

In other words, I have tried to acknowledge that unveiling ideology cannot be done with the purpose of searching for some other, purer or more benevolent form of knowledge and power. Foucault puts this well:

> The notion of ideology appears to me to be difficult to make use of, for three reasons. The first is that, like it or not, it always stands in virtual opposition to something else that is supposed to count as truth. Now, I believe that the problem does not consist in drawing the line between that which, in a discourse, falls under the category of scientificity or truth, and that which comes under some other category; rather, it consists in seeing historically how effects of truth are produced within discourses that, in themselves, are neither true nor false. The second drawback is that the concept of ideology refers, I think necessarily, to something of the order of a subject. Thirdly, ideology stands in a secondary position relative to something that functions as its infrastructure, as its material, economic determinant, and so on. For these three reasons, I think that this is a notion that cannot be used without circumspection.[47]

Ideology is a difficult notion because, as Althusser shows, we are always already in it. There is no outside ideology, nor can we oppose it with

[47] Foucault, 'Truth and Power', vol. III, p. 119.

something that would not be ideological. What we can do is show that ideological constructions exist and have effects.

Hopefully, the analysis has shown that in addition to the selfsame, autonomous individual, privacy and personal data law *can* protect other kinds of persons as well. We have seen such alternatives in older forms of privacy protection and we have also seen them emerge in passing in various contemporary judgments. No doubt, these other conceptions of the person come with inherent problems as well – and they too are definitely ideological in their own ways.

Why Privacy Is Valuable

There is no one Europe, no one ideology and, hence, no singular purpose of privacy protection either. Many actors and institutions collectively produce the European private person, sometimes with conflicting goals and ideologies. A different ethos prevails for different actors. The Court, for instance, does not necessarily adhere to the same goals as legislative bodies, nor are the different legislating institutions always aligned. Tensions between Member States and the Union also play their role in the plurality of ideologies colliding in the law.

I argued in the introduction that the concept of privacy itself is ambiguous. The effects it has on us are not straightforward, either. The productions of personhood achieved through privacy rights can be alienating and they can be exploitative, as in the economic data usage undertaken by corporations in surveillance capitalist models. On the other hand, privacy and data protection rights can enable emancipation and resistance.

Privacy and data protection can, just like any other rights, be operationalised in a variety of ways. These rights do not have an intrinsic essence or fixed meaning that would always stay the same. In this sense, they are neither good nor bad, neither liberating nor constraining. I have shown in this book, however, that privacy rights are often understood as solely the rights of an atomised individual. Other alternatives are possible and may cause different results in everyday legal practice.

For privacy to be valuable, it is not necessary that we presuppose pre-existing clear-cut persons, whose identity is the object of protection. On the contrary, the most important value of privacy rights might be that they allow fluid personhood to remain fluid. When privacy and personal data protection work, they provide a space for people to stay conditioned by otherness and to remain complicated in their plurality. If privacy rights are breached, there is a risk that a person becomes defined as a specific kind of subject. They are frozen into something with a name or a category, or a role that they are cast in without a say. Privacy rights are important because they give us the possibility to live out the myriad facets of singular plurality that constitute a human being.

Privacy law is one way of protecting the stories we tell of ourselves – private stories that we hold on to. Those stories may be true or less so, and they may even be lies. Privacy rights give us a right to make up stories about ourselves, and to lie.

This book has only considered privacy and personal data regulation and selected case law, mostly from the ECJ. The picture painted is hopefully compelling, if not necessarily exhaustive. There are always other examples, other sources, other views. Nevertheless, it has been my aim to discuss various kinds of persons that emerge from the source material without any pregiven typology. Individualising tendencies have been discovered, but also other trends. The book does not argue that there would be one person of privacy rights, for there are many.

Another caveat is that this book only deals with privacy regulation in the EU. It does not say anything general about the way legal persons are constructed in the Union. Nor does it say anything general about privacy. It focuses on one area of law, albeit a significant one, and investigates only that. Of course, another reading with a different focus or other source material will give different results.

There are obvious methodological difficulties with drawing critical claims from a selection of case law.[48] Already the selection, any selection, comes with an inbuilt bias that scholars tend to be painfully aware of. I have discussed many of the landmark cases in personal data protection, but there are other cases that have been left out because they do not directly deal with personal data or privacy. In this sense, I approached the material looking for privacy, and privacy is what I found. I have also chosen to limit the material to recent cases where privacy is defined, and these cases deal predominately with personal data protection. Other privacy issues have not been on the agenda as much of late.

[48] For comparison, see Marie-Bénédicte Dembour, *Who Believes in Human Rights?: Reflections on the European Convention* (Cambridge: Cambridge University Press, 2006), p. 8.

This book has questioned the way privacy issues are framed by the EU Court. The framing of a case can always be done in various ways as the law never applies itself. Any court will always have some space within which to apply the law.[49] The choices that are made will be value-laden in some way or another, even in those situations where a court claims only to re-affirm settled interpretations.[50]

In the EU legal system, there are certain established ways to interpret the law, according to which, for instance, teleological interpretation is one of the main methods to be applied. Nevertheless, there is room for choice, classification, interpretation, definition and balancing. What has come to the fore in the analyses in this book is that in addition to the chosen interpretation methods, an understanding of the privacy needs of individuals plays a large role in the Court's reasoning. By emphasising protection of individuals, the Court has taken a stand that can be regarded as ethical as well as ideological.

The most important thing about privacy rights is that they offer means of regulating relations between people, and people as relational beings. As such, privacy should not be used to protect individuals alone, but rather as part of sharing a world. To share a world is not easy and conflicts arise. Privacy rights can influence the ways in which the world is shared and community upheld.

What changes in the law if this kind of thinking is upheld? In my view, conceptual re-configuration has the potential to influence legal reasoning in privacy law. Firstly, privacy and data protection should not be seen in isolation. There is a need to include balancing in most cases, if the relational aspects of these rights are considered in full. Other rights and values need to be taken into account to a further extent than the ECJ has usually done. Furthermore, data protection should not only be understood as a right of the individual. Case-by-case analysis should be undertaken, focusing on the ways in which persons are in relation with others, which makes their lives entangled and their data often shared.

Privacy rights can be a means of protecting the community against totalitarian tendencies. This is one of their valuable functions. They enable the community to hold on to singularity and the freedom that makes singularisation possible. This requires, however, that there is no

[49] See Lindroos-Hovinheimo, *Justice and the Ethics of Legal Interpretation*, for an extensive discussion of legal interpretation.

[50] See e.g. Duncan Kennedy for ways in which judges are never neutral in Duncan Kennedy, *A Critique of Adjudication (fin de siècle)* (Cambridge, MA and London: Harvard University Press, 1997).

unifying essence into which all singularities are summed up. Such thinking is compatible with privacy rights when understood in the singular–plural framework. The point of these rights is to protect singularity and the space of freedom in which singularisation happens.

No matter how much we fear that we lose our selves with breaches of privacy, law does not and cannot protect our individual, subjective personhood. Law is common law. It connects us with community, and even when drawing limits on that community's intrusions into our lives, it operates with a communal logic.

Conclusions

We started off with two provisos. Firstly, we considered the statement that privacy is under threat. For the sake of argument, we experimented with not seeing privacy as something about to be lost. This has enabled us to take a step back and discuss privacy protection from different angles. We have not been stuck in thinking that privacy is an intrinsic value, or that the more privacy is protected, the better. Rather, we have analysed privacy in a societal context focusing on the ideologies that go with it. Secondly, we began by distancing ourselves from the idea of a pre-existing person, whom privacy rights are meant to protect. This brought us to the central question that has guided this book: What kind of person is constructed in contemporary privacy law?

The urge to protect privacy in new ways has caused considerable effects in the law. This has become visible in EU legislation as well as case law. The societal conditions that correspond to these legal developments, especially in data protection law, are too numerous to map out in full on the pages of one book. I have concentrated on personhood, where I have argued that an individualised view plays a large role. The selfsame autonomous person traverses legal thinking, where it affects how privacy rights operate.

Is it necessary to hold on to the individual as a grounding figure of law in order to achieve justice and equality? Is it necessary that individualism, as it appears in contemporary privacy and personal data law, be kept intact? Naturally, there are very good reasons to cherish the individual. Vulnerable people should be protected and the oppressed empowered. These are the benefits of law, including privacy law.

We have seen that privacy regulation both produces autonomy through emancipation, and presupposes it while protecting the person in control. That way, the autonomous individual is the assumption as well as the goal of privacy law. In tandem with such a person there appears, however, a vulnerable, sometimes deeply passive person, whom privacy rights also protect. The GDPR shows clearly that the data subject has this double character.

Privacy rights are valuable in many ways. Nevertheless, the need for privacy and the strengthening of its protection by regulatory means should be questioned. They correspond to a major feature of contemporary societies. Personhood is understood in more individual and less communal ways.

The main critique of the book has focused on the individualism inherent in privacy protection. Control of privacy and personal data often implies that there exists a person who controls, can control and should control their data. This is especially visible in the self-management ideology of data protection, where consent is emphasised. The law presupposes that there is a person who knows themselves, their own preferences and opinions. A conception of a selfsame and autonomous subject thus lies at the heart of privacy rights. The problem is that this view is based on a rather simple and self-contrary understanding of what it means to be a person. Privacy law has difficulties in grappling with the ways in which we are all incomplete and uncontrollable beings embedded in society.

Privacy is valuable when it protects the parts of ourselves that we control, as well as the parts that we do not control. Arguably, some of the most intimate data about a person relates to situations where they are not in full control of themselves. Health data, data about sexual relationships or data about sleep, for instance, includes information about personal matters that people do not control. Our bodies are not completely ours to master, nor is our subconscious. The important task of privacy rights then becomes to help us control what we cannot control.

At the beginning of the book, I discussed the person of privacy rights as a liquid modern subject. Undoubtedly, life was never easy, but the life of a person in late-modern global capitalism is certainly confusing. There is increasing freedom to consume, to define oneself and to live an individually meaningful life. This freedom, however, turns into an obligation to choose.

Simultaneously, we are increasingly helpless, as global economic power relations are beyond anybody's grasp. Political subjectivity in well-to-do Western societies contains an odd combination of a free subject who experiences themselves as wholly responsible for themselves as well as a subject whose wider economic and political conditions are beyond their control.

Privacy rights can be understood as rights that deflect attention from all the issues that are beyond our control, such as a democratic say in government or an economic say in the material conditions of our lives. What we can control – and what the law wants to enable us to control – is the stories we tell of ourselves and the digital portraits that we reveal to others.

Hence, privacy law turns our attention to our own affairs. Protection of privacy becomes a way for an individual to focus on themselves. With this turn inwards comes a need to protect oneself from outside intrusion. Immunisation is one of the main tasks of privacy regulation.

This form of regulation goes well together with the kind of liberalism that presupposes the freedom of a self-conscious agent, who is at full liberty to choose the kind of life they want to lead, and is therefore responsible for their actions and omissions. Every individual is seen as an autonomous agent. Privacy rights tend to reflect this view.

An alternative would be to see privacy not as an individual entitlement but as something that is born in relation. The relational nature of privacy should also be the starting point of regulation. I do not suppose that this would mean a revolution in privacy and personal data law. In fact, the openness and ambiguities of the legal texts themselves do allow for different interpretations even now. The issue concerns, rather, the way in which these regulatory instruments are used. The *telos* of interpretation, especially in the EU Court, has very often, although not always, been protection of persons as individuals. This has led to clashes with other values, most notably freedom of speech, access to information and transparency of government.

It is important to note that when regulating privacy, definitions of what is public are also drawn. These two 'spheres', the private and the public, are crude categories but still useful to some extent. As we have seen in case law, the problem of where to draw the line between the private and the public – or the common – is very much alive. Today, in the EU at least, it is the era of the private sphere. Political pressure as well as rights-based legal rhetoric tends to give more weight to the private than the public. And in personal data law, the private turns into the personal.

An alternative view of privacy would be one where privacy is seen as a vital means of protecting people *as social beings*. Privacy rights, when understood in this way, would be seen as predominately an instrument by which we can protect interaction and communication. Privacy entails not only a right to private life, but a right to shared life.

Privacy rights are valuable because they can protect our being-with. This means, however, that their primary target is not immunisation or closure of private individuals. Nor should privacy rights be used to trump all other rights and values. Protection of individuals as social beings means that other rights need careful balancing in all cases. The weight of privacy claims requires evaluation on a scale containing many values, not just individualist ones.

The social value of privacy has been noted many times. I argue, though, that in order to take into account all the nuances of this aspect of privacy, we need to re-think the person protected. Many theories that see privacy as valuable for societal reasons still hold on to the autonomous selfsame being as the primary object of privacy protection. When it turns out, in case law, that we are neither completely autonomous nor completely individual but much messier in our being, the logic of privacy regulation becomes problematic.

In deconstructing the person of privacy rights, this book has sought ways to re-think privacy. One opening for new conceptualisation lies in the idea that privacy rights presuppose the possibility to keep things hidden, as well as the possibility to lie. These rights can be used to protect the selfsame ego for sure. But they can also be compatible with an understanding of human beings with aspects of themselves hidden, even from themselves. This may be the dark underside of privacy rights – because it is so seldom acknowledged – or it may be the light. It may be the way to discuss privacy in a more nuanced manner, allowing for inconsistencies, incompleteness and uncertainty at the heart of the legal person.

Privacy rights, when understood this way, protect people who do not know themselves, and often have no idea of what they are doing and why. This way of thinking goes against the picture of the individual as a selfsame intelligible person.

In some legal cases, we already see that the law protects something other than the autonomous individual. The law protects persons who might be completely clueless, or careless when they use technology or engage in other forms of mediated communication. Perhaps the person is aware of the fact that their data is being processed, perhaps not, perhaps they do not care. The law does not have to presuppose that they know what they are doing.

Privacy rights, as the rights of the messy and opaque people that we are, need to admit the incapability of persons to fully understand themselves. Perhaps privacy law can also help with the difficulties we have in sharing our lives and expressing ourselves to others. In that light, the need for privacy includes a demand of the law to acknowledge the fundamental risk of miscommunication inherent in human relationships.

Privacy rights are therefore valuable because they offer possibilities for regulating relations between people as incomplete beings. Hence, privacy should not be used to protect individuals left alone, but rather as sharing a world.

Bibliography

Althusser, Louis, *Lenin and Philosophy and Other Essays* (New York: Monthly Review Press, 1971).

Amendola, Adalgiso, 'The Law of the Living: Material for Hypothesizing the Biojuridical' (2012) 8 *Law, Culture and the Humanities* 102–18.

Andre, Steven J., 'Privacy As an Aspect of the First Amendment: The Place of Privacy in a Society Dedicated to Individual Liberty' (1988) 20 *University of West Los Angeles Law Review* 87–112.

Aristodemou, Maria, 'Freedom in the Free World: The Extimate Becomes the Law' (2016) 48 *International Journal of Law and Psychiatry* 85–91.

Armstrong, Philip, Smith, Jason E. and Nancy, Jean-Luc, 'Politics and Beyond: An Interview with Jean-Luc Nancy' (2015) 43 *Diacritics* 90–108.

Augenstein, Daniel, 'We the People: EU Justice as Politics', in Dimitry Kochenov, Gráinne De Búrca and Andrew Williams (eds.), *Europe's Justice Deficit* (Oxford: Hart Publishing, 2015), pp. 153–64.

Ausloos, Jef and Dewitte, Pierre, 'Shattering One-Way Mirrors – Data Subject Access Rights in Practice' (2018) 8 *International Data Privacy Law* 4–28.

Azoulai, Loïc, 'The European Individual as Part of Collective Entities (Market, Family, Society)', in Loïc Azoulai, Ségolène Barbou des Places and Etienne Pataut (eds.), *Constructing the Person in EU Law: Rights, Roles, Identities* (Oxford: Hart Publishing, 2016), pp. 203–24.

Azoulai, Loïc, Barbou des Places, Ségolène and Pataut, Etienne (eds.), *Constructing the Person in EU Law: Rights, Roles, Identities* (Oxford: Hart Publishing, 2016).

Balibar, Étienne, *We, the People of Europe?: Reflections on Transnational Citizenship* (Princeton, NJ: Princeton University Press, 2003).

Bauman, Zygmunt, *Liquid Modernity* (Cambridge: Polity Press, 2000).

Bauman, Zygmunt, *The Individualized Society* (Cambridge: Polity Press, 2001).

Beck, Gunnar, *The Legal Reasoning of the Court of Justice of the EU* (Oxford: Hart Publishing, 2012).

Bengoetxea, Joxerramon, *The Legal Reasoning of the European Court of Justice: Towards a European Jurisprudence* (Oxford: Clarendon Press, 1993).

Bernal, Paul, *Internet Privacy Rights: Rights to Protect Autonomy* (Cambridge: Cambridge University Press, 2014).

Blanc, Nicolas, 'Wirtschaftsakademie Schleswig-Holstein: Towards a Joint Responsibility of Facebook Fan Page Administrators for Infringements to European Data Protection Law' (2018) 4 *European Data Protection Law Review* 120–6.

Bradford, Anu, 'The Brussels Effect' (2012) 107 *Northwestern University Law Review* 1–68.

Brkan, Maja, 'The Concept of Essence of Fundamental Rights in the EU Legal Order: Peeling the Onion to Its Core' (2018) 14 *European Constitutional Law Review* 332–68.

Buitelaar, J. C., 'Privacy: Back to the Roots' (2012) 13 *German Law Journal* 171–202.

Buonamano, Roberto, 'The Legal Subject in Althusser's Political Theory' (2014) 25 *Law & Critique* 231–48.

Butler, Judith, 'Giving an Account of Oneself' (2001) 31 *Diacritics* 22–40.

Butler, Judith, *Giving an Account of Oneself* (New York: Fordham University Press 2005).

Campbell, Timothy, '"Bios", Immunity, Life: The Thought of Roberto Esposito' (2006) 36 *Diacritics* 2–22.

Campbell, Timothy and Luisetti, Federico, 'On Contemporary French and Italian Political Philosophy: An Interview with Roberto Esposito' (2010) 75 *Minnesota Review* 109–18.

Cavell, Stanley, *Conditions Handsome and Unhandsome: The Constitution of Emersonian Perfectionism: The Carus Lectures* (Chicago, IL: University of Chicago Press 1990).

Cohen, Julie, *Configuring the Networked Self – Law, Code, and the Play of Everyday Practice* (New Haven, CT and London: Yale University Press, 2012).

Corcoran, Steven, 'Editor's Introduction', in Jacques Rancière, *Dissensus: On Politics and Aesthetics* (New York: Continuum, 2010), pp. 1–24.

Coser, Lewis, *Introduction in Durkheim: The Division of Labour in Society* (Basingstoke: Palgrave, 1984).

Cotterrell, Roger, 'Justice, Dignity, Torture, Headscarves: Can Durkheim's Sociology Clarify Legal Values?' (2010) 20 *Social & Legal Studies* 1–18.

Cover, Robert M., 'Nomos and Narrative' (1983–4) 97 *Harvard Law Review* 4–68.

Davies, Gareth, 'Social Legitimacy and Purposive Power: The End, The Means and the Consent of the People', in Dimitry Kochenov, Gráinne de Búrca and Andrew Williams (eds.), *Europe's Justice Deficit* (Oxford: Hart Publishing, 2015), pp. 259–74.

Dembour, Marie-Bénédicte, *Who Believes in Human Rights?: Reflections on the European Convention* (Cambridge: Cambridge University Press, 2006).

Derrida, Jacques, *Dissemination* (Chicago, IL: University of Chicago Press, 1981).

Derrida, Jacques, *Limited Inc* (Evanston, IL: Northwestern University Press, 1988).

Derrida, Jacques and Stiegler, Bernard, *Echographies of Television: Filmed Interviews* (Cambridge: Polity Press, 2002).

Durkheim, Émile, *The Division of Labour in Society*, W. D. Halls and Lewis Coser trs., introduction by Lewis Coser (Basingstoke: Macmillan, 1984).

Esposito, Roberto, 'Totalitarianism or Biopolitics? Concerning a Philosophical Interpretation of the Twentieth Century' (2008) 34 *Critical Inquiry* 633–44.

Esposito, Roberto, 'The Dispositif of the Person' (2012) 8 *Law, Culture and the Humanities* 17–30.

Esposito, Roberto, *Third Person: Politics of Life and Philosophy of the Impersonal* (Cambridge: Polity Press, 2012).

Esposito, Roberto, *Immunitas: The Protection and Negation of Life* (Cambridge: Polity Press, 2013).

Esposito, Roberto, *Terms of the Political: Community, Immunity, Biopolitics* (New York: Fordham University Press, 2013).

Esposito, Roberto, Nancy, Jean-Luc and Campbell, Timothy, 'Dialogue on the Philosophy to Come' (2010) 75 *Minnesota Review* 71–88.

Etzioni, Amitai (ed.), *New Communitarian Thinking: Persons, Virtues, Institutions, and Communities* (Charlottesville, VA: University Press of Virginia, 1995).

Eubanks, Virginia, *Automating Inequality: How High-Tech Tools Profile, Police, and Punish the Poor* (New York: St. Martin's Press, 2018).

Ferretti, Federico, 'Data Protection and the Legitimate Interest of Data Controllers: Much Ado about Nothing or the Winter of Rights?' (2014) 51 *Common Market Law Review* 843–68.

Foucault, Michel, 'Truth and Juridical Forms', in Michel Foucault, *Power*, James D. Faubion ed., Robert Hurley et al. trs., *The Essential Works of Foucault 1954–1984*, vol. 3 (New York: New Press, 2000), pp. 1–89.

Foucault, Michel, 'Truth and Power', in Michel Foucault, *Power*, James D. Faubion ed., Robert Hurley et al. trs., *The Essential Works of Foucault 1954–1984*, vol. 3 (New York: New Press, 2000).

Foucault, Michel, *The Birth of Biopolitics: Lectures at the Collège de France, 1978–1979*, Michael Senellart ed., Graham Burchell trs. (New York: Palgrave Macmillan, 2008).

Fried, Charles, 'Privacy' (1968) 77 *The Yale Law Journal* 474–93.

Fuller, Lon L., *The Morality of Law*, revised ed. (New Haven, CT: Yale University Press, 1969).

Gadamer, Hans-Georg, 'Subjectivity and Intersubjectivity, Subject and Person' (2000) 33 *Continental Philosophy Review* 275–87.

Gavison, Ruth, 'Privacy and the Limits of Law' (1980) 89 *The Yale Law Journal* 421–71.

Gellert, Raphael, 'On Risk, Balancing, and Data Protection: A Response to van der Sloot' (2017) 3 *European Data Protection Law Review* 180–6.

Giddens, Anthony, 'The "Individual" in the Writings of Émile Durkheim' (1971) 12 *European Journal of Sociology / Archives Européennes de Sociologie / Europäisches Archiv für Soziologie* 210–28.

González Fuster, Gloria, *The Emergence of Personal Data Protection as a Fundamental Right of the EU* (Cham: Springer, 2014).

Guinchard, Audrey, 'Taking Proportionality Seriously: The Use of Contextual Integrity for a More Informed and Transparent Analysis in EU Data Protection Law' (2018) 24 *European Law Journal* 434–57.

Hallward, Peter, 'Staging Equality: On Rancière's Theatrocracy' (2006) 37 *New Left Review* 109–29.

Harman, Graham, 'On Interface: Nancy's Weights and Masses', in Peter Gratton and Marie-Eve Morin (eds.), *Jean-Luc Nancy and Plural Thinking: Expositions of World, Ontology, Politics, and Sense* (Albany, NY: State University of New York Press, 2012), pp. 95–107.

Hijmans, Hielke, *The European Union as Guardian of Internet Privacy: The Story of Art 16 TFEU* (Cham, Heidelberg, New York, Dordrecht and London: Springer, 2016).

Hixton, Richard F., *Privacy in a Public Society: Human Rights in Conflict* (Oxford: Oxford University Press, 1987).

Hoofnagle, Chris Jay, van der Sloot, Bart and Zuiderveen Borgesius, Frederik, 'The European Union General Data Protection Regulation: What It Is and What It Means' (2019) 28 *Information & Communications Technology Law* 65–98.

Hurri, Samuli, *Birth of the European Individual: Law, Security, Economy* (Oxon and New York: Routledge, 2014).

Hutchens, B. C., 'Archi-Ethics, Justice, and the Suspension of History in the Writing of Jean-Luc Nancy', in Peter Gratton and Marie-Eve Morin (eds.), *Jean-Luc Nancy and Plural Thinking: Expositions of World, Ontology, Politics, and Sense* (Albany, NY: State University of New York Press, 2012), pp. 129–42.

Ieven, Bram, 'Heteroreductives: Rancière's Disagreement with Ontology' (2009) 15 *Parallax* 50–62.

Johnston, Adrian, *Žižek's Ontology: A Transcendental Materialist Theory of Subjectivity* (Evanston, IL: Northwestern University Press, 2008).

Johnston, Adrian, *Badiou, Žižek, and Political Transformations: The Cadence of Change* (Evanston, IL: Northwestern University Press, 2009).

Käll, Jannice, 'A Posthuman Data Subject? The Right to Be Forgotten and Beyond' (2017) *German Law Journal* 1145–62.

Käll, Jannice, *Converging Human and Digital Bodies. Posthumanism, Property, Law* (Gothenburg: University of Gothenburg, 2017).

Kapur, Ratna, 'In the Aftermath of Critique We Are Not in Epistemic Free Fall: Human Rights, the Subaltern Subject, and Non-Liberal Search for Freedom and Happiness' (2014) 25 *Law & Critique* 2–45.

Kennedy, Duncan, *A Critique of Adjudication (fin de siècle)* (Cambridge, MA and London: Harvard University Press, 1997).

Koivisto, Ida, 'The anatomy of transparency: the concept and its multifarious implications' Working Paper EUI MWP 2016/09, 1–29.

Kokott, Juliane and Sobotta, Christoph, 'The Distinction between Privacy And Data Protection in the Jurisprudence of the CJEU and the ECtHR' (2013) 3 *International Data Privacy Law* 222–8.

Koops, Bert-Jaap, 'The Trouble with European Data Protection Law' (2014) 4 *International Data Privacy Law* 250–61.

Kurki, Visa, *A Theory of Legal Personhood* (Oxford: Oxford University Press, 2019).

Lenaerts, Koen and Gutierrez-Fons, Jose A., 'To Say What the Law of the EU Is: Methods of Interpretation and the European Court of Justice' (2014) 20 *Columbia Journal of European Law* 3–61.

Lindroos-Hovinheimo, Susanna, *Justice and the Ethics of Legal Interpretation* (Oxon and New York: Routledge, 2012).

Lindroos-Hovinheimo, Susanna, 'Excavating Foundations of Legal Personhood: Fichte on Autonomy and Self-Consciousness' (2015) 28 *International Journal for the Semiotics of Law* 687–702.

Lindroos-Hovinheimo, Susanna, 'There Is No Europe – On Subjectivity and Community in the EU' (2017) 18 *German Law Journal* 1229–46.

Lindroos-Hovinheimo, Susanna, 'Ranciere and the Legal Subject – Coming to Terms with Non-Existence', in Mónical López Lerma and Julen Etxabe (eds.), *Rancière and Law* (Oxon and New York: Routledge, 2018), pp. 73–91.

Lindroos-Hovinheimo, Susanna, 'Data Protection Does Not Always Override Authorities' Need to Obtain Data' (2019) 4 *European Data Protection Law Review* 568–72.

Lindroos-Hovinheimo, Susanna, 'Who Controls Our Data? The Legal Reasoning of the European Court of Justice in Wirtschaftsakademie Schleswig-Holstein and Tietosuojavaltuutettu v Jehovan todistajat' (2019) 28 *Information & Communications Technology Law* 225–38.

Lynch, Michael P., 'Privacy and the Threat to the Self', *The New York Times*, 22 June 2013, http://opinionator.blogs.nytimes.com/2013/06/22/privacy-and-the-threat-to-the-self/.

Lynskey, Orla, 'From Market-Making Tool to Fundamental Right: The Role of the Court of Justice in Data Protection's Identity Crisis', in Serge Gutwirth et al. (eds.), *European Data Protection: Coming of Age* (Dordrecht: Springer, 2013), pp. 59–84.

MacCormick, Neil, 'My Philosophy of Law', in L. J. Wintgens (ed.), *The Law in Philosophical Perspectives* (Dordrecht: Springer, 1999), pp. 121–45.

MacCormick, Neil, *Institutions of Law* (Oxford: Oxford University Press, 2007).

MacPherson, C. B., *The Political Theory of Possessive Individualism: Hobbes to Locke* (Oxford: Clarendon Press, 1962).

Mantelero, Alessandro, 'Regulating Big Data. The Guidelines of the Council of Europe in the Context of the European Data Protection Framework' (2017) 33 *Computer Law & Security Review: The International Journal of Technology Law and Practice* 584–602.

Marks, Susan (ed.), *International Law on the Left: Re-Examining Marxist Legacies* (Cambridge: Cambridge University Press, 2008).

Marshall, Jill, *Personal Freedom through Human Rights Law?* (Leiden: Martinus Nijhoff, 2009).

Marshall, Jill, 'The Legal Recognition of Personality: Full-Face Veils and Permissible Choices' (2014) 10 *International Journal of Law in Context* 64–80.

Marshall, Jill, *Human Rights Law and Personal Identity* (Oxon and New York: Routledge, 2014).

Marx, Karl, *Capital: A Critique of Political Economy*, Friedrich Engels ed., Samuel Moore and Edward Aveling trs., 3 vols. (London: Penguin Books, 1992).

May, Todd, 'Wrong, Disagreement, Subjectification', in Jean-Philippe Deranty (ed.), *Jacques Rancière: Key Concepts* (Durham: Acumen, 2010), pp. 69–79.

Mayer-Schönberger, Viktor and Cukier, Kenneth, *Big Data: A Revolution That Will Transform How We Live, Work, and Think* (New York: Hachette, Eamon Dolan/ Mariner Books, 2014).

Moore Jr., Barrington, *Privacy: Studies in Social and Cultural History*, reprint ed. (Armonk, NY: M. E. Sharpe, 1984).

Morin, Marie-Eve, '"We Must Become What We Are": Jean-Luc Nancy's Ontology as Ethos and Praxis', in Sanja Dejanovic (ed.), *Nancy and the Political* (Edinburgh: Edinburgh University Press, 2015), pp. 21–42.

Moyn, Samuel, *Not Enough: Human Rights in an Unequal World* (Cambridge, MA: Belknap Press, 2018).

Naffine, Ngaire, 'Who are Law's Persons? From Cheshire Cats to Responsible Subjects' (2003) 66 *Modern Law Review* 346–67.

Nancy, Jean-Luc, *The Inoperative Community*, Peter Connor ed., foreword by Christopher Fynsk (Minneapolis, MN: University of Minnesota Press, 1991).

Nancy, Jean-Luc, *The Experience of Freedom*, Bridget MacDonald trs., foreword by Peter Fenves (Stanford, CA: Stanford University Press, 1993).

Nancy, Jean-Luc, *Being Singular Plural* (Stanford, CA: Stanford University Press, 2000).

Nancy, Jean-Luc, *The Creation of the World or Globalization*, François Raffoul and David Pettigrew trs. (Albany, NY: State University of New York Press, 2007).

Nancy, Jean-Luc, *The Truth of Democracy*, Pascale-Anne Brault and Michael Naas trs. (New York: Fordham University Press, 2010).

Nancy, Jean-Luc, 'From the Imperative to Law', in B. C. Hutchens (ed.), *Jean-Luc Nancy: Justice, Legality and World* (New York: Continuum, 2012), pp. 11–18.

Neyrat, Frédéric, 'No/Us: The Nietzschean Democracy of Jean-Luc Nancy' (2015) 43 *Diacritics* 66–87.

Nippert-Eng, Christena, *Islands of Privacy* (Chicago, IL: The University of Chicago Press, 2020).

Nissenbaum, Helen, *Privacy in Context: Technology, Policy and the Integrity of Social Life* (Stanford, CA: Stanford University Press, 2010).

Norris, Andrew, 'Jean-Luc Nancy and the Myth of the Common' (2000) 7 *Constellations* 272–95.

Norris, Andrew, 'Jean-Luc Nancy on the Political after Heidegger and Schmitt', in Peter Gratton and Marie-Eve Morin (eds.), *Jean-Luc Nancy and Plural Thinking: Expositions of World, Ontology, Politics, and Sense* (Albany, NY: State University of New York Press, 2012), pp. 143–58.

Nussbaum, Martha C. and Levmore, Saul (eds.), *The Offensive Internet: Speech, Privacy, and Reputation* (Cambridge, MA: Harvard University Press, 2010).

Ojanen, Tuomas, 'Making the Essence of Fundamental Rights Real: The Court of Justice of the European Union Clarifies the Structure of Fundamental Rights under the Charter' (2016) 12 *European Constitutional Law Review* 318–29.

Øverenget, Einar, 'Heidegger and Arendt against the Imperialism of Privacy' (1995) *Philosophy Today* 430–44.

Parker, Andrew, 'Editor's Introduction: Mimesis and the Division of Labor', in Jacques Rancière, *The Philosopher and His Poor* (Durham, NC: Duke University Press, 2003), pp. ix–xx.

Paunio, Elina and Lindroos-Hovinheimo, Susanna, 'Taking Language Seriously: An Analysis of Linguistic Reasoning and Its Implications in EU Law' (2010) *European Law Journal* 395–416.

Petkova, Bilyana, 'Privacy as Europe's First Amendment' (2019) 25 *European Law Journal* 140–54.

Post, Robert C., 'The Social Foundations of Privacy: Community and Self in the Common Law Tort' (1989) 77 *California Law Review* 957–1010.

Rancière, Jacques, 'Politics, Identification, and Subjectivization' (1992) 61 *October* 58–64.

Rancière, Jacques, 'The Community of Equals', in Jacques Rancière, *On the Shores of Politics*, Liz Heron trs. (London: Verso, 1995), pp. 63–91.

Rancière, Jacques, *Disagreement: Politics and Philosophy*, Julie Rose trs. (Minneapolis, MN: University of Minnesota Press, 1999).

Rancière, Jacques, 'From Politics to Aesthetics?' (2005) 28 *Paragraph* 13–25.

Rancière, Jacques, 'The Janus-Face of Politicized Art: Jacques Rancière in Interview with Gabriel Rockhill', in Jacques Rancière, *The Politics of Aesthetics: The Distribution of the Sensible* (New York: Continuum, 2006), pp. 50–2.

Rancière, Jacques, 'The Aesthetic Dimension: Aesthetics, Politics, Knowledge' (2009) 36 *Critical Inquiry* 1–19.

Rancière, Jacques, 'A Few Remarks on the Method of Jacques Rancière' (2009) 15 *Parallax* 114–23.

Rancière, Jacques, *Dissensus: On Politics and Aesthetics*, Steven Corcoran ed. and trs. (New York: Continuum, 2010).

Rancière, Jacques, 'Democracies against Democracy: An Interview with Eric Hazan', in Giorgio Agamben et al. (eds.), *Democracy in What State?* (New York: Chichester, 2011), pp. 76–81.

Rancière, Jacques, 'Work, Identity, Subject', in Jean-Philippe Deranty and Alison Ross (eds.), *Jacques Rancière and the Contemporary Scene: The Philosophy of Radical Equality* (New York: Continuum, 2012), pp. 205–16.

Rancière, Jacques, *The Method of Equality: Interviews with Laurent Jeanpierre and Dork Zabunyan*, Julie Rose trs. (Cambridge: Polity Press, 2016).

Rancière, Jacques and Panagia, David, 'Dissenting Words: A Conversation with Jacques Rancière' (2000) 30 *Diacritics* 113–26.

Rancière, Jacques et al., 'Jacques Rancière: Literature, Politics, Aesthetics: Approaches to Democratic Disagreement' (2000) 29 *SubStance* 3–24.

Raz, Joseph, *The Morality of Freedom* (Oxford: Oxford University Press, 1986).

Richardson, Janice, *Law and the Philosophy of Privacy* (Oxon and New York: Routledge, 2016).

Ricoeur, Paul, 'Althusser's Theory of Ideology', in Gregory Elliott (ed.), *Althusser: A Critical Reader* (Oxford: Blackwell, 1994), pp. 44–72.

Roessler, Beate and Mokrosinska, Dorota, 'Privacy and Social Interaction' (2013) 39(8) *Philosophy and Social Criticism* 771–91.

Rubenfeld, Jed, 'The Right to Privacy' (1989) 102 *Harvard Law Review* 737–807.
Rundle, Kristen, *Forms Liberate: Reclaiming the Jurisprudence of Lon L Fuller* (Oxford: Hart Publishing, 2012).
Sangiovanni, Andrea, 'Solidarity in the European Union: Problems and Prospects', in Julie Dickson and Palvos Eleftheriadis (eds.), *Philosophical Foundations of European Union Law* (Oxford: Oxford University Press, 2012), pp. 384–411.
Sankari, Suvi, *European Court of Justice Legal Reasoning in Context* (Groningen: Europa Law Publishing, 2013).
Sarat, Austin (ed.), *A World Without Privacy: What Law Can and Should Do?* (Cambridge: Cambridge University Press, 2015).
Seubert, Sandra and Becker, Carlos, 'The Culture Industry Revisited: Sociophilosophical Reflections on "privacy" in the Digital Age' (2019) 45 *Philosophy and Social Criticism* 930–47.
Solove, Daniel J., *Understanding Privacy* (Cambridge, MA: Harvard University Press, 2008).
Somek, Alexander, *Individualism: An Essay on the Authority of the European Union* (Oxford: Oxford University Press, 2008).
Somek, Alexander, 'Integration without Emancipation: Reflections on "Social Europe"', in Bjarne Melkevik (ed.), *Standing Tall: Hommages à Csaba Varga* (Budapest: Pázmány Press, 2012), pp. 419–36.
Somek, Alexander, 'The Preoccupation with Rights and the Embrace of Inclusion: A Critique', in Dimitry Kochenov, Gráinne de Búrca and Andrew Williams (eds.), *Europe's Justice Deficit* (Oxford: Hart Publishing, 2015), pp. 295–309.
Tsakyrakis, Stavros, 'Disproportionate Individualism', in Dimitry Kochenov, Gráinne de Búrca and Andrew Williams (eds.), *Europe's Justice Deficit* (Oxford: Hart Publishing, 2015), pp. 235–46.
Van der Sloot, Bart, 'Do Data Protection Rules Protect the Individual and Should They? An Assessment of the Proposed General Data Protection Regulation' (2014) 4 *International Data Privacy Law* 307–25.
Van der Sloot, Bart, 'Ten Questions about Balancing' (2017) 3 *European Data Protection Law Review* 187–94.
Van der Sloot, Bart, *Privacy as Virtue: Moving beyond the Individual in the Age of Big Data* (Cambridge: Intersentia, 2017).
Vincent, David, *Privacy: A Short History* (Cambridge: Polity Press, 2016).
Warren, Samuel D. and Brandeis, Louis D., 'The Right to Privacy' (1890) 4 *Harvard Law Review* 193–220.
Watkin, Christopher, 'Rancière Now: Current Perspectives on Jacques Rancière (Review)' (2014) 68 *French Studies: A Quarterly Review* 418.
Weiler, J. H. H., 'Deciphering the Political and Legal DNA of European Integration: An Exploratory Essay', in Julie Dickson and Pavlos Eleftheriadis (eds.), *Philosophical Foundations of European Union Law* (Oxford: Oxford University Press, 2012), pp. 137–58.
Weinstein, W. L., 'The Private and the Free: A Conceptual Inquiry' (1971) 13 *NOMOS: Yearbook of the American Society for Political and Legal Philosophy* 27–55.

Westin, Alan F., *Privacy and Freedom* (New York: Atheneum Publishers, 1967).
Wyatt, D., 'The Anaemic Existence of the Overriding Public Interest in Disclosure in the EU's Access to Documents Regime' (2020) 21 *German Law Journal* 686–701.
Žižek, Slavoj, *The Sublime Object of Ideology* (London: Verso, 1989).
Žižek, Slavoj, *The Ticklish Subject: The Absent Centre of Political Ontology* (London: Verso, 2008).
Žižek, Slavoj, *Less than Nothing: Hegel and the Shadow of Dialectical Materialism* (London: Verso, 2012).
Žižek, Slavoj, *Like a Thief in Broad Daylight: Power in the Era of Post-Human Capitalism* (London: Allen Lane 2018).
Zuboff, Shoshana, *The Age of Surveillance Capitalism – The Fight for a Human Future at the New Frontier of Power* (London: Profile Books 2019).

Index

www.ingramcontent.com/pod-product-compliance
Lightning Source LLC
LaVergne TN
LVHW011814200926
848484LV00005B/1192
* 9 7 8 1 1 0 8 4 7 8 8 8 5 *